The Foundation for Digital Twins

The Foundation for Digital Twins

An Architectural, Technical, and Software Perspective

Roberto Minerva

Institut Polytechnique de Paris
Telecom SudParis

Noel Crespi

Institut Polytechnique de Paris
Telecom SudParis

IEEE Press
WILEY

Published by John Wiley & Sons, Inc., Hoboken, New Jersey.

Library of Congress Cataloging-in-Publication Data

Names: Minerva, Roberto, 1958- author | Crespi, Noel author | John Wiley & Sons publisher
Title: The foundation for digital twins : an architectural, technical, and software perspective / Roberto Minerva, Noel Crespi.
Description: Hoboken, New Jersey : IEEEPress : Wiley, [2026] | Includes bibliographical references and index.
Identifiers: LCCN 2026006445 | ISBN 9781394298303 hardback | ISBN 9781394298327 adobe pdf | ISBN 9781394298310 epub
Subjects: LCSH: Digital twins (Computer simulation)
Classification: LCC QA76.9.C65 M565 2026
LC record available at https://lccn.loc.gov/2026006445

Cover Design: Wiley
Cover Image: © innni/Shutterstock

To our beloved families

Contents

Foreword

Digital Twin technology has emerged as a groundbreaking method for representing and simulating physical systems within the digital realm. As we navigate an era marked by rapid advancements in artificial intelligence, Digital Twins are evolving to become not only smarter but also increasingly responsive to real-time data and contextual changes.

This comprehensive volume is designed to serve as both a foundational resource and a practical guide. Within these pages, you will encounter a rich tapestry of theoretical insights alongside actionable strategies. The book delves deeply into the foundational principles and core concepts that underpin Digital Twin technology, while also providing robust implementation strategies that are crucial for leveraging this transformative approach. In addition, you will find an array of relevant use cases and the latest trends shaping the future landscape of Digital Twins across various industries.

It is my sincere hope that this book will serve as a catalyst for inspiring innovative approaches, fostering collaborative endeavors, and accelerating advancements within a field that has the potential to profoundly influence our understanding of and interactions with the physical world. By providing both rigor and accessibility, we aim to empower readers to actively participate in the evolution of Digital Twin technology and its application in real-world scenarios.

Khaled B. Letaief
New Bright Professor of Engineering, HKUST, Hong Kong
Member, US National Academy of Engineering

About the Authors

Roberto Minerva is an Emeritus Associate Professor at the Institut Polytechnique de Paris – Télécom SudParis. His career bridges decades of research in industrial innovation with academic contributions, focusing on the convergence of distributed systems, the Internet of Things (IoT), and advanced platforms driven by artificial intelligence (AI) and Digital Twin technology.

Dr. Minerva's academic foundation includes a master's degree in Computer Science from the University of Bari (Italy), a PhD in Computer Science and Telecommunications, and an HDR from Sorbonne University (France).

From 1987 to 2016, his industrial tenure was spent at CSELT/TILAB (the advanced research branch of TIM – Telecom Italia), a historical hub for Italian telecommunications innovation. He began as a researcher and served as a Research Manager from 1996 on, leading groups dedicated to pioneering foundational technologies, including SDN/NFV, 5G, Big Data, and IoT. He contributed to international cooperative efforts such as TINA-C (Service Architectures) and provided global leadership as Chairman of the IEEE IoT Initiative between 2013 and 2016.

In 2017, he transitioned to the academic sector, joining Télécom SudParis before achieving emeritus status. His current research remains centered on IoT, Digital Twin platforms, and the strategic exploitation of AI techniques. He is the author of numerous influential papers published across leading international venues.

Noel Crespi Prof. Noel Crespi holds Masters degrees from the Universities of Paris-Saclay (formerly Orsay) and Kent (UK), a diplome d'ingénieur from Telecom Paris, and a Ph.D and an Habilitation from Sorbonne University. From 1993 he worked at CLIP, Bouygues Telecom and then at Orange Labs in 1995. He took leading roles in the creation of new services with the successful conception and launch of Orange prepaid service (15M+ subscribers), and in standardization (from the rapporteurship of IN standard to the coordination of all mobile standards activities for Orange). In 1999, he joined Nortel Networks as telephony program manager, architecting core network products for the EMEA region. He joined Institut Mines-Telecom, Telecom SudParis in 2002 and is currently Professor and Program Director at Institut Polytechnique de Paris, leading the Data Intelligence and Communication Engineering Lab. He coordinates the standardization activities for Institut Mines-Telecom at ITU-T and ETSI. He was an adjunct professor at KAIST (South Korea), a guest researcher at the University of Goettingen (Germany) and an affiliate professor at Concordia University (Canada). He is the scientific director of AI^2, a French-Korean laboratory. As a Principal Investigator or Co-Investigator, he has secured research grants added up to 8M+ euros. His current research interests are in Edge Intelligence, IoT, Digital Twin, Artificial Intelligence and NLP.

http://noelcrespi.wp.tem-tsp.eu/

Preface

This book explores the architectural, technical, and software-oriented foundations of Digital Twin (DT) technology. DTs offer a powerful means to represent and interact with physical systems in the digital realm, enabling advanced analysis, optimization, and decision-making. While general-purpose sensing served as an initial inspiration for the authors, the core motivation was to investigate whether, starting from general measurement data of the environment, it is possible to derive meaningful insights about a system and ultimately determine its behavior.

A central theme of this volume is the integration of data-driven and model-based approaches in DT development. The book examines the benefits of combining "bottom-up" (data-driven) and "top-down" (model-based) methodologies, with the goal of achieving a more comprehensive understanding of DT systems and the increasingly complex physical systems they represent. The discussion emphasizes a software-oriented perspective, focusing on the definition of DT software architectures that support the design, structuring, and reusability of components to enhance adaptability and scalability.

A key aspect addressed is the definition and modeling of system behavior. Methods for deriving behavior models from observational data are explored, as well as strategies for integrating model-based behavioral modeling with available data streams.

Further motivation comes from the need for development environments that provide essential components and behavior templates, as well as the integration of artificial intelligence (AI) as a core element of DT architectures.

Another important consideration is the support for the entire DT life cycle, with particular attention to continuous software improvement across all phases.

This book aims to provide readers with a structured overview of DT, encompassing core concepts and software architecture considerations.

It is intended for researchers, practitioners, and all those interested in the development and application of DT technology.

10th May 2025

Noel Crespi and Roberto Minerva
Paris, France

Acknowledgments

The authors owe their gratitude to Dr. Adam Drobot for the invaluable insights he has shared over many years of friendly collaboration on Digital Twin topics.

Special thanks are extended to colleagues at Institut Polytechnique de Paris – Telecom SudParis, especially Prof. Djamal Zeglache, Head of the Networks and Mobile Multimedia Services Department, Dr. Hrishikesh Dutta, and all the others, for their support and for the stimulating discussions that enriched our exploration of Digital Twin concepts.

The authors are deeply grateful to their students, whose curiosity and questions have highlighted the challenges of software representations of physical systems and have provided valuable suggestions and ideas that contributed to this book.

Appreciation is also due to our editor, Veena Rajendran, and to everyone involved in the production of this book for their dedication and professionalism.

Last but not least, the authors thank their families, who once again have given them the time, love, and calm needed to pursue this objective.

Noel Crespi and Roberto Minerva

Acronyms

AI	Artificial Intelligence
ANN	Artificial Neural Network
API	Application Programming Interface
ARIMA	Autoregressive Integrated Moving Average
BIM	Building Information Modeling
CBR	Case-based Reasoning
CNN	Convolutional Neural Network
CPS	Cyber-Physical System
DDOS	Distributed Denial of Service
DDS	Data Distribution Service
DES	Discrete Event Simulation
DiffServ	Differentiated Services
DL	Deep Learning
DT	Digital Twin
DTDL	Digital Twin Definition Language
EDA	Event-driven Architecture
EDSM	Evidence-driven State Merging
ETSI	European Telecommunications Standards Institute
FIFO	First in - First out
FSM	Finite State Machine
GenAI	Generative Artificial Intelligence
GB	Global Balance
GoS	Grade of Service
GRU	Gated Recurrent Unit
ICT	Information and Communication Technology
IFC	Industry Foundation Classes
INCOSE	International Council on Systems Engineering
IntServ	Integrated Services

IoT	Internet of Things
IT	Information Technology
IP	Internet Protocol
ITU-T	International Telecommunication Unit – Standardization Sector
JSON	JavaScript Object Notation
JSON-LD	JavaScript Object Notation - Linked Data
KPI	Key Performance Indicator
LB	Local Balance
LHS	Left-hand Side
LIFO	Last in - First out
LLM	Large Language Model
LSTM	Long Short-term Memory
MBSE	Model-based System Engineering
MMPP	Markov Modulated Poisson Process
ML	Machine Learning
MOSA	Modular Open Systems Approach
MRM	Multi-retry Model
MTM	Multi-threshold Model
NDT	Network Digital Twin
NGSI-LD	Next Generation Service Interfaces - Linked Data
NLP	Natural Language Processing
O&M	Operations and Maintenance
OT	Operational Technology
OWL	Web Ontology Language
PART	Partial Decision Trees
PDF	Probability Distribution Function
PFS	Product Form Solution
PLM	Product Life-cycle Management
PO	Physical Object
PS	Physical System
QoS	Quality of Service
r.v.	Random Variable(s)
RBAC	Role-based Access Control
RDF	Resource Description Framework
RED	Random Early Detection
RHS	Right-hand Side
RIPPER	Repeated Incremental Pruning to Produce Error Reduction
RL	Reinforcement Learning
RLA	Reduced Load Approximation
RNN	Recurrent Neural Networks
ROI	Return of Investment
RUL	Remaining Useful Life

SIRO	Service in Random Order
SLA	Service Level Agreement
SRM	Single-retry Model
STM	Single-threshold Model
SPIME	SPace-tiME
SYSML	Systems Modeling Language
TCP	Transport Control Protocol
TEVV	Testing, Evaluation, Verification, and Validation
TH	Threshold(s)
UDP	User Datagram Protocol
UML	Unified Modeling Language
WOT	Web of Things
XAI	Explainable Artificial Intelligence
XAI-DT	Explainable AI Digital Twins

Introduction

Expectations about the usage of Digital Twin concepts and platforms are extraordinarily high in several problem domains and related applications. The potential capabilities and properties of Digital Twins are attracting more and more researchers, practitioners, and developers. This leads to an increased coverage of the possible problem domains and yields a better specification of Digital Twin features, platforms, and execution environments. The Digital Twin definition is no longer confined to the 3D representation of an object, product, system, or environment. Instead, the evolution of supporting technologies (modeling and artificial intelligence) is pushing towards new DT capabilities and properties. This book focuses on the aspects inherent to the modeling and implementation of effective software Digital Twins solutions. While the visualization capabilities remain important and relevant, it is the modeling and implementation of a full logical representation of a system that is presented here. The purpose is to provide hints and guidelines to developers for realizing compelling Digital Twin solutions for the management, optimization, improvement, and exploitation of virtualized systems.

1

What Is a Digital Twin?

What a Digital Twin Is: The Digital Twin (DT) is a software counterpart of a system or process. It is reproducing its major features and characteristics for analyzing or controlling the physical system (PS). The relations between the DT and the PS are described in terms of properties to achieve a representation that is meaningful also from a software perspective. The properties defined in this chapter will be used in the book to describe, rationalize, and lead the definition of a software platform supporting the implementation and execution of DTs for several problem domains.

1.1 Introductory Concepts

The Digital Twin (DT) concept is built upon a broad knowledge base encompassing systems engineering, software engineering, and software technology. Defining a common base of discourse is essential to clarify important concepts discussed in this book.

1.1.1 Basic Definitions

Several fundamental systems engineering concepts, as defined by [1], provide a foundational understanding of the problem domain. They define what a system, its behavior, and its properties are and provide a context for describing software architecture. These are preliminary concepts that will be used throughout the book.

1.1.1.1 System Definition

A system is an integrated set of elements (physical, software, etc.) organized to achieve a specific purpose. It encompasses components, their interactions, and the context within which they operate. In Cyber-Physical Systems (CPS), systems often integrate physical components with software and networked elements to execute complex functions [1, 2].

1.1.1.2 Behavior of a System

Behavior refers to the observed or expected actions, responses, and states of a system as it operates and interacts with its environment. Behavior can be modeled and analyzed to predict system performance, detect faults, or optimize operation (behavior model). It includes dynamic changes and reactions to stimuli or inputs.

1.1.1.3 Characterization of Behaviors: Intrinsic and Extrinsic Properties

In systems engineering, behaviors and system attributes are often classified as intrinsic or extrinsic properties:

- **Intrinsic properties (attributes)** are inherent characteristics that define the system itself, independent of its operational context. These include physical dimensions, material properties, design constraints, or structural configurations. Intrinsic properties are constants or semi-constants that affect but do not directly demonstrate performance behaviors.
- **Extrinsic properties (performance)** refer to observable performance outcomes, behaviors, or responses resulting from operation in a given environment or under specific conditions. They describe how the system acts or reacts, such as response time, throughput, durability under load, or fault tolerance. Extrinsic properties depend on intrinsic attributes and environmental interactions.

1.1.1.4 Software Architecture

Software Architecture is a basic organization of a software-intensive system embodied in its components, relationships among those components and the environment, and the principles guiding design, evolution, and realization. It provides an abstraction enabling understanding, engineering, and management of software aspects within broader system contexts. The architecture defines significant elements of the software system, their externally visible properties, and their interactions, serving as a blueprint for construction and validation of system requirements and quality attributes. Integration with system architecture ensures alignment with overall system goals and constraints [1].

1.1.1.5 Digital Twin (DT)

A DT is a software representation of a PS that reflects its structure, behavior, and state in real or near-real time. It is constructed by integrating system and software models with data collected from the physical entity (via sensors, actuators, etc.). The DT facilitates analysis, simulation, testing, and decision-making—enabling insights into system performance and behavior throughout life-cycle stages [1, 2].

1.1.2 Formalized Definitions

The previous definitions can also be formalized to provide a sound conceptual framework for further discussion.

1.1.2.1 System

Formally, a system S is a structured composition of interacting components (physical, software, human, or organizational) organized to achieve well-defined purposes within specified operational contexts. It is modeled as a tuple:

$$S = (C, I, E)$$

where:

- C is the set of components,
- I is the set of interactions/interfaces among components,
- E is the environment in which the system operates.

It is important to note that system engineering recognizes the impact that the environment can exert on the PS and its behavior.

1.1.2.2 Behavior of a System

The behavior B of a system S consists of state transitions and outputs generated in response to inputs and environmental conditions over time:

$$B : (S_t, u_t) \rightarrow (S_{t+1}, y_t)$$

where S_t is the system state at time t, u_t is the input, S_{t+1} is the subsequent state, and y_t is the output.

1.1.2.3 Characterization of Behaviors

Intrinsic properties $P_{\text{int}} \subseteq \text{Attributes}(S)$ are inherent system attributes independent of operation (e.g., physical dimensions). Extrinsic properties $P_{\text{ext}} = B(S, E)$ capture observable performance and behavior dependent on the environment E.

1.1.2.4 Digital Twin

A DT is a software implementation DT of a system S maintaining a continuously updated digital representation of the system's structure, state, and behavior using real-time or historical data D and formal models M. Formally:

$$\text{DT} = f(S, M, D)$$

where f denotes the software functions enabling synchronization and simulation.

1.2 DT: A Rationale

There are many definitions of the DT concept. They range from the initial ones focused on defining the concept, e.g., [3, 4], to more recent definitions, such as [5–7], concerned with its formalization, especially with respect to software architectures. Various definitions try to emphasize aspects and features of the DT concept with respect to specific goals or characteristics of the intended problem domains. The DT essence is a capability to represent a system or a process by means of descriptive data and a behavior model. The system is then embodied and implemented as software. The supporting model should represent the changing state of the system and explain its actions and behavior with respect to actual data. In this book, the prevailing interpretation is that a DT representation typically pertains to a large PS. It should also be noted that the development of an effective DT requires a lot of knowledge and representation of concepts pertaining to the specific problem domain, its peculiarities, and the current understanding of it. One important consequence is that the models used to represent the system and implemented by the DT are important and convey up-to-date knowledge of specific fields or applications.

1.2.1 Models and Modeling

In the context of the DT definition, the terms **model** and **modeling** have distinct meanings. A **model** is a physical, mathematical, formal, or logical representation of a system, entity, phenomenon, or process. It is an abstraction that captures the essential features needed to represent, analyze, or predict aspects of the real system at a given time. For the time being, these definitions can be used to describe the models characterizing a DT:

- **Descriptive Model:** The descriptive model represents the necessary data and their conceptual organizations and relationships needed to describe the relevant features and states of a PS.
- **Behavior Model:** The behavior model represents why and how a PS responds to events within its operating environment. It is a representation of the PS aiming to explain and specify the dynamic actions of a DT.

Modeling is the process of creating this representation. It involves selecting which elements to include or exclude, how to represent them, structuring the model, and defining its parameters. Modeling is a conceptual process aimed at designing a suitable and understandable representation of the system through formalization techniques such as rules, descriptions, and constraints.

A **simulation** is the execution or implementation of a model to study system behavior and the interactions of its components using computational tools. Simulation **evaluates** scenarios and use cases to predict results, supporting decision-making based on the defined behavior model and starting from initial conditions.

Prediction models play a crucial role in DTs by leveraging historical and real-time data (framed into a well-structured data model) along with machine learning techniques to forecast future states or events of the PS. These models enable the DT to anticipate changes of status that can be used to tackle failures, optimize operations, and guide proactive maintenance, enhancing decision-making capabilities beyond what static simulations offer.

A **DT**, however, is more than a static model, a one-off simulation, or a predictive model. It is an executable model of a physical object or system that is **continuously updated with real-time data** from its physical counterpart through data flows such as sensors. Thus, a DT functions as a combination of **continuous simulation and predictive modeling**, persistently mirroring the processes and states of the PS throughout its life-cycle phases. Unlike typical simulations that focus on limited processes or predefined scenarios, or predictive models based on consolidated data sets, DTs must **adapt and justify themselves to real-world data continuously**, also in the presence of rare situations.

Because of this dynamic nature, the underlying model supporting a DT must be characterized by **adaptation**—it must evolve and recalibrate as new data arrives, reflecting changes in the PS to maintain accuracy and relevance over time, also in critical occurrences. An adaptive model is critical to the twin's ability to provide actionable insights, predict failures, and optimize system performance in an ongoing, real-time context.

For formal definitions and more detailed descriptions, good starting sources include the ISO 23247 standard and the W3C Digital Twin Community Group documentation [8, 9].

1.2.2 DT as a Combination of Models

DTs leverage a model (often comprising data, predictive, simulation, and behavioral features) as part of their architecture and integrate real-time data feeds and two-way communication to reflect ongoing conditions, enabling enhanced monitoring, analysis, prediction, and optimization. A key distinction is scale and connectivity: while simulation studies curated scenarios with static data, DTs operate as dynamic, responsive digital counterparts synchronized with their physical twins.

The system's model should always be aligned with the status and actions of the physical objects it represents and be able to timely anticipate or substantiate future changes. The availability of PS data is essential for determining and understanding its current status, as well as for its logical representation. The expected and intended behavior of the system, on the other hand, must be represented by rules or laws describing how the system is reacting to the course of events and what actions are executed or responsible for the changes of status.

A first assumption is that a DT is a software implementation of a model capable of representing the actions performed by or on a system and its changes of status. Sometimes, the interpretation of a DT leans toward a data-driven perspective. Actually, if there are one or more data sets representing historical data, then the PS's behavior can be analyzed as a sequence of states' changes over time. The adoption of statistical or artificial intelligence techniques may lead to a mere data-based representation of changes of DT status [10], potentially overlooking the important behavioral features that contributed to those changes.

Data analysis actually is a fundamental part of the DT construction. Data availability enables two important DT features: **prediction** and **simulation**. For the time being, these assumptions can hold: prediction relies on leveraging data to forecast future states of the PS using statistical methods or advanced Machine/Deep Learning (ML/DL) techniques; simulation utilizes a behavior model to describe possible behaviors of the PS based on initial conditions or data, which may differ from its current or most probable states.

The combination of different modeling capabilities is central to creating a powerful DT and will be explored in greater detail in this and subsequent chapters.

Example: A descriptive model of a thermostat collects its current temperature. A behavior model contains the rule to turn on the heat if the temperature drops. When combined, the digital twin can not only monitor but also act upon the PS, as well as predict and diagnose issues, moving beyond simple data display.

Although the visualization capabilities of a digital twin are considered important, they will be discussed only marginally in the book, because they are seen as features that must be supported by accurate behavior models (reflecting the PS actions) and descriptive models (capturing its status changes). These models are essential for monitoring, predicting, or simulating the expected behavior of the target system. Visualization and a fully fledged model of a system are two fundamental components of a DT. Their integration will drive a broader adoption of the digital twin approach.

The DT's application domains are many, and new applications are already numerous, and new implementations are continuously emerging [11, 12]. The DT will soon become a relevant asset [13] for many different enterprises and organizations that are interested in softwarization, i.e., the transformation of services and business features into software applications [14, 15]. An example of a real-world digital twin is the one used by Siemens to create a virtual replica of its factories [16]. This twin allows them to optimize production, predict maintenance needs, and simulate changes to the factory layout without disrupting physical operations.

A particular aspect is the application of DT representations in the context of the Operational Technology (OT) domain. In this field, the ability to monitor, control, and optimize the usage and behavior of resources is particularly relevant, and it is evident the correlation between OT goals and the possibilities offered by DT solutions. A well-formed general-purpose model of OT monitoring capabilities can be considered as a global goal of DT technology.

Developing, deploying, and managing a DT solution is a challenging and complex task [13]. The aspects of designing, implementing, and operating a DT are relevant for each organization that wants to exploit the capabilities offered by this approach. Design and development is a critical step that needs cooperation and support of several parts of the organization. The challenge lies in the need to create benefits for all parties involved in the detailed representation of a system's data and behavior. One positive point is that knowledge about a system and views on it can be shared and made available to different groups. This can lead to a better understanding of the value and requirements of a system from many different perspectives. The deployment and operation of a DT solution is also very challenging: it involves the identification of distributed computing resources, their management, and the continuous integration of real-world data into a large software system. Changes or improvements of software capabilities can make a DT model and its supporting technologies obsolescent. Hence, the need for technology improvements as well as the software upgrade of salient characteristics of the solution (changes or updates to the DT supporting model) arises. All these requirements introduce new degrees of complexity at the process definition level, and it's modeling for improving and updating the logical representation.

Design, implementation, and operation are big challenges for actual use and exploitation of a DT solution.

1.3 DT Definition: A Step Further

Despite the numerous definitions of the DT (e.g., [4, 5, 13, 17–19]), a consensus is emerging in the literature around a set of core characteristics. These include the software replication of a physical object, the capacity to model the system as a "system of systems," the necessity of real-time data for status updates, and the ability to simulate potential behaviors under specific conditions.

A definition that aligns closely with several authoritative academic and industrial sources on DT technology (e.g., [20] and [21]) is as follows:

> A digital twin is a virtual representation of a physical object or system, designed to accurately mirror its real-world counterpart. It acts as a digital replica that allows for simulation, monitoring, and analysis of the physical twin throughout its life-cycle.

Some key characteristics underpinning this definition are:

- **Virtual Representation:** Software-based models that mirror physical objects, systems, or processes.

- **Dynamic and Interactive:** Continuously updated with real-time data, enabling responsive analysis.
- **Life-cycle Span:** Covers the entire life cyclefrom design and development to operation and decommissioning.
- **Real-time Data Integration:** Sensors and data sources feed continuous information into the twin.
- **Simulation and Analysis:** Enables scenario testing, performance optimization, and predictive insights.
- **Applications:** Used across manufacturing, healthcare, transportation, and infrastructure.
- **Key Benefits:** Supports predictive maintenance, improved design, operational efficiency, and cost reduction.

All these definitions are adding new features or clarifying some aspects with respect to this concept. From a practical perspective, the INCOSE definition provided in Section 1.1.2 provides a simple, clear, and formalized definition of it. It will be used as a baseline in this book. In spite of its simplicity, there is a need to characterize the DT by means of properties that can help in capturing features, requirements, and constraints for development and operation. There is a need to describe a DT in terms of properties that span the foundational, software, business aspects of it.

1.3.1 DT Properties

The definition guiding this book is derived from [7]: "The digital twin is the constant association between a (physical) object and its software representations within a virtualized environment. Events, actions, features, status, data, and all the other information characterizing the object are to be timely reflected by the logical (software) object (and vice versa)." The association between the physical object[1] and the DT can be characterized by properties. In this definition, the environment in which the physical object operates is an important element to consider and represent. The following properties are not mandatory, but at least some are needed to adequately qualify the relationships between physical and software counterparts. They can be categorized into different classes:

1. **Foundational Properties:** These represent major features that characterize the relationships between the physical object, its environment, and the representing DT. They are foundational because they characterize the most important aspects of a DT.

1 The object can be a system, a concept, a process, or other entities that can be described by data and behavior.

- Representational Capacity: The capability to represent by means of an effective model the physical object and the important aspects of the environment in which it is operating. This property is designed to achieve the highest possible *Representativeness and Contextualization* of the physical object and its different aspects that are associated with the model's objectives.
- Reflection: The DT ability to exactly mirror the status and behavior of the physical object under the circumstances dictated by the environment. In principle, observing the DT should provide the same information that can be found by observing the physical object. This expressive capability strongly relies on acquiring status data and structuring them into a model.
- Entanglement: The property of promptly reflecting changes in the physical object's status or environmental features that impact the DT representation. In principle, each change in the physical object and its environment should be immediately mirrored in the DT [7, 22–24].

2. **Software Properties:** The DT, as a software implementation, should benefit from some specific properties that characterize it as a system. In particular:
   - Communication: It is a software property strongly related to entanglement, i.e., the ability to timely communicate changes in status between the physical and software instances. This communication can be unidirectional (typically from the physical entity to the software one) or bidirectional. In the first case, the DT functions as a digital shadow of a physical asset [25, 26]. In other cases, it serves as a medium for exchanging information between the two counterparts, implicitly enabling the transmission of requests and commands from the software element to the physical one.
   - Replication: If needed, a DT (or parts of it) could be replicated several times for serving user demand. Still, the coordination (and sometimes consistency) between the different replicas must be maintained. This property can be useful when a specific replica is devoted to specific goals, or it can be used for studying particular behavior or is allocated to a specific client.
   - Persistency: The DT must remain available even if the physical object fails or communication is lost, as it serves as a persistent, digital representation of the system. The DT should guarantee at least the possibility to represent the latest available information. In some cases, the expected behavior could be predicted by means of AI technologies [27] or by interpolation even in the absence of direct communication between the DT and the physical object.
   - Memorization: The DT should collect and maintain historical data that can be used to understand and evaluate the DT behavior over time. The data could be stored with timestamps and location indications to allow an interpretation in time and space [28–31]. This property can be exploited for predictive analysis of the state evolution of the physical object.

- Composability: This is the possibility to aggregate different parts (as DTs) and to build a larger and consistent DT representing a complex physical object [32, 33]. Composability is useful to separate concerns about the parts of a physical object and to recompose them into an entity that maintains the consistency of itself and that of its constituents. Components can also be individually analyzed and reused in other DTs.
- Accountability/Manageability: A DT must be managed along an entire object life cycle and, in different forms, it should be integrated and managed as a software entity within platforms. This property ensures that a DT can be managed as a software entity throughout the entire life cycle of the physical object [13]. Additionally, it accounts for system resources required to support the software representation and the users accessing its services [34].
- Augmentation: Assures that when a DT is implemented, a well-defined interface is always included. A DT Application Programming Interface (API) allows for structured interactions between different parts of the DT system as well as for its usage and control of DT by external applications [35]. The APIs support the integration and reuse of the DT or parts of it, and they contribute to extending and augmenting functionalities offered by the DT over those provided by the physical object. In fact, the DT, being a software entity, can be improved and enriched with new functionalities quicker and more often than a physical entity. This property is important for exploiting the possibility to incrementally add new functions and capabilities to the DT.
- Predictability: A core capability of a DT is its ability to predict a PS's future behavior. This is achieved through two complementary methods. First, as a defining characteristic of DTs [36], simulation allows for modeling the object's behavior in various hypothetical contexts. Second, by leveraging its memorization property, a DT can store large historical datasets (typically time series). This enables the application of Artificial Intelligence (AI) algorithms [37] to predict future states based on past data. The integration of these two convergent capabilities—simulation and AI—significantly enhances the DTs overall predictive power [27, 38].

3. **Business Properties:** A DT can be used to satisfy the business requirements of several actors. Replication and augmentation properties can help in developing different replicas of the DT designed to fulfill the business requirements of stakeholders. In addition, due to the possibility of executing different instances of DT, it is also important to keep track of their usage. This yields to some business-related properties:
   - Ownership: This property is useful to associate specific stakeholders or users to their specific DT replica. This association may be needed to specialize DT functions and data to specific responsibilities or ownership. A DT instance, running for a government, can be different than one running for

a citizen. Ownership attribution can also be useful for restricting the scope or capabilities enabled by augmentation, as well as for accessing privileged historical data. A DT can thus extend the challenges related to "data ownership"; [39] to include behavioral and usage-related aspects.

- Servitization: This is the ability to transform a product into a service by means of software. Servitization is increasingly important in many enterprises and systems [40, 41]. Due to its capabilities, a DT aligns well with this perspective, as it facilitates the creation of new services and applications by means of APIs and augmentation. A DT serves as a key enabler in supporting servitization [42–44].

4. **Additional Properties:** The listed properties are only a few examples of the features that can be associated with the relationship between a physical object and its software counterpart. This list is not exhaustive, as new properties can and will be incorporated based on the evolving needs for representing the physical object within a DT. On the other hand, they are not necessarily mandatory; some may be selected based on the type and objectives of the software implementation. Examples of additional properties are as follows, which may also point to previously discussed features:
   - Suitability: Evaluates how well the DT definition, its functionalities, and its interfaces align with the needs and requirements of applications. The combination of representational capacity, reflection, and augmentation can align to the applications' requirements. Extensibility of the DT could be seen as another complementary property.
   - Scalability: This property, together with manageability, replication, and ownership, guarantees that the DT system can support the growing needs of applications.
   - Responsiveness: Is strongly related to entanglement and augmentation. It ensures that the response time of the entire DT system is satisfactory with respect to applications' needs.
   - *Other properties* can be progressively identified and added to the list.

A DT architecture and implemented frameworks, see Figure 1.1, should accommodate these properties and should also be designed to incrementally add new emerging properties aligned with applications' requirements. In other words, the DT should be a means to permit applications to interact as if they were interacting with the physical object but with some guaranteed quality of service (QoS) determined by the selected properties.

The environment plays a crucial role. The DT definition and its supporting software framework should facilitate the development of a model representing both the physical object and, when necessary, the environment in which it operates. This ensures that if the environment influences the behavior or representation of the physical object, the DT can accurately capture and reflect these key features.

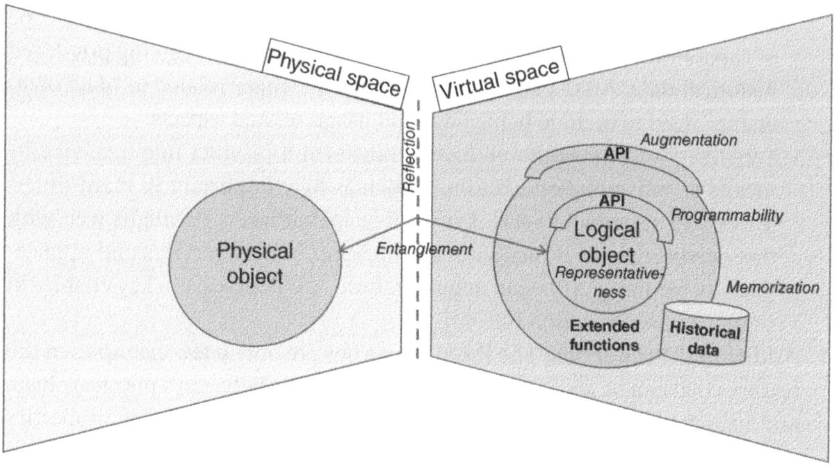

Figure 1.1 A representation of some DT properties.

1.4 DT Representation, Model, and More

A DT represents the key features of a physical entity, system, or object. This definition is closely linked to the concept of a model, which serves as an abstract representation of a system. The model incorporates archetypes, concepts, laws, rules, and relationships to represent the essential properties, components, and interactions of a system. Through these fundamental concepts, the model effectively characterizes the system.

Abstraction or conceptualization help in simplifying nonessential aspects of the system while representing the fundamental concepts that exemplify its functioning, life cycle, and relationships with other systems or environments. Many papers investigate the relationships between conceptual models and their physical world counterparts [45]. The representational capacity could have a dual meaning, i.e., the ability to describe and represent in a consistent way at a conceptual level (abstracting some details) the status and behavior of a PS; and/or the possibility to design a conceptual model that can be used to realize, implement, and use PSs according to a set of laws, rules, functions that satisfy specific needs and requirements.

The concept of a model and the activity of modeling have a very long history, and they were fundamental for defining cybernetics as the "science of models" [46]. In this context, Herbert Stachowiak [47] stated the basic properties of a model, which are:

1. Representation/reflection/mapping, i.e., the capability to represent the status and characteristics of "something" (e.g., a system).
2. Reduction, the model will describe and represent only the concepts, mechanisms, and relationships that are relevant to the modeler.
3. Pragmatism, models are not built *per se*, they allow a system to be conceptualized to serve a scope, for someone to use, and for a certain timeframe.

These definitions or conceptualization of a model fit well with the concept of DT as a model serving the scope of different stakeholders over a period of time (e.g., the life cycle of a product).

The properties described in Section 1.3 are aligned with these concepts. In fact, they extend and further characterize the DT from several viewpoints comprising representational capacity, software implementation, and business aspects.

The definition of a DT includes different model views of a system. There is an increasing interest in the separation of concerns between different aspects of the representational capacity: descriptive, behavior, and predictive modeling are emerging, especially in the field of business analytics and decision-making [48–50]. These aspects have also risen, with different peculiarities, in the manufacturing problem domain [51]. The progress in this area also has an influence on the DT modeling [52] and the consolidation of viable models.

The need to focus on behavior models of a system in a data-driven era has also emerged [53, 54]. They highlight a modern shift in DT development. Instead of simply creating a static, descriptive replica of a physical object, the focus is now on building a **behavioral model**. This means the DT is designed to simulate and predict the system's dynamic responses to various inputs and conditions. This approach allows for a more efficient and effective analysis and control of complex, real-world systems by focusing on what the system *does* rather than just what it *is*.

ETSI has identified and classified DT abstractions (or types). This classification focuses on models usable for representing a physical entity as a DT [55–58], yielding to basic definitions that can be used to clarify some of the different capabilities of DT model types:

1. **Descriptive:** Represents the different data needed and their conceptual organization to describe relevant features and states of a PS [59]. Different data models may be needed to feed the representation of a DT [60].
2. **Predictive:** Is the ability to use a combination of statistics, ML and general artificial intelligence algorithms to predict the expected behavior of a physical object tied to a DT [61].
3. **Prospective:** Is the ability to represent the system aiming at analyzing special cases starting from different initial states or by altering some basic conditions of the DTn. This type of model is used to create and observe "what-if" situations, exploiting the historical data and the expected behavior of the DT.

4. **Prescriptive:** This representation capability is based on historical datasets, current data, and behavior analysis to support decision-making processes. A prescriptive model will determine what are the best possible actions that the DT (and its corresponding physical object) should perform to optimize the DT response to the current situation and circumstances.
5. **Diagnostic or Prognostic:** Is the ability to identify and understand the causes of diversion of the DT and the physical object from the expected states and results.

A fundamental requirement for creating a DT, however, is the availability of a **behavior model**, i.e., the ability to represent a physical object's contextualized behavior within its operating environment. Behavior representation is crucial for understanding how a PS and its corresponding DT respond to events under specific conditions, which are characterized by descriptive state data. Designing a behavior model is difficult, in fact, behavior modeling is a critical activity in the software engineering of large systems, encompassing the creation, maintenance, and continuous updating of models that represent and predict the dynamic interactions and responses of a system [62]. One of the aspects to be modeled in a DT is the dynamic behavior of the physical entity (and hence of the DT) in response to events and changes of status [52, 63, 64]. Also, Model-based Systems Engineering (MBSE) methodologies are being increasingly investigated for their potential ability to represent system behavior using DTs [65].

During the design phase, it is essential to develop an actionable, effective, and complete model of the expected and intended DT actions, ensuring they accurately reflect the real behavior of the corresponding physical object. For this purpose, different methods can be used and integrated: behavior modeling [66, 67]; methodologies like Unified Modeling Language (UML), or Systems Modeling Language (SYSML), or others [68–70]; state, data flow, and action diagrams (e.g., [71]); and modeling tools [72–75]. The definition of a behavior model is an essential aspect, i.e., the goal that has to be considered in the design, implementation, and testing of a DT. Many tools and methodologies are focusing on ways and procedures to facilitate the process of behavior modeling of DTs [76–78].

A continuous behavior modeling process is considered in this book as a fundamental necessity for DTs definition and construction. The modeling process can align with ETSI standards to accurately describe a physical object through an updatable and evolving model in which descriptive and behavior models together form the foundation of an actionable DT [79], enabling real-time representation of the asset's condition and dynamic behavior.

However, there is a difference in perspective between the data-driven modeling approach, as represented by ETSI, and the behavior-oriented methodology, such as MBSE, in how they define and construct a DT. At a high level, the former emphasizes a data-centric approach (descriptive modeling) focusing on continuous data flows from existing systems, while the latter serves as a comprehensive methodology for defining and designing new systems through behavior models.

For the modeling of a DT, it is important to recognize that it is a multi-component system integrating physical assets, communication layers, data management middleware, and software models. These components together form a virtual representation that should accurately reflect the physical object's properties, behavior, and interactions.

The approach advocated and adopted in this book for modeling a DT—defined as the process of defining, developing, and refining its representation—is based on integrating various model aspects using dedicated modeling tools and methodologies. This approach combines organized data and corresponding usable data models with the explicit formulation of intended and expected system behavior within a behavior framework. Two critical and integrated aspects must be addressed: ensuring availability of up-to-date data supported by well-structured data models and providing a sound description of the system's expected behavior. By integrating data and behavior in the DT architecture, a richer and more actionable representation of the PS's operation is achieved.

A DT that only captures and visualizes the physical object's data—such as its current and historical states—can be characterized as a passive DT. While useful for monitoring, this approach lacks the ability to interpret or predict system behavior. Conversely, a DT that relies solely on behavior models, without alignment to real-time or historical data, functions as a theoretical DT: it describes possible behaviors in theory but cannot accurately reflect the actual state or dynamics of the PS.

A truly effective DT emerges from the integration of both data and behavior models, as depicted in Section 4.1. This integration supports advanced predictive models, where historical and current data are leveraged to forecast future states and behaviors of the physical object. By initializing simulations with real data and applying behavior models, the DT can not only predict outcomes but also explain the underlying causes of past events—enhancing both diagnostic and prospective analysis.

Such capabilities enable the DT to evolve beyond monitoring, supporting diagnostic functions (identifying malfunctions based on observed and simulated data), and prospective functions (recommending actions to optimize performance). When these predictive and prescriptive features are combined with autonomous decision-making, the DT transitions into an autonomic DT, capable of self-management and adaptation to changing conditions [27]. The fusion of data-driven and behavior-driven approaches is fundamental to realizing the full potential of DTs, enabling systems that are descriptive, predictive, prescriptive, and ultimately autonomous.

However, the adoption of different models characterizes various types of DTs. A DT can be designed and developed by leveraging the capabilities and relationships of these diverse models, as illustrated in Figure 1.2. It is crucial to decide early in the design process which type of DT to implement, as the functions and components required by a passive DT differ significantly from those needed for an autonomic DT. Scaling up a DT may not always be straightforward or feasible. The choice of model greatly influences the complexity and approach of the modeling activities and their subsequent implementation.

The use of different models, along with their potential applications and utilization, is outlined in Sections 2.2 and 4.1. Further details on descriptive and behavior models are respectively provided in Chapters 3 and 4. The implementation patterns for these models are illustrated in Chapter 5.

Despite the strong relationship between DTs and models, a DT relies on the continuous availability of data, requiring its behavior to adapt to reality. However, the discrepancy between real data and expected values generated by the behavior model presents an opportunity to refine the model and determine corrective actions to reconcile theoretical and real data. This can be achieved by adjusting the behavior model and guiding the PS toward the expected range of values. The ability to interact with and control its physical counterpart allows the DT to go beyond a mere static model, making it a more powerful, adaptive, and dynamic tool, as discussed in Refs. [80, 81].

The nature of a DT can be elusive, ranging from a simple data model to a purely behavioral representation of a physical object. However, its true power lies in the integration of a data model, capturing current and past data, and offering the possibility to predict future states, with a behavior model that represents the actions and events driving state changes. This integration forms the foundation for more advanced DTs, capable of achieving high levels of autonomy in their behavior.

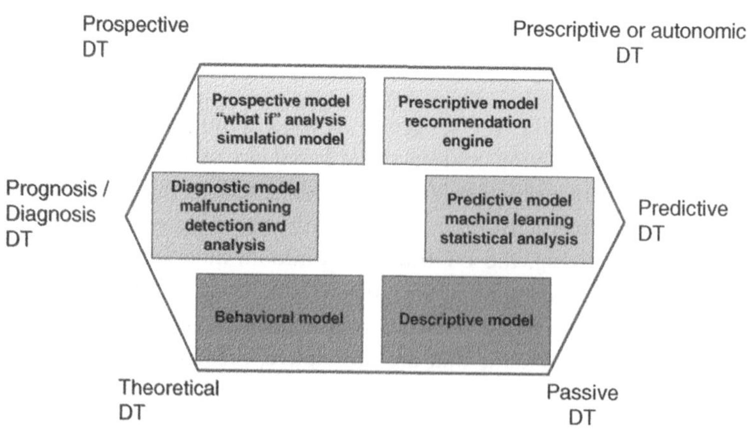

Figure 1.2 Models and different types of DT.

1.5 The Software Part of a DT

The DT is a software-intensive system; as such, it should be developed and operated in an optimized manner. A software architecture, in the terms described in Section 1.1.1, is a means to optimize the development of a large software system by exploiting existing guidelines and organizing its components according to segmentation or layering that introduces separation of concerns and reusability. A software architecture is an important aspect of DT development because a DT should last over time and, generally, is a large project that needs continuous update and extension. A proper and flexible service architecture can serve to the scope of easing the evolution and reuse of functions, components, and interfaces of the DT. A software implementation of a DT represents the dynamic state of its corresponding physical object by leveraging available data and a digital model of the relevant phenomena. Usually, the DT is tied and constrained by the peculiar physical object's characteristics and specificity in such a way that limits generality and reuse of components and approaches. The strong correspondence and interdependence between the physical object's unique characteristics and its software implementation present both benefits and drawbacks: the software representations are easier to understand and fully aligned with the real world; however, they emphasize diversity over generality and specialization. A DT implementation risks failing to leverage key principles of software reuse and design, including generalization, abstraction, and specialization-based reuse. DT software approaches are striving to maintain objectivity and strong ties to reality as well as to create a large library of reusable parts, concepts, and tools for supporting the creation and evolution of large DT projects [77].

There are several platforms claiming the capability to help the quick development of DTs [33, 82]. Some of them also support different facets of the design and specification of DTs and identify and provide patterns of development [67, 83, 84]. A truly complete platform has not yet emerged and current propositions are either generic or they focus on specific aspects (e.g., data management, or visualization) and lack important capabilities with respect to relevant facets of the DT implementation. The identification of actionable patterns of representation is a major goal for DT platforms.

1.5.1 D Architecture and Development Approach

To achieve the goal of rapid and comprehensive DT development, a well-structured architecture is essential. Throughout this book, an exemplary DT architecture will be utilized to illustrate key requirements and possible solutions. Then Chapter 2 will introduce modeling concepts and their implications for architectural models and components. Chapters 3 and 4 will explore descriptive and behavioral aspects, identifying relevant architectural functional decomposition and separations of concerns. Finally, Chapter 5 will provide insights into defining a fully-fledged architectural vision for DTs.

1.5.2 An Introductory DT Architecture

At a high level, a DT architecture comprises several core containers and subsystems, as illustrated in Figure 1.3. The representation follows a simplified architecture model based on the system context level definition of the C4 software methodology [85].

While C4 provides an initial representational framework, other methodologies can also be applied. In fact, the incremental definition of this architecture will utilize various methodologies, prioritizing a conceptual emphasis over strict

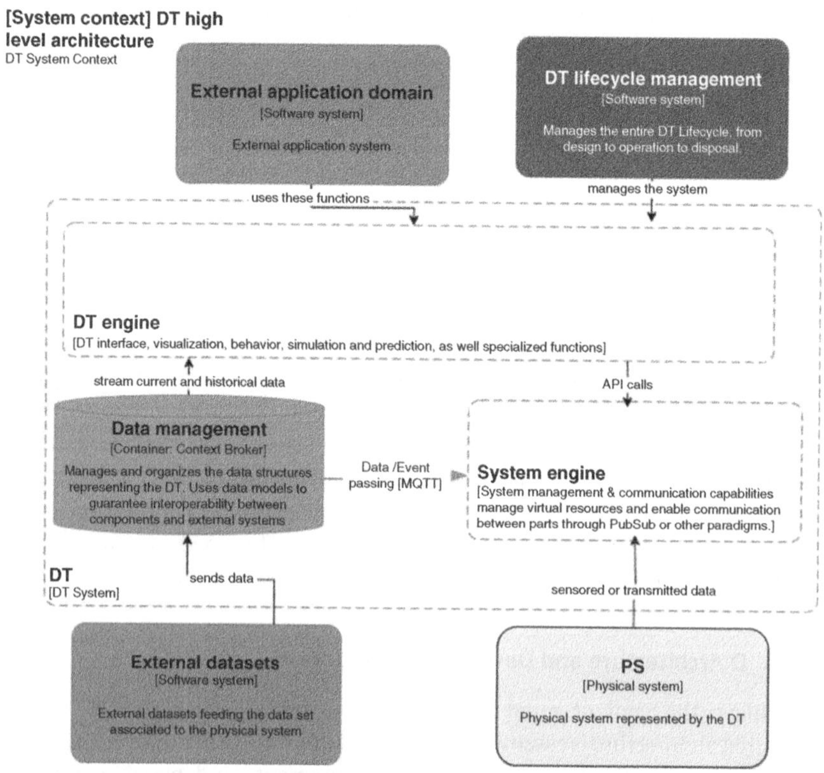

Figure 1.3 System context view of a DT architecture.

adherence to any single framework. This approach ensures that the architectural representation highlights fundamental driving concepts rather than enforcing consistency with a specific methodology.

The envisaged architecture is based on the segmentation of subsystems and their functionalities. Each of them should be capable of interacting with the other by means of well-defined interfaces and passing of messages. Some subsystems are aimed at supporting enabling functionalities like communication and interactions between modules, allocation, orchestration, and management of computing resources. Others are focusing on the core functions like mapping real-time data to well-formed data models, or the execution of actions and functions in synchronous with the behavior of the PS. Since the DT is defined to serve the goals of different stakeholders, specialized logic exploiting data or behavior of the DT can be executed on top of the framework by means of well-formed APIs. The **external application domain** represents a set of applications that use or add additional functions to the **DT system**.

A DT architecture should offer a **data management subsystem** capable of managing the required data by capturing them through interactions with the physical object, its environment, and other data sources that can provide meaningful data to characterize it. These data will be organized into well-defined data models. Data models are also important for dealing with attributes and data types utilized to represent the PS as well for supporting the exchange of parameters internally and externally to the whole DT platform in a standardized and clear way. The contextualized data are made available for usage by the **DT engine**. This subsystem is devoted to the integration of the behavioral, predictive, and simulation parts of the DT. It also includes additional functions specific to the application domain or PS, such as prescriptive analysis, diagnosis, visualization, and interfaces for external applications. The communication, system and resource management is provided by a **system engine subsystem**. It is in charge of supporting the management of the infrastructure supporting the DT, guaranteeing the resource optimization and the manageability of the entire system. A **DT lifecycle management subsystem** covers the different phases of DT's life-cycle: it supports design and implementation (a sort of DT development environment) of DT components; it provides requirements and descriptions for controlling and optimizing the execution of the DT system with respect to the capabilities offered by the system engine during operations; and it intervenes for critical events management allowing humans to determine or choose actions to be executed (proposed, suggested by the DT itself or proactively selected by humans). Further details of a DT supporting architecture are provided in Section 5.1.

1.6 Specification Methodologies

The DT can be supported by modern methodologies that assist in the design and specification of large systems. MBSE [86, 87] is a branch of system engineering strongly related to the definition and specification of DTs. It provides methodologies and tools for the design and specification of systems and their parts. A set of different views of such systems are defined and supported by languages and tools (see, for instance, SYSML [88]). This methodology can also be complemented by other approaches such as Modular Open Systems Approach (MOSA) [89]. It requires an extended system componentization and the identification of well-defined interfaces for each component. This is very aligned with the needs of an open, extensible, and flexible architecture. It also focuses on open interfaces. The combination of system design methodologies plus modularization and interface definition can push toward the consolidation of approaches and tools for creating more general-purpose DT platforms. SYSML 2.0 [90] goes in this direction. However, a few points related to system design methodologies should be emphasized:

- The main goal of these methodologies is to support the design and specification of new systems and, if possible, their integration with existing ones. These methodologies have an implicit **top-down approach** that is particularly useful for new products or objects.
- Due to their generality, these methodologies do not explicitly address the need to complete the specifications with software code. Even if some tools are closing this gap, the MBSE technologies have, as main goal, the system design and specification.
- They do not pursue the goal to support the integrated development of a DT representation alongside the specification of the PS.
- A bottom-up approach, i.e., the modeling of existing systems, is not necessarily supported or easy to implement.
- AI functions are typically integrated into a system as modular components, failing to be considered as an integral part of the specification process or a fundamental element of a DT.

These issues may have an impact on the design and definition of software platforms that can help in the construction of DTs. There is still a need to focus on current methodologies and technologies, and to reuse and compose them to create a viable DT architecture and development environment.

1.6.1 Designing a DT Based on Available Specifications of a PS

Designing a DT based on system specifications involves defining and detailing various aspects that are under the control of designers. These aspects determine the DT's behavior, rules, and interfaces in accordance with explicit requirements and purposes, ensuring alignment with the PS's definition. In a way, they describe why and how a system (and its DT) behaves in a certain manner. In this approach, DT creation can be facilitated by incorporating specific interfaces within the PS specification—such as data structures and related APIs—that represent essential information characterizing the DT. A key advantage of this method is that the PS's state transitions and behavior models can be shared, enabling the DT to fully mirror the PS.

These interfaces—built-in data communication mechanisms between the PS and the DT, shared model specifications, and defined data endpoints—not only allow seamless interaction but also enable the DT to exert control over the physical object. This approach follows an inside-out design strategy, where the internal details of the PS are specified to achieve the desired and acceptable behavior for the DT.

1.6.2 Designing a DT Without Previous System Specifications

Designing a DT for a PS that has not been specified with these technologies, e.g., the specifications are not shareable, or they do not even exist at all, needs a different approach. The designers are observers of an existing system, and they have to determine the rules and data governing the system's functioning. Data are captured by measuring system behavior's effects on the environment, and they are used to capture the rules and laws that govern these actions. A DT, in this case, is a representation of how a system is behaving and how it is impacting the environment. Sometimes, it can be very difficult to understand and represent different parts of the system to be monitored and controlled. This is a sort of outside-in design, i.e., observing a system to understand and determine the internal functions of its parts and subsystems. Governing the PS can be extremely difficult under these conditions, because the DT has very few means to drive or control the physical object's behavior.

1.6.3 Understanding the Physical System Behavior

Another differentiation emerges in these design approaches: the ability to clearly understand and specify the system's behavior. In the first case, the expected behavior is defined by means of shared specifications. Some unintended effects can emerge, but they can be reconducted to the expected behavior carried out under uncertainty or border circumstances [3]. Simulations or checks on constraints and requirements can help mitigate these issues. On the other case, there are no specifications. Representing the behavior and data transformation by observations introduces different issues. Grasping the emerging behavior of a system can take a long time to be well-understood and adequately represented by a DT. In this case, determining or simulating the system behavior under critical circumstances or difficult situations can be very complex and hard to achieve. A sort of bottom-up approach in the identification of salient DT's characteristics can be conceived for this situation. It is based on a progressive refinement and consolidation of the PS model and, consequently, of its DT aiming at approaching a factual and actionable specification and implementation.

These two approaches represent the "extremes" that are possible in the characterization of a DT, they stress the possibility of exploring its design considering "inside-out" vs. "outside-in" methods as well as a "top-down" vs. a "bottom-up" modeling.

1.7 Domain Knowledge and Operation in DTs

Two other topics are relevant in this introductory chapter. They are related to the transposition of domain-specific knowledge into the DT and the way in which enterprises need to operate processes and systems to fully exploit the DT capabilities. A successful DT project needs to integrate in-house knowledge as well as to prove its value and show the advantages of transforming processes and consolidated procedures in an enterprise for better efficiency and responsiveness.

1.7.1 The Role of Domain-specific Knowledge and Technologies

Domain-specific knowledge and technologies are central to the effective construction, validation, and operation of DTs. This knowledge spans the entire system life cycle—from initial concept and design, through deployment and operation, to maintenance and decommissioning. Embedding domain expertise ensures the DT accurately models the PS's behaviors, constraints, and environmental interactions, enabling high-fidelity representation and predictive capabilities.

Domain knowledge involves multiple facets, including physical characteristics, regulatory requirements, safety constraints, and operational processes unique to the system's context. Systems engineers and domain experts collaborate to elicit, formalize, and maintain this knowledge, ensuring the DT evolves consistently with its physical counterpart. In order to optimize system requirements elicitation and extract relevant knowledge needed for the definition, construction, and operation of a DT in enterprises, the usage of large language models has been considered [91]. This approach could minimize the effort of personnel required to formalize knowledge while simultaneously enabling the capture of relevant information and its formal representation. However, for the time being, human supervision is recommended to avoid false information and hallucinations.

Equally important is the full involvement of enterprise management and operational personnel. Their engagement facilitates alignment of the DT with established workflows and corporate culture, fostering acceptance, and effective use. Lack of such organizational integration has been identified as a key failure factor in several DT initiatives [92]. Conversely, exemplars like Rolls-Royce's DT implementation demonstrate that embedding DT within operational processes and securing stakeholder buy-in are vital to realizing measurable business value, such as predictive maintenance and reduced downtime [93, 94].

1.7.2 Operational Context: Bridging IT and OT Domains

The operation of DTs is positioned at the intersection of IT and OT domains, each with distinct characteristics and requirements. IT encompasses data management, analytics, security, and software life-cycle support, while OT focuses on real-time control, safety, and physical process monitoring.

The operational environment is shaped by the enterprise's technology platform, its traditional operational processes, and organizational culture. Successful DT operation demands accommodating these heterogeneities through adaptable integration architectures, robust data governance, and operational workflows that bridge both IT and OT domains.

Ensuring interoperability, real-time responsiveness, and security in combination with scenario simulation and assessment of possible options requires collaboration across software engineering, systems engineering, domain expertise, and operations. The combined influence of technological infrastructure, process maturity, and organizational practices makes the operational dimension a fundamental factor in DT adoption and sustained effectiveness [1, 93].

An adaptable software architecture capable of exposing diverse facets and functions of a DT to multiple organizational groups is crucial. For example, running "what-if" analyses alongside normal DT execution requires duplication and coordination of functionalities, while meticulous data acquisition, curation, and tagging ensure traceability and facilitate knowledge sharing. The operational model must therefore reflect the enterprise's readiness, culture, and collaborative ethos [95].

1.8 Clarifying Scope and Terminology for DT Architectures

The definition of architectures, functions, and platforms supporting DTs is shaped by a variegated panorama of efforts spanning standardization, consortia initiatives, and diverse industrial and research activities. Standardization efforts include the ISO 23247 framework [8] and ISO/IEC 30173 [96], which provide foundational terminology and architectural guidelines essential for interoperable DT deployment. Active consortia, such as the Digital Twin Consortium (DTC) [97] and the Industrial Digital Twin Association (IDTA) [98], coordinate industry collaboration to accelerate adoption and generate best practices. Complementing these, institutional organizations like the National Institute of Standards and Technology (NIST) [99] and the Industrial IoT Consortium (IIC) [100] contribute white papers and innovation forums that bridge academic research with practical applications.

Recent reports, such as the NIST Internal Report 8356 [101], emphasize the evolving and diverse definitions of DTs and stress the critical role of standards and cybersecurity in achieving interoperable and trustworthy implementations.

Industrial contributions from global leaders such as General Electric provide extensive documentation of DT implementations, combining physics-based modeling with AI to optimize asset performance and operations [102]. Dassault Systèmes advances the field through their virtual twin experiences, integrating simulation, AI, and collaboration tools in sectors from aerospace to manufacturing [103].

These efforts are enriched by other industrial and research contributions focusing on implementations, governance, and integration [104–106]. Leading cloud platforms, including Microsoft Azure DTs and AWS IoT TwinMaker, embody these standards and consortia-driven practices in current commercial solutions. This diverse literature complements academic studies by providing a comprehensive and applied view on current efforts to define and build reliable, scalable DT solutions for real-world development and usage. The focus of the next chapters is on progressing and extending the applicability of the DT concepts, enlarging applicability to additional problem domains as well as promoting newer approaches focusing on programmability and broader access to the DT technologies. These goals require extensions of concepts related to DT representation aiming at the identification of horizontal architectures and platforms. These goals aim at enlarging the possibility of building DT by reusing components and require additional research and experimentation.

1.8.1 D Architecture and Scope Definition

This work primarily focuses on software architecture, data and behavior representation, and software aspects applied to DTs. While these components are essential, it is important to note that they appear in a wide range of related domain solutions. However, the presence of such components does not necessarily constitute a DT. For example, control system engineering shares overlapping concerns, such as system definition and representation capabilities, but it is not necessarily considered a DT. The definitions and property identifications presented in this chapter aim to help classify solutions as DTs or as belonging to related fields such as control systems.

1.8.2 Evolving Terminology in DT Research

Authors refer, wherever possible, to existing academic literature, established standards, and current industrial approaches to define terminology consistently. However, the definition of a DT remains elusive and differentiated [107], transcending its original domain, i.e., manufacturing, and extending to new fields and application domains. The interpretation and concept of a DT have evolved significantly, especially with the increasing integration of AI models and tools.

Another major influence shaping the evolving concept of the DT is software architecture and service platform design. The aim is to transform the DT into a reusable framework composed of programmable components, enabling the creation of new applications and services. This evolution represents a departure from the traditional focus on modeling PSs.

For example, notions such as APIs and functional segmentation stem more from software architecture than from classical systems modeling. In addition, specific domains such as smart cities require tailored explanations of DT concepts suitable for systems that have evolved organically with limited initial design. Advances in the Internet of Things (IoT) and CPS continue to drive and expand the scope of DTs. Further evolution is anticipated as the DT concept is applied increasingly in medicine and physiology (modeling the human body) and in cultural heritage (digital humanities). This expansion will further enlarge the scope of DT representations and the associated terminology required to describe concepts specific to these problem domains. In the future, the scope of DTs is expected to expand beyond PSs, objects, products, and processes to include abstract concepts. This broader application reflects the growing capability of DT technology to represent, simulate, and analyze increasingly complex and intangible phenomena across diverse domains.

Consequently, terminology must adapt to this broadening scope and evolving objectives. The authors take the liberty of extending the meanings of established terms or introducing new terminology to improve conceptual clarity and enhance readers' understanding of the wide-ranging nature and applications of DTs.

This disclaimer is intended to clarify the authors' conscientious approach to terminology, aiming to fulfill standards of academic rigor while acknowledging the dynamic and interdisciplinary nature of this emerging field.

2

Models and Modeling Aspects of a DT

After reading this chapter, you should be able to:

- Understand the profound relationships between descriptive and behavior models.
- Identify different types of DT with respect to models.
- Identify different phases of modeling supporting the DT evolution and life cycle.
- Integrate models to support multi-facet representation of the physical system.

2.1 The Representational Aspects of a DT

The key constituent of a Digital Twin (DT) is an underlying representation of what the physical system (PS) is, its planned and expected behavior, its interactions with the environment, and its reactions to external conditions (see Section 1.1.2). The choice of a model influences the DT capabilities and its functions, as well as its possible evolution toward more complex representations. Depending on the goals and intended use of a DT, the modeling activity can be more or less complex. In many cases, the modeling should consider the PS's properties, its requirements and constraints, and the environment and its influence on the system's behavior.

A foundational step in designing a DT is establishing a cohesive governing logic that dictates how the PS operates under various conditions. This logic serves as a control structure for defining rules, states, and conditions, ensuring structured and predictable system behavior. Within this framework, key operating parameters, expected state transitions, and functional constraints are systematically outlined.

The system is designed to handle both expected and unexpected events efficiently. Expected events, such as routine sensor updates and predefined triggers, follow structured state transition logic, ensuring smooth progression based on known conditions.

For unexpected events, such as anomalies or system failures, the DT relies on predefined recovery actions to mitigate disruptions. These include fallback mechanisms, adaptive control strategies, and error-handling routines that restore functionality while maintaining stability. Sensors and real-time data continuously feed into the control logic, enabling the system to evaluate incoming information, determine necessary responses, and either trigger an expected state transition or execute a corrective action.

The hooks—built-in data communication mechanisms between the PS and the DT, shared model specifications, and defined data interfaces—not only enable seamless interaction but also allow the DT to exert control over its physical counterpart. This approach refers to an inside-out design strategy, where the internal details of the PS are specified to achieve resilient, adaptive, and goal-oriented behavior for the DT.

For large-scale systems organized in this way, sensors and real-time data continuously feed into the control logic, providing situation awareness that helps the system evaluate when actions must be taken. Transition mechanisms must also account for interdependencies between components, ensuring smooth coordination as the system moves from one state to another without disruptions. By embedding a holistic control framework, the DT ensures that state changes and operational commands follow a structured, logical progression—allowing for adaptive behavior, precision in execution, and alignment with real-world dynamics.

In an "outside-in" DT approach for large systems, control logic is minimal and primarily driven by observation of system behavior. Instead of enforcing predefined rules, the DT monitors real-world data, evaluates the effects of system actions, and refines future responses. The DT relies on pattern recognition, probabilistic decision-making, and machine learning (ML) to improve predictions and recommendations over time. Rather than directly controlling the PS, it serves as an advisory model, influencing optimizations based on observed trends. This method is widely applied in complex environments such as smart cities, industrial systems (for optimization), and environmental monitoring.

2.1.1 The Importance of Environment Representation

A PS may be influenced by environmental changes to varying degrees. For instance, modeling a fruit plant must account for the orchard structure, geographical location, and weather variations, as these factors significantly impact its behavior. In contrast, a crash test may be minimally affected by environmental conditions such as temperature or humidity, as they have little relevance to the primary measurements being taken. A critical aspect of DT modeling involves determining which environmental features are relevant and should be integrated into the PS's representation (the model). Identifying these key influences ensures that the resulting DT model accurately captures the system's behavior under real-world environmental conditions, enhancing its fidelity and usefulness.

2.1.2 Physical System Life cycle and Development of DT

An important challenge in DT design is the lack of complete methodologies or tools that fully support its development and extensions across the entire life cycle of a PS. The relationships between the DT and its life cycle are discussed in Section 6.2, focusing on operational aspects.

Four major phases are considered:

- **Creation and Design Phase**, where the PS is conceived, designed, and prototyped.
- **Production Phase**, covering development, testing, and deployment.
- **Operations Phase**, involving system management, maintenance, and continuous improvements.
- **Disposal Phase**, where the system is decommissioned.

Each of these phases impacts the DT. Being a software artifact, the DT is continuously updated and refined to enhance its manageability and increase its functionality (manageability and augmentation properties) and to improve its representation of the PS (reflection property).

A key design principle is: **If the goal is to develop both the PS and its DT, it is preferable to design them in parallel throughout the entire life cycle of the PS.** This approach helps in early identification of key interactions, data structures, and models that should be shared between the PS and its DT, ensuring alignment and minimizing later modifications.

The interaction aspect is particularly important, as it serves as a key distinguishing characteristic of the DT, closely linked to the concept of entanglement. If the PS only transmits data to the DT, its design impact remains limited compared to the potential of bidirectional communication. In a bidirectional setup, the DT can send messages that actively modify the state of the PS, enabling operational control. This capability necessitates structuring the PS to receive and implement commands or policies issued by the DT. In essence, the DT acts as a supervisor overseeing the PS, which, in turn, functions as an autonomous agent within its operating environment.

Attempting to first design the PS and then its DT separately may lead to misalignment of models and functionality, requiring costly changes that may render the initial PS design obsolete. A best practice is to integrate DT development as a core part of the PS design process, ensuring continuity and adaptability. Even if the DT is not immediately implemented, designing the PS with a mock DT model can bring future advantages without significant upfront investment.

Another critical decision is the type of DT to develop: a passive DT is relatively simple to realize, focusing on monitoring and representing the PS. An autonomic DT introduces complexity by actively influencing system operations and decision-making. Changing the scope from passive to autonomic can significantly impact the design process and entire life cycle of the PS, requiring careful planning.

2.1.3 Modeling Aspects and Their Relationships

The actual design, specification, and implementation of a DT involve significant integration between different modeling activities [108–110]. Because DT modeling spans the entire life cycle, backpropagating changes from a later DT phase to earlier design stages, or adjusting corresponding PS phases, can be time-consuming and costly. To improve efficiency without overburdening the PS development cycle, avoiding unnecessary backpropagation of modifications across phases is crucial for maintaining consistency and optimizing workflow [111–113].
Figure 2.1 shows that changes in behavior, descriptive, or other models will create the need to change characteristics of their dependent aspects. This is particularly true for basic modeling: changes in behavior or in data representations

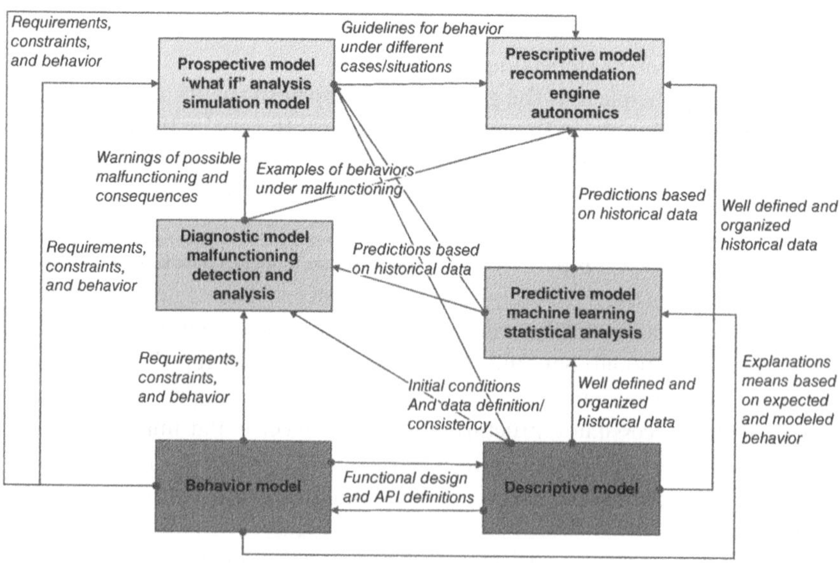

Figure 2.1 Relationships and dependencies between different models for a DT.

will rapidly propagate to other modeling aspects, requiring updates and adaptations to the entire modeling chain. While changes in predictive or simulation tools and technologies may have a limited effect, modifications to behavior or data representation, or the addition of new functions, can have a more significant impact on other models.

2.1.4 Cascade and Parallel Life cycles

A PS designed to natively interact with its DT will perform actions (e.g., state information collection and its forwarding to the DT) and execute additional functions that increase the PS's functional complexity and, thus, make it substantially different from an isolated PS. Two examples of the execution of life-cycle-related activities can simplify the differences between a cascade and an integrated approach to the construction, deployment, operation, maintenance, and disposal of a twinned PS.

In the construction and operation of large systems, changes to support new or needed operations and management processes can have a significant impact on the design and production phases of the PS itself, requiring, for example, improvements in specifications and implementation. Keeping the design of a PS and its DT separated increases the possibility that a change required for one of the two systems could have an unclear impact on the other. Figure 2.2 shows a simplified case in which a PS is designed before conceiving and developing its DT. In this example, the construction and deployment (product phase) of the PS ends and the DT construction begins. Typically, this implies that the PS has been defined without considering the required interactions and exchange of data between the physical and twin systems. The consequences of adding a DT can lead to the need to modify the specifications and, more importantly, require the modification of a consistent part of the PS's implementation. Both of these changes can disrupt operations and management processes.

An integrated development and operational approach that treats the DT as a subsystem of the PS ensures their life cycle phases remain closely linked. By considering the DT's requirements, such as data acquisition, interactions, and functionality, from the outset, the need for later modifications to the PS can be significantly reduced.

These requirements also relate to key properties of the DT definition. For example, the model features should be consistent between the DT and its physical counterpart, ensuring seamless interaction and accurate representation. Additionally, mechanisms should be in place to support reflection, entanglement, and state memorization, reinforcing the DT's ability to mirror and respond to changes in the PS. These and other fundamental properties should be natively embedded into the specification and implementation of the twinned system to maintain fidelity and operational effectiveness.

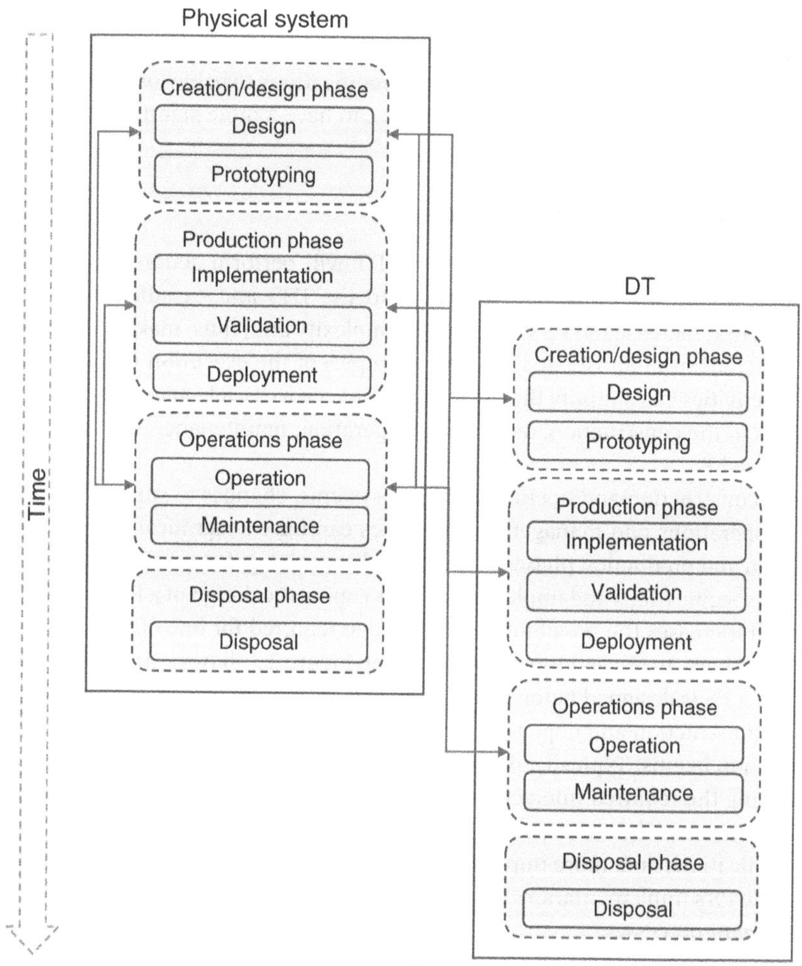

Figure 2.2 Separated life cycles of a PS and its DT.

Figure 2.3 shows an integrated construction of a PS and its DT. Changes to one subsystem can be quickly implemented on the other one. The single arrows indicate the flows of changes triggered by new needs in Operations and Maintenance (O&M). They propagate to implementation and design activities and from here to the same activities in the DT counterpart till they reach the operations phase activities. On the other side, changes in operation and management in the DT could have impacts on the PS. For instance, adding maintenance capabilities for improving DT functions could have consequences on the PS management process, requiring more operations and pushing for extra attention from maintainers.

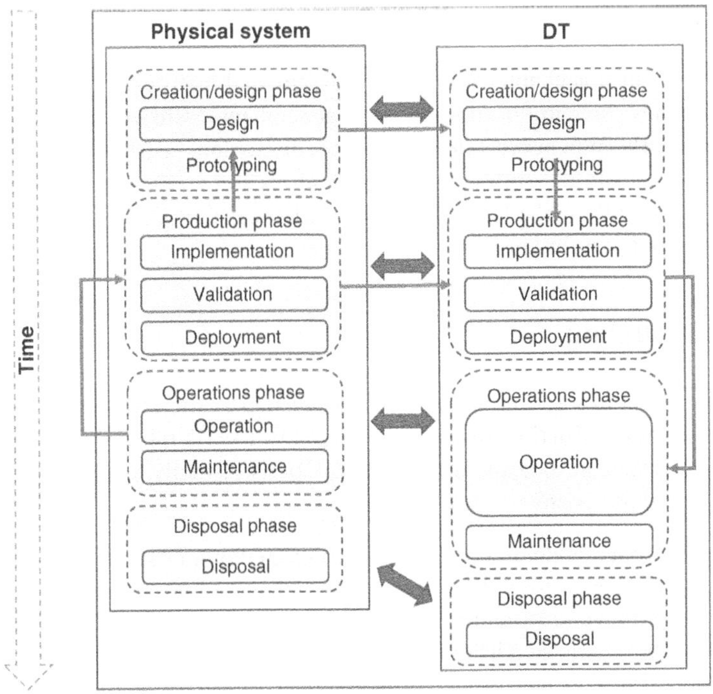

Figure 2.3 A PS and its DT as two integrated subsystems during the life cycle.

The relationships between operations, maintenance, and disposal of a PS, and its DT, may differ due to the DT's persistent property. Unlike the PS, which follows a finite life cycle, a DT can extend beyond the PS's operational lifespan, necessitating specialized and long-term maintenance. This extended maintenance ensures the DT remains relevant and functional even after the PS is decommissioned, allowing for historical analysis, optimization insights, and potential reuse. Moreover, these prolonged DT activities can contribute to the development of an enhanced next-generation PS by leveraging accumulated knowledge, refined models, and improved operational strategies.

Even if a specific methodology is not formally applied, SYSML, especially in its v.2.0, is considered as a basis for illustrating some features or issues in the modeling and in the general construction of DT. As discussed in Ref. [88], SYSML offers different functionalities for supporting specifications. A special attention is devoted to the definition of behavior and structure features that are instrumental to behavior model and architecture definition, with particular attention to the decomposition and identification of interfaces between the components. In this interpretation, the structuring also comprises the use of data models, i.e., descriptive capabilities.

The second part of this chapter introduces fundamental features of DT modeling and examines their implications for the general representation of a DT software framework. Whenever relevant to the discussion, aspects such as requirement and constraint capture, as well as analysis and verification, will be considered—particularly when focusing on simulation capabilities for assessing system behavior and performance.

2.2 Data Modeling

Data modeling structures and organizes the data related to the representation, functioning, and results of actions of a system [114, 115]. The DT representation is strongly based on available data and their representations. Actually, a data model, from a more formal perspective, is described as [116]:

> **Data Model**: A data model is a conceptual representation of data, its relationships, and its constraints within a particular domain or information system. It serves as a precise structure that defines what data is to be collected and how it will be organized. The model is typically technology-independent and provides a common, consistent, and predictable way of managing data resources.
>
> **Data Modeling**: Data modeling is the formal, structured, and iterative process of creating a data model. This process involves analyzing an organization's data requirements and representing them visually or textually to facilitate communication among stakeholders. The goal is to ensure the data structures are completely and accurately represented, reducing redundancy and improving data integrity.

The data modeling process generally comprises three levels of abstraction:

- **Conceptual**: A high-level view that identifies the main business concepts and their relationships, independent of any specific database technology.
- **Logical**: A more detailed representation that defines entities, attributes, and relationships, but remains independent of a specific database management system.
- **Physical**: The final, technology-specific structuring that specifies how the data will be stored, including tables, columns, data types, and constraints for a chosen database.

In this section, we consider, mainly, the logical level. Modeling and its results (a well-defined data model) are an important facet of the system specification, and it is complementary to the identification of behavior and structuring of a system into subsystems and components capable of interacting with each other.

2.2.1 Data and Behavior Modeling

A simple PS, shown in a style similar to SYSML diagrams, consists of a controller, a sensor, and an actuator, as illustrated in Figure 2.4. The controller is able to send commands to the actuator and the sensor by means of commandPorts. The actuator also provides a port (a communication means) for checking its status. The sensor offers a port for collecting the measures it takes in the environment.

Figure 2.4 presents the system structure and its interfaces. The control flows are intuitive: the controller sends commands and reads results. However, because commands, measurements, and status are generic, this basic representation only offers an initial insight into the system's intended goal and the operations required to achieve it. Also, considering a deeper specification of data and messages (as represented in Figure 2.5), the expressiveness of the representation does not capture the full PS's richness.

The system represented is flexible and capable of supporting several use cases. It could support a simple case in which a controller receives liquid level measures in a tank and commands the actuator to open a valve after reception of a preset measurement. It can also command the same actuator to close that valve after a few seconds and request the sensor to take a new measure of the level. In another scenario, this same system could also represent a sensor that measures temperature and an actuator that controls the volume of cold or hot water flowing into conduits.

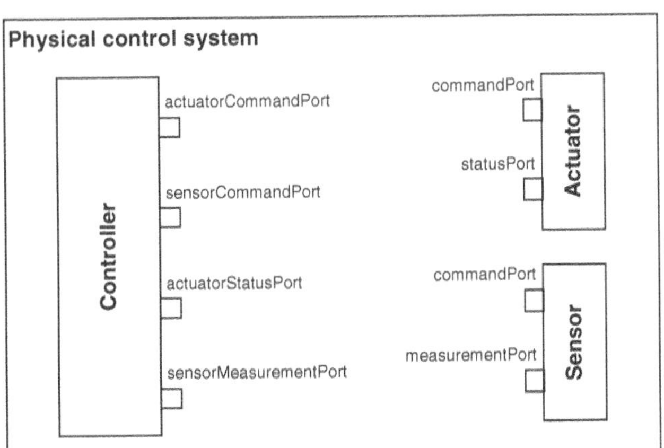

Figure 2.4 A simple representation of a PS with components and ports.

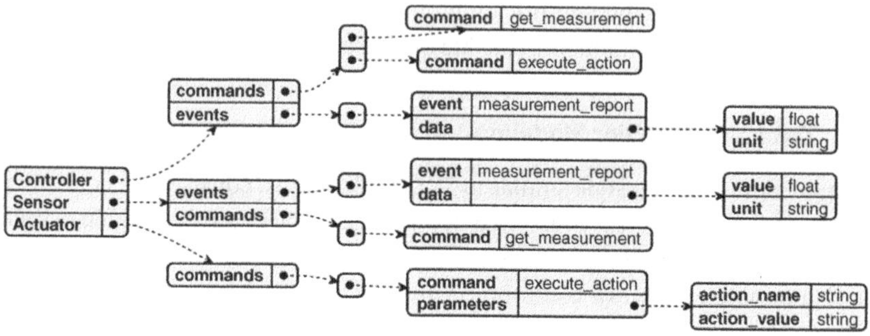

Figure 2.5 A data representation of generic commands and events for a simple PS.

This representation offers a structural view, i.e., the elements involved in an activity and the way they can communicate by messages. It is a sort of template that should be specialized for a specific use case. What needs to be added is content. A representation, a formalization of the messages, i.e., the data, their structure, and their constraints as they relate to an actual problem domain, is needed to specialize the template. A data model provides constructs to represent the problem domain data that the PS is intended to control. The data model allows a description of the context, the specific features and characteristics of the environment that the PS is trying to govern/orchestrate. Adding a data model to the PS representation enables designers to better determine the actions and rules that are to be applied and when.

Considering a specific example, e.g., a home automation framework and its expected capabilities and data, the PS behavior can now be better determined with rules, constraints, and actions that can be applied by the system itself:

Examples of rules and constraints enabled by data

```
if temperature > 10 C then sendCommand(increase)
temperature should always be in [a,b] range
```

As an example, the system representation of Figure 2.4 can be augmented by a specific data model (see Figure 2.6) that represents a simple home automation system.

By combining the simple representative structure with a basic data model, it becomes possible to design the expected behavior of the PS (and thus its DT) by leveraging the available data models. They constitute a sort of dictionary that can be used to describe the intended results of actions, the commands and responses (events that can be seen as changing status requests and notifications), the requirements, and the constraints of the PSs.

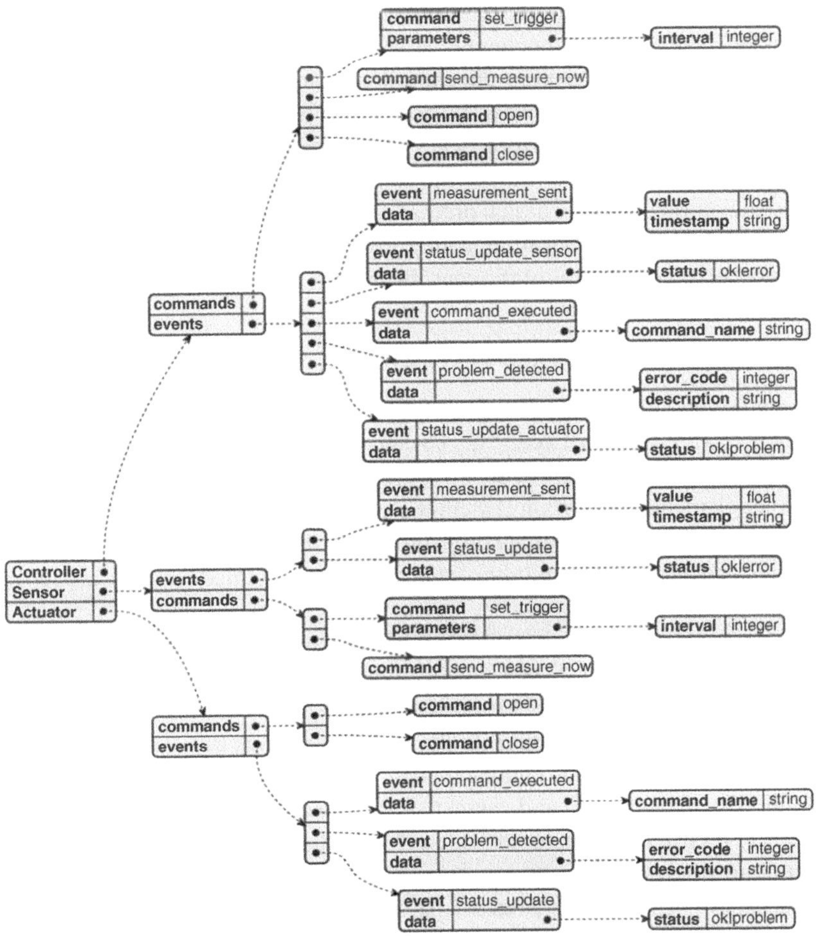

Figure 2.6 A data representation of basic commands and events for a simple home automation PS.

Data models are not always readily available, which makes system structuring and identifying relevant data closely interconnected activities that continually influence and refine each other. As a best practice, specifying the PS should proceed in parallel with identifying data models to ensure consistency and adaptability throughout the design process.

When suitable data models are available, they can serve as a baseline that can evolve through extension, modification, or enrichment to align with system requirements. In cases where no predefined models exist, the creation of new ones should be pursued alongside the definition of interfaces and data exchange mechanisms between system components.

Because data models heavily depend on the nature of the problem domain, system specifications must evolve in close coordination with the structuring of components and the identification of key requirements. This ensures that the PS's representation remains aligned with an adaptable, evolving data model, fostering consistency throughout the design process. Figure 2.7 represents the rich relationship between data and behavior modeling, each one contributing to improving the PS representation by means of the consolidation of models.

2.2.2 Data Models as Enablers of Passive DTs

The representation of a PS through a DT requires an organized framework for defining relationships between the PS and its DT according to fundamental properties. As discussed in Section 2.1, the representation capability, reflection, and entanglement properties are essential features of a DT. The power of data models lies in their ability to facilitate these properties through structured data frameworks and components, even in the absence of a fully defined behavior model for the PS or DT.

In practice, the PS continuously generates data that reflect its status and operational changes. These data alone can provide meaningful insights into system functionality, enabling a data-driven representation of the DT with minimal or nonexistent behavior model. The PS (and, in many cases, its surrounding environment) produces raw data, which are collected, processed, and structured through data management and contextualization components, such as a Context Broker [117, 118]. This structured data can feed visualization tools directly or serve as input for a lightweight behavior representation.

This data-driven DT, referred to as a passive DT, primarily functions as a mirror of a PS, displaying its current status and historical information without actively representing, anticipating, justifying, or simulating its behavioral aspects. While the core DT properties remain present, they are implemented in a simplified manner, focusing on state representation rather than behavioral interaction.

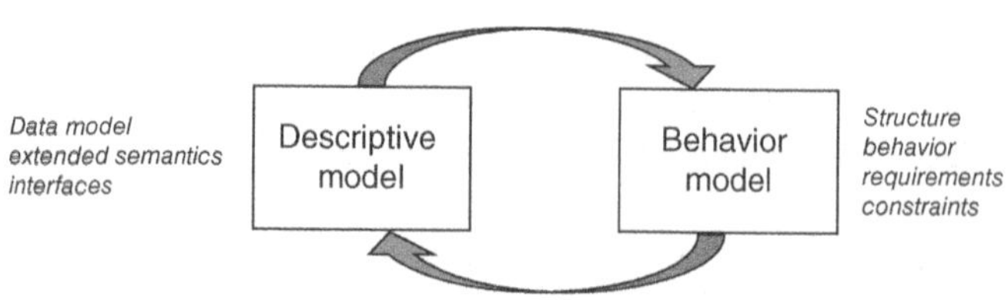

Figure 2.7 Interrelationships between data and behavior models.

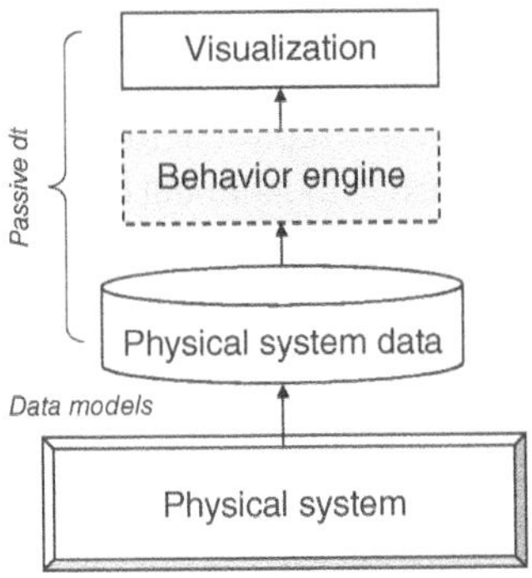

Figure 2.8 Data models supporting a passive DT.

Figure 2.8 shows the case for a passive DT. The PS generates data that are collected and formatted in well-formed data by aligning to one or more specific data models. These data are then used to visualize the current evolution of the DT. If historical data are used, the passive DT can provide a representation of past states of the PS. A simple behavior engine (in gray in Figure 2.8) can provide some hints about the behavior of the PS.

While the functionalities and services provided by this arrangement are valuable, they do not fully harness the capabilities of DT representation. In particular, the ability to govern the PS's behavior through the DT remains underutilized. Additionally, key properties such as augmentation and servitization, which enable the DT to extend its functionality beyond mere representation, are not fully realized. Addressing these gaps would allow the DT to move from a passive monitoring tool to an active, adaptive system capable of influencing and optimizing the physical counterpart.

2.3 Behavior Modeling

A fundamental aspect of DT development is behavior modeling in terms of structured mapping to subsystems, components, interfaces, and operational logic. This process results in a model that captures the expected behavior of the entire PS while maintaining consistency in the behavior of its parts. PSs can be viewed at various levels of detail, which requires identifying, at each level of abstraction, the relevant components, their dependencies and interrelations, and the internal and emergent behaviors arising from their interactions. The DT should support the desired level of representation and provide meaningful insights into the PS's states and behavior.

The DT representation is strongly based on available data and their representations. From a more formal perspective, a model can describe a specific instance of a system, such as a DT for a single car. However, a DT can also represent the characterizing features of many instances of a PS. In this context, a MetaModel defines the concepts, rules, relationships, and constraints that are used to build and represent the characteristics of these several instances. A MetaModel can be seen as a model of models or as a means to derive a specialized model from a fully specified, yet generic, model.

According to this, a DT can represent either a single instance of a PS or multiple instances in the form of a MetaModel. In the first case, the focus is on a specific PS, enabling the identification of policies and improvements tailored to that individual entity. In the latter case, the DT represents features common to a class of PS, allowing comparison between the actual behavior of a single system and the MetaModel, which aggregates information collected from many entities. For instance, this approach can be especially useful for detecting malfunctions in a specific aircraft by comparing its behavior with similar cases and solutions observed in other entities. This MetaModel representation capability could also refer to different phases of the PS's life cycle. The DT should represent

- The requirements and constraints characterizing the PS.
- The salient aspects and components of the environment in which the PS is operating.
- The flow of control between internal and external parts.
- The components and elements (possibly at different levels of abstraction and aggregation) that describe and make evident the relevant parts of the system and their behavior.
- The different representations (activity, finite state machine, message sequence diagrams) that can help in understanding and implementing the expected behavior.
- The integration with applicable data models.

During execution, the DT receives contextualized data—that is, data specific to the environment in which the PS operates. This data enables the DT to determine the system's specific situation (Situation Awareness[1] [119]) and provides a continuous dataflow for real-time monitoring. Leveraging the behavior model, the DT can mimic the PS's actions, offering insights into why certain behaviors occur. This may lead to specific commands or policy requests sent to the PS to govern and orchestrate its behavior. Additionally, the DT can impose new constraints on the PS, either temporarily or permanently. Finally, by analyzing a class of entities, the

1 Differences between context and situation with respect to DT are presented in Section 2.7.4.

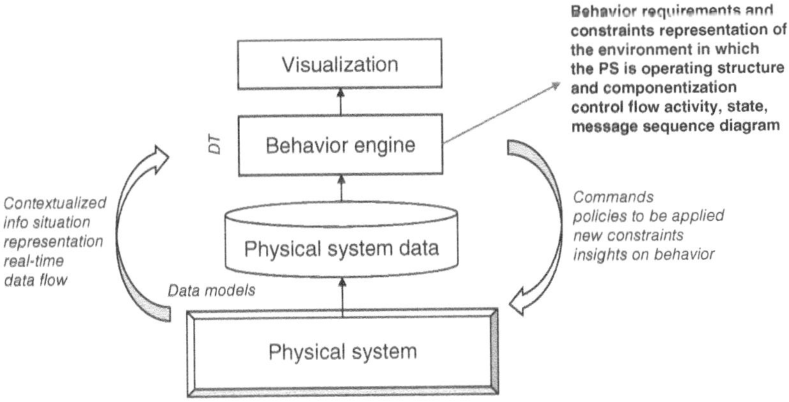

Figure 2.9 Basic behavior model representation for a DT.

DT can extract valuable insights, rules, and constraints on their collective behavior. Figure 2.9 simplifies the complexity of DT execution in relation to the PS, the system's data, and other components.

The behavior of a system can change over time, including cyclical variations. The DT should be capable of capturing these dynamic changes and translating them into constraints or rules that define the expected behavior.

2.4 Predictive Models

The ability to predict future events or outcomes of the PS is an important aspect of a DT. Two features can help in this endeavor: the availability of descriptive and behavior models.

Due to the current trend toward the usage of ML/DL technologies, based on large datasets, the DT offers the possibility to apply these technologies independently from the usage of an actual behavior model. This possibility is linked to the fact that a PS can be represented by means of the data it produces. A Passive DT can be augmented with predictive capabilities to become a simple Predictive DT, as shown in Figure 2.10.

A predictive DT is characterized by the use of historical and real-time data to forecast the future states of a PS. It employs AI algorithms, particularly those based on time series analysis like long short-term memory (LSTM) [120] or others, to identify the most likely state transitions and provide a basis for informed decision-making. A key challenge with these algorithms, however, is that while they can provide accurate predictions, they often do not clearly explain the reasons for the changes in state. The lack of this "why" and "how" is a critical limitation that is addressed by more advanced DT concepts.

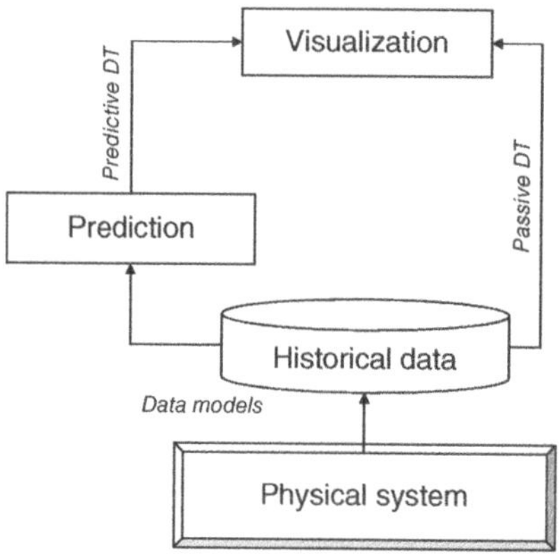

Figure 2.10 Adding prediction capabilities to a passive DT to create a predictive DT.

Having a solid behavior model can provide useful and precise insights on the expected evolution of the PS based on its own rules, laws, and internal logic. This can be instrumental in anticipating critical situations or providing the ability to cope with them by establishing and imposing policies on the PS by means of interaction with the DT. In addition, well-organized historical data and structured streams of (real-time) actual data can be exploited by means of statistical or artificial intelligence tools and functions to predict future states. These two abilities enable forecasting of future conditions for the physical object and the identification of measures to counter undesired behavior or mitigate external influences on its operation. For instance, anticipating special weather conditions enables the DT to implement mitigation policies, adjusting constraints, such as reducing maximum speed, or modifying requirements to minimize potential impacts. These could also imply some further restrictions on constraints (e.g., reduce the max allowed speed) or requirements. The interaction between DL/ML capabilities and behavior representation can help provide explanations for expected PS's behavior, addressing a well-known deficiency of current AI tools in supporting Explainable AI [27, 121]. Figure 2.11 represents a prediction function that interacts with the PS data function (i.e., the Context Broker) to collect data and create data-driven predictions of future system states. The behavioral side of the DT, the behavior engine, operates in sync with the predicted states to identify the policies, rules, or laws that govern them. In doing so, it can provide explanations about the expected resulting states.

In more detail, the predictive engine forecasts the transition from one state to another, while the behavior engine applies a set of rules to achieve the same transition. The identification of these rules, laws, and policies provides a foundation for understanding the "how" and "why" of the PS's transition to a new state and under what specific conditions and constraints the change occurred.

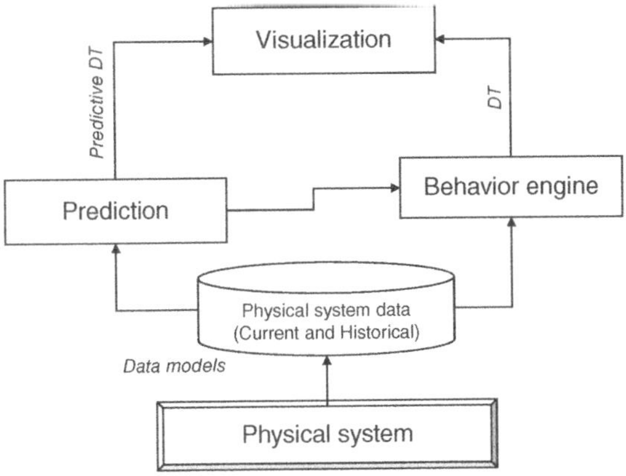

Figure 2.11 Explainable DT: combining the behavior and predictive capabilities.

This represents a powerful DT that can be termed an "explainable DT," which highlights its capability to provide clear explanations of the PS's future behavior.

Choosing between a simple predictive DT and a more complex explainable DT depends on the specific requirements and the ability to implement sophisticated systems. The advantage of an explainable DT lies in its capacity to provide humans with meaningful insights into the expected behavior, enabling human-in-the-loop decision-making. This facilitates more informed decisions and the implementation of corrective policies to steer the PS back to its desired state. However, integrating behavior and predictive models requires significantly more effort compared to using established AI techniques that primarily handle time-series data. Therefore, the benefits must justify the complexity and effort involved in the integration.

2.5 Prognosis Model

A DT can monitor, analyze, predict, and detect malfunctions in a PS. To support these functions, a dedicated prognosis model should be established. This prognosis model may cooperate with a behavior model and/or be based on a predictive model.

Prognosis DTs often include predictive capabilities to foresee future states and anticipate malfunctions. They identify approaching measurements or actions near critical thresholds and issue warnings or requests for intervention to external systems or humans.

Ideally, the prognosis DT not only detects malfunctions but also, leveraging predictive capabilities, anticipates issues and, utilizing behavior model insights, determines corrective policies. When possible, it applies them directly; otherwise, it alerts humans to act, helping steer the PS back to its expected behavior or execute recovery actions. A fully developed prognosis DT can predict and send policies—directly or via a Context Broker—to the PS, enabling both to collaboratively execute a coordinated plan to mitigate and control malfunctions.

A detailed behavior model is useful for assessing deviations between the PS's actual behavior and the modeled expectations. Discrepancies in measurements or events exceeding defined thresholds can trigger responses guided by the prognosis model. The availability of this behavior model offers the possibility to apply rules, laws, and specialized logic to different initial conditions and to analyze how the PS reacts (or reacted) to events. Differences between expected results and those achieved (or recorded in historical data) can be used to determine behavioral malfunctions or divergences in expected results, providing insights on possible causes that triggered the anomalous behavior. Different instances of the behavior model can be used for this goal.

In addition, the predictive engine can provide insight about expected events to be compared with those determined by the behavior model. Mismatches can be the subject of further analysis and can be used to refine the behavior model. Figure 2.12 represents how a prognosis function can cooperate with behavior and prediction functions to govern the malfunctions and to record them in the Context Broker (possibly with recovery actions to be executed by the PS) and the ability to visualize problems to external systems.

The prognosis functions are intentionally separated and isolated from the primary DT execution. This ensures they do not disrupt the normal operation of

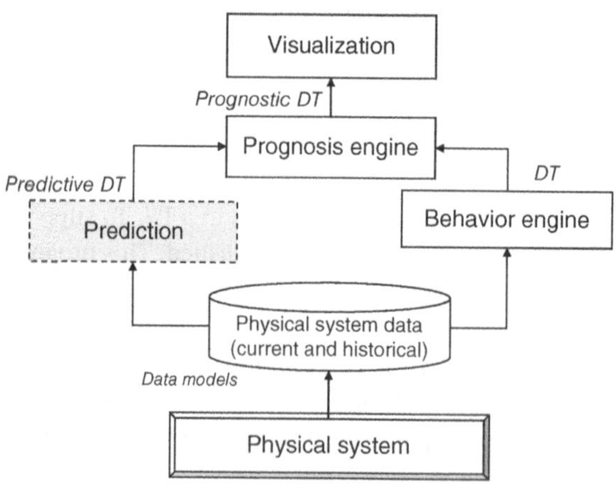

Figure 2.12 Prognosis DT capable of using behavioral and predictive functions to govern malfunctions.

the prediction and behavior engines. These core engines are designed for con tinuous execution, with the prediction engine forecasting future states and the behavior engine explaining the transitions based on its rule set, while a prognosis function determines possible malfunctions and helps to anticipate and mitigate their effects.

The Replication Property allows for a powerful capability: the entire prediction and behavior engines can be replicated and used in conjunction with a dedicated prognosis engine instance. This allows the system to:

- **Conduct Root Cause Analysis:** By applying historical data, these replicated instances can determine the root causes of past faults, helping to understand why certain events occurred.
- **Study "What-if" Scenarios:** By setting up special initial conditions, these replicas can anticipate and analyze possible malfunctions under unique or critical circumstances.

This strategic isolation and replication ensures that deep, complex studies can be performed without impacting the real-time functionality and integrity of the main DT.

The prognosis DT is characterized by these possible behaviors: **monitoring**, a continuous action to identify actions or values that deserve attention (warning) or immediate intervention (malfunctioning); **detection**, the action of determining the type of error or issue; and **governance**, i.e., the set of actions to put in place for governing the problem and reconducting it to normal behavior. The prognosis DT can also be classified as proactive, i.e., capable of autonomously taking actions for resolving or mitigating the problems; or passive, i.e., capable of monitoring, detecting problems, and requesting external systems or humans for intervention or indications on the policies to apply. In fact, the prognosis DT can mix these approaches and, for instance, take initial mitigation actions while waiting for a more appropriate strategy to cope with the issue to be elaborated or executed by the external system. The prognosis DT is characterized by different interactions and levels of cooperation with the PS itself (which can be capable of executing some corrective actions) and external systems, as shown in Figure 2.13.

The prognosis DT is a focal point of control for allowing the possibility to interact with the PS and to instantiate global recovery or prevention policies to mitigate malfunctioning. For instance, a prognosis DT can allow interaction with the PS (e.g., by automatically adjusting the turbine's operational parameters) and instantiate global prevention policies (e.g., scheduling maintenance based on a predicted failure date) [122].

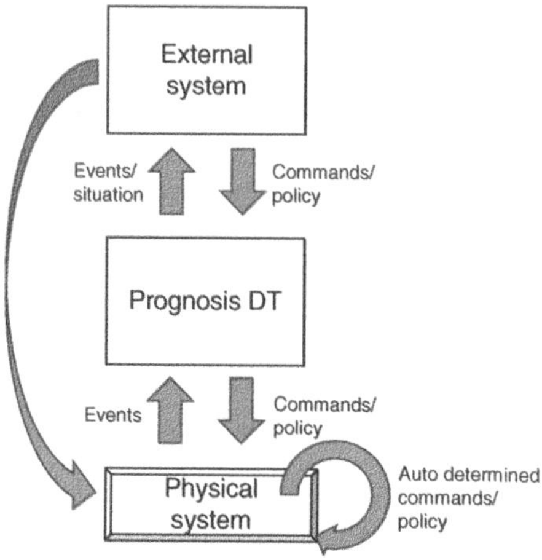

Figure 2.13 Prognosis DT interactions with other systems for coping with malfunctioning.

2.6 Prescriptive Model

A prescriptive DT is based on a combination of the previous functions plus the ability to generate scenarios by means of AI to generate the intended behavior of the DT and PS in rarely occurring or very critical situations. The prescriptive DT can be seen as a specialized recommendation system capable of analyzing, simulating, and predicting the PS behavior in several hypothetical or real situations and recommending optimized actions to keep the behavior within expected limits as determined by requirements and constraints. The prescriptive DT is, therefore, not only focused on malfunctions but also on the continuous monitoring and optimization of the behavior of the PS (and DT) according to the needs of users and stakeholders (see Figure 2.14).

Artificial intelligence functions (and in particular generative AI) can be used to create scenarios and to evaluate different "responses" of DT and PS to optimize their behavior with respect to stakeholders' requirements. Simulations and predictive functionalities can be extremely useful to determine how to properly react in an optimized manner to different situations that the PS may encounter.

The ability to generate scenarios (represented by the gray box, "generation and prediction of future events/conditions" function) in terms of correlated events and conditions can be leveraged in a powerful way. These generated scenarios can produce meaningful time-series data, which can then be injected into the PS data as if it were historical data. This data is then provided as input to a simulation DT (which is an instance of a DT Behavior Engine).

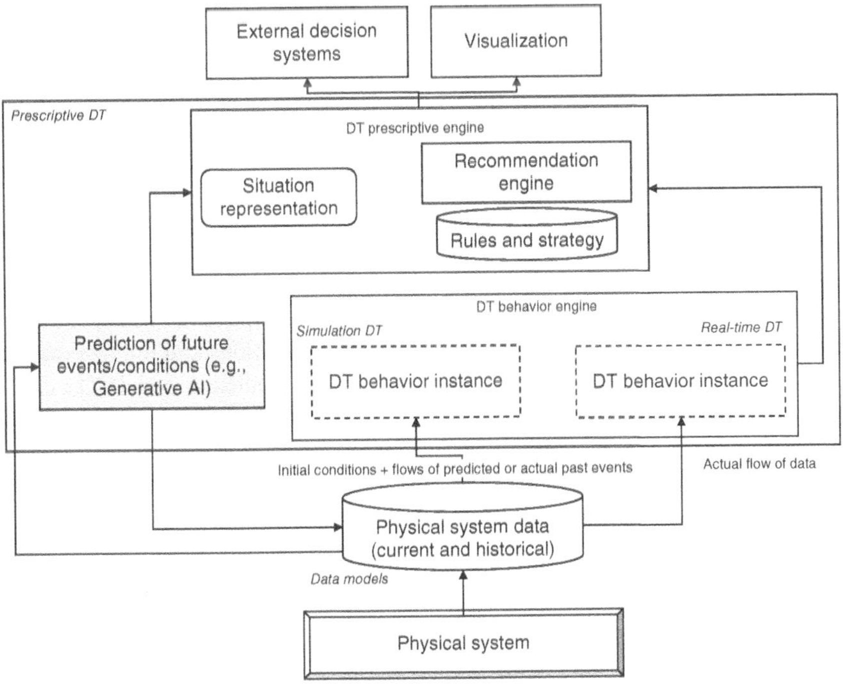

Figure 2.14 Prescriptive DT integrating generative AI, simulation, real-time data representation, situation, and decision-making.

In this manner, the simulation DT can represent and predict actions and changes in the PS's status. If the simulated behavior is undesirable, it can be corrected by changing the logic within the behavior engine. This process allows for the proactive testing and refinement of the DT's behavioral rules in a virtual environment before they are applied to the PS.

Another important aspect of a prescriptive model is the DT level of autonomy. If the DT is only recommending solutions to external decision systems or humans, the final resolution about policies to apply will be taken outside of the DT system. If the prescriptive DT can determine the optimized policies and autonomously govern their implementation in the PS, the predictive DT is autonomic. In this case, the prescriptive DT engine can encompass functions for situation representation, rules and strategies to determine the most effective actions, and a recommendation engine to suggest to humans or other external decision system the policies to implement.

2.7 A Flexible Approach to Multi-facet Models

The previous sections have presented different types of DTs, differentiated by their complexity and the models they adopt. The availability and interplay of these models are essential for characterizing and defining the diverse capabilities of a DT. The specific combination of these models fundamentally characterizes the type of DT. There are both dependencies and a degree of freedom in combining them to fulfill specific objectives and requirements. Figure 2.15 represents the possible relationships and the choices that a designer of a DT may consider.

Single arrows point to a direct dependence (e.g., prescriptive model depends on the existence of a Data Model). Dotted lines point to relations and improvements (e.g., the behavior model improves the capabilities of a predictive model). The double arrows indicate a reciprocal influence (e.g., predictive model and simulation model can improve each other).

2.7.1 Relationships Between Different Models

As discussed, the relations between descriptive and behavior models are profound, and they determine the effectiveness of a DT. The descriptive model provides data representations that are processed and elaborated by the behavior engine to pose the "system" in the subsequent correct states. The interplay and alignment of data and actions in the model embodied by the DT are essential for a good representation of the PS. All the data needed by the behavioral part should be provided, and all the actions should result in data that represent a step in the functioning of the PS. Figure 2.16 illustrates the interplay between a descriptive and behavior model.

Figure 2.16 underscores the importance of a well-coordinated definition and integration between the data model, which describes the properties and states of the PS, and the behavior representation, which defines how actions lead to state

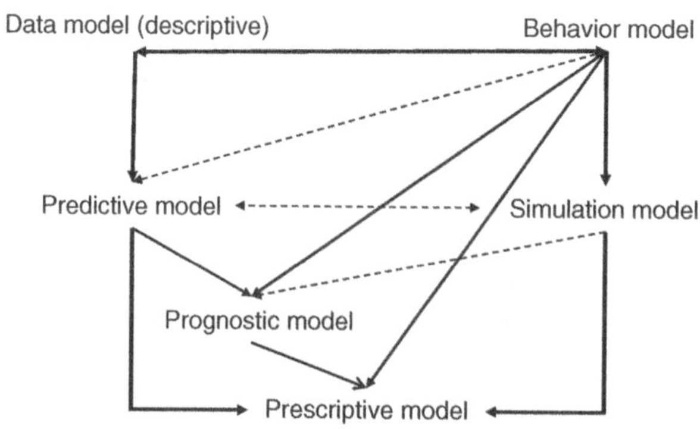

Figure 2.15 Major relations between model capabilities.

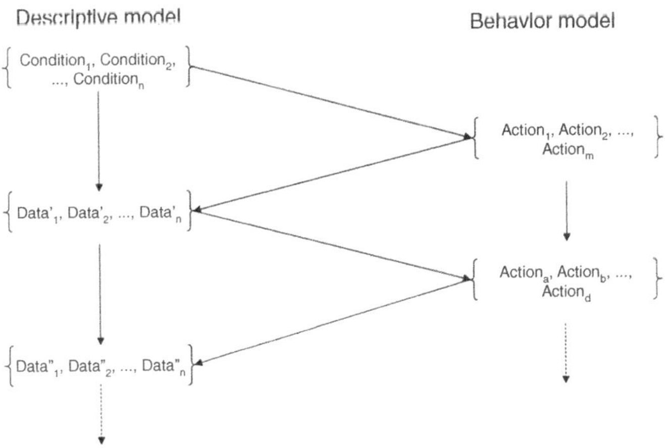

Figure 2.16 Interplay between a data and a behavior model of a DT.

and property changes. Designing this interplay is a fundamental step in shaping the DT.

The prediction of future states is another relevant DT function. It can be achieved in different ways: by applying DL/ML algorithms and by means of simulation. A structured DT can even exploit both. Figure 2.17 shows the possibilities offered by the different prediction methods.

On the right side, the availability of data as determined by the historical sequence of events can be used to predict future states of the DT by means of AI tools and techniques. Given the same initial conditions and the same sequence of injected events, an instance of a simulation model (i.e., a behavior model instance)

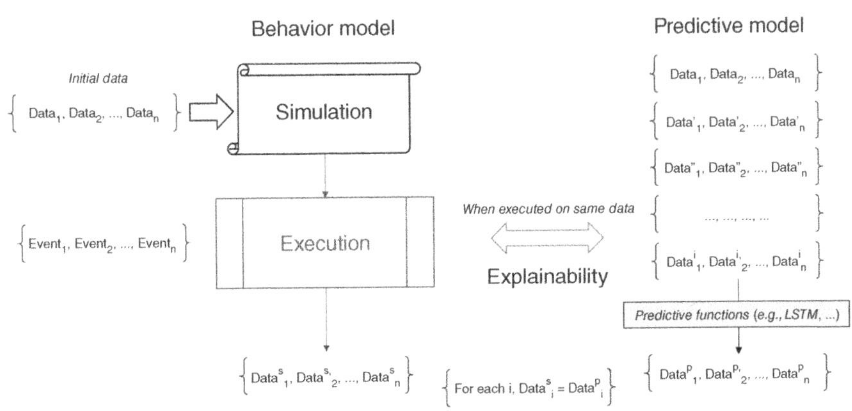

Figure 2.17 Predictive capability: simulation, data-driven prediction, and their interrelation.

should produce the same sequence of states as observed historically and as predicted by the model.

The integration of these functionalities can be used to check the validity and accuracy of the prediction method and the simulations (as well as the behavior model). Their combination can provide "explanations" for the predicted states of the system. This approach also leads to some considerations related to the links between simulation and execution of the behavior model. There is a strong constraint toward the alignment of the two. A simulation engine should support exactly the same logic and resulting behavior (except a few add-ons for allowing the simulation execution) of the behavior model executed in parallel with the PS. Discrepancies could result in different representations that undermine a major property of the DT: the ability to simulate the PS. To this end, executing simulations as instances of the behavior model should be required to avoid the parallel development of two similar models. Figure 2.18 represents the case for a perfect alignment between the two instances and the need for a unique model.

The modeling instance can temporarily diverge because it can be used to determine and analyze the behavior in particular cases. It can be used to forge the behavior to desired reactions in particular situations. It is a way to continuously update the behavior model for new occurrences. But in principle, the modeling, execution, and simulation instances should converge when committed by designer/developers.

As noted above, the simulation capability can be used to determine (and adjust) the behavior in critical or difficult-to-replicate situations. The simulation can identify and suggest modifications to the design and implementation of the behavior of PS and its DT. These changes will need to be implemented and verified in the simulation engine and, when consolidated by proof and tests, be committed in

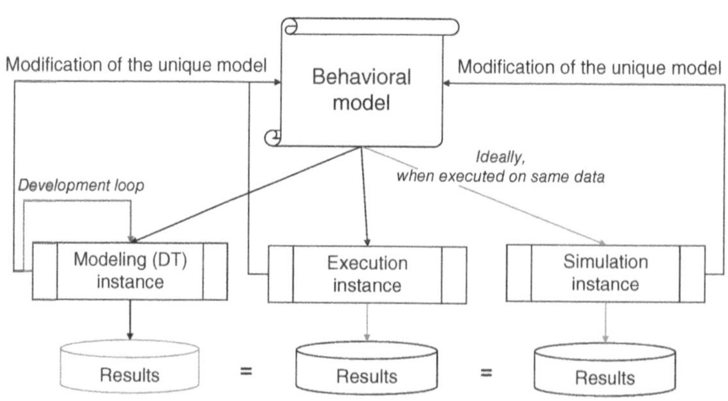

Figure 2.18 Alignment between behavioral and simulation functions.

the behavior model (of the PS and DT). On the other hand, designed changes to the behavior model of the PS or DT must be aligned, and the simulation model should constantly reflect them. This is an alignment requirement: the behavior model is the unique element that integrates the modifications due to advances in the PS specification or improvements required by results of simulations that grasp additional and important characteristics of the PS. Object-oriented methodology defines relationships between classes and objects. These relationships highlight the need to manage different instances of the same behavior model across physical execution, enhanced DT modeling, and simulation of the PS.

2.7.2 Models and Design, the Complexity of DT Modeling

From the beginning, designers should clearly define the DT goals and, consequently, determine the types of models that best support them. The initial choices have direct consequences on the modeling and the related design and implementation aspects. Choosing a fully fledged DT requires a considerable amount of modeling activities supported by the ability of the PS to receive and actuate commands suggested by the DT. Major changes to the PS are requested to support this bidirectional entanglement. For a passive DT, the PS needs only to send data. In any case, DT development necessitates a considerable investment in modeling and implementation. A successful DT development is based on well-structured processes that can involve several parts of an enterprise [13, 17]. Modeling and operating a Prescriptive Autonomic DT can require a considerable level of involvement, participation and contribution from people in terms of shared knowledge, skills, and dedication, in contrast to a simpler Passive DT. Conversely, the functions and richness that a prescriptive DT can offer compared to simpler ones are many: for instance, people can be focusing on real and new issues while repetitive situations are well-optimized by the DT. The engagement and major effort will then be on improving and making the DT even more autonomic and capable of coping with more situations. For enterprises or organizations entering the field, a Prognosis DT (as represented in Figure 2.19) can be a good starting point, avoiding some complexity of the higher-level DTs while still providing meaningful functions useful within an organization, retaining a set of important hooks for future evolution of the model. Descriptive and behavior models are essential to create a prognosis

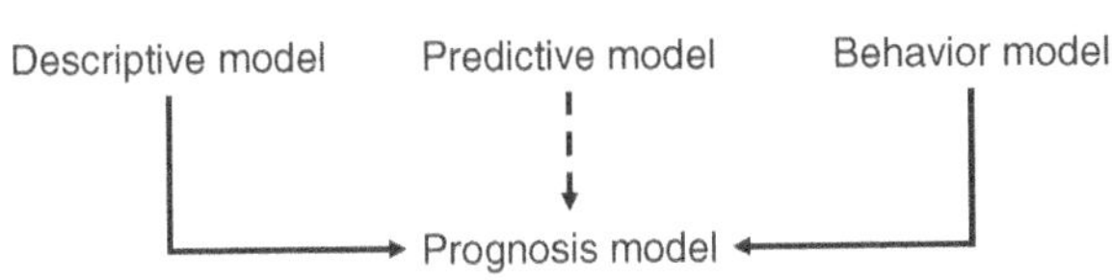

Figure 2.19 Prognosis model aspects.

model (plain lines in figure), while a predictive model can greatly contribute to improve the capabilities of foreseen issues and prevent them (dotted lines).

This example introduces the problem of DT scalability. Upgrading a simple DT (e.g., a passive one) to a more powerful one, e.g., a prognosis DT, requires re-engineering of the system starting from the need to introduce bidirectional control and the introduction and use of new data models for representing new facets of the PS to model. In addition, predictive models as well as a more detailed behavior engine must be introduced or redesigned. Scaling up to a prescriptive DT can require a complete re-engineering because of the need for detailing the situations in which the PS can incur and the level of detail and precision needed for an automatic system for making or suggesting decisions.

2.7.3 Modeling the Environment

The environment in which a PS is operating may have a major impact on its behavior. In this case, a representation of the environment (of the salient aspects impacting on the PS) must be modeled and integrated in the DT design. Sometimes, the environment can be instrumented to provide measures or data that have an impact on the PS. For instance, modeling a roundabout (as represented in Figure 2.20) in an accurate manner can lead to a better understanding of the traffic behavior and its anomalies.

A simple model representing the entries and dimensions of the roundabout could not suffice for a reasonable level of representativeness of the PS. A model of the roundabout representing the sense of rotation or the forward direction of the road can also be useful to detect anomalies. Cars stopped in the center of the roundabout, or at its edges, can be considered as unusual situations that deserve attention and warning. Analyzing traffic behavior in relation to the environment can allow us to determine the actual behavior of users beyond the stated rules and laws. The environment modeling and its detailing as a part of the DT behavior model can also be an aspect to consider when scaling up the whole DT representation. In addition, studying its behavior can provide insights on laws or rules not explicitly stated in the DT design.

2.7.4 Context and Situation

It is important to make a distinction about the *context* and *situation*. In fact, context and situation are related but distinct concepts in DT systems. *Context* refers to the background information and conditions about a PS at a given time. In DTs, the context includes all relevant data describing the environment, state, and relationships of the physical entity, such as location, operational parameters, environmental conditions, and historical data [123]. With reference to Figure 2.20,

Figure 2.20 An example of modeling the environment.

a data model can describe the context of the roundabout (in terms of its features like entries, size, number of lanes). Context provides the foundational "what" and "where," i.e., a consistent, real-time representation of all relevant elements and their status.

Situation is a concept that enriches the context definition. It is a representation of the current state of the context (with additional information, if needed) to understand what is occurring and what are the possible issues or problems for operations or corrective actions to adapt the behavior to the current conditions. Situation awareness typically involves three levels: perception (recognizing the current context), comprehension (understanding the meaning and implications), and projection (anticipating future developments based on the present situation) [124]. In DTs, situation awareness integrates contextual data to provide actionable insights [123], predict outcomes (predictive functionalities of DT), and support rapid, informed decisions in complex environments (e.g., prescriptive DT). With respect to Figure 2.20, the situation uses the context information for determining where cars are (in normal position, taking a wrong direction, and the like). The goal is to provide a current representation of what is happening in the context. As an analogy, the situation provides a richer understanding, addressing "what is going on," "how," "where," and "to whom."

2.7.5 From Top or Bottom?

The roundabout example also provides insights on the typical way in which DTs are designed. A top-down approach is prevalent for new systems: the PS and its DT are designed and progressively detailed to grasp more features to consider and represent. Referring to Figure 2.3, the integrated development of the PS and DT is essential for reducing the need to redesign part of the PS. There are, however, many cases in which the PS exists, yet it has not been designed and built according to a well-established methodology (e.g., a roundabout). In this case, there is a need to derive the logic of functioning in a different way. A bottom-up approach allows to progressively determine the rules and behavior of an environment and its components. This possibility has been pursued in [38]. For instance, the large Shibuya crossroad has been studied by [125] and [126] in the realm of studies about DT and general-purpose sensing [119, 127]. The application of DT modeling supported by behavior capture through sensing and integration with AI can lead to a methodology that incrementally defines and formalizes the behavior of an environment.

The DT approach has been incrementally applied to large systems such as cities [128–131], transport systems [132–135], network systems [136–138] or even to human bodies [139, 140]. These systems have been developed without a precise and comprehensive top-down approach. Instead, they are the result of a long-term evolution. Creating a model for them is difficult and complex because they are influenced by different factors. Several applied sciences and related methodologies are needed to capture their complexity. In such cases, the bottom-up approach is the only possibility to model them. Observation and general-purpose sensing for data and behavior capture are essential activities that contribute to an expanding corpus of information, rules, and actions. These elements progressively enhance the system's description and enable the implementation of a DT [38, 119, 131]. The starting point is a descriptive modeling process, i.e., the ability to identify, extend, or create data models that can represent meaningful data. On top of these data, the behavior and predictive functions can be designed in an open way, i.e., leaving space to increase the number of components and functions to be integrated as needed by new technological possibilities (e.g., new algorithms or rules) or new data. The bottom-up approach is where the DT meets complex systems. These topics will be further discussed in Chapter 4 and, in particular, Sections 4.2 and 4.4.

3

Foundational Data for a Digital Twin

After reading this chapter, you should be able to:

- Understand how to build a data-driven Digital Twin.
- Understand the needed data and how to organize it for supporting a data-driven Digital Twin.
- Understand the importance and use of data models and contextualized information for representing Digital Twins.
- Understand the use of data models to support the definition of application programming interfaces.

3.1 Descriptive Models

Data play a central role in modeling Digital Twins (DTs) [141–143]. A data model is an abstract framework that defines, organizes, and standardizes the structure, relationships, and constraints of data that represent a system. A data model represents and dictates how data elements relate to each other and to real entities. This structure is used for abstract, formal, and current representation of the system: a data model abstracts the types and relations of data characterizing the physical object, but it also instantiates the actual and current "values" of the salient features of the physical system in a well-formed manner. These capabilities are at the basis of data models' exploitation as the foundations on top of which to build and use complex representations of a physical system. They are essential for at least a few major reasons:

- To define a *reference frame* for relating the data, their relationships, and constraints for describing the salient features and states of a physical system and its environment.

- Help in defining a *contextualized representation* of the physical system under specific conditions posed by the system itself and the environment.
- To continuously *update*, a stream of data can constantly adjourn relevant features and states of the physical system, allowing a continuous synchronization between the real and software counterparts of the physical system.
- They are *collections of well-formed and structured data* that can be used for prediction purposes.

The data-driven paradigm for modeling a DT is well-established and widely adopted in practical implementations. It builds on two core concepts originating from the Internet of Things (IoT) and manufacturing domains: first, the ability to monitor and quantify the states and outcomes of physical elements through sensing (and actuation); second, the capacity to create and analyze an interconnected flow of relevant data that traces a product throughout its life-cycle—commonly referred to as the digital thread (e.g., [144, 145]). These capabilities enable the creation of datasets containing current and historical values, organized according to well-structured data models.

The availability of these datasets, structured as well-formed attributes representing key system and environmental aspects such as relationships and value types, facilitates the creation of comprehensive data models (e.g., [55, 58, 114, 146, 147]), which underpin effective DT operation and analysis.

On the other hand, the availability of these datasets, structured as well-formed attributes representing key system and environmental aspects such as relationships and value types, facilitates the update and extension of more comprehensive data models. This virtuous loop enables the continuous improvement of data models and their specialization for specific use cases.

This data-driven approach focuses on a multistep process: first, acquiring data in a timely manner; second, formatting it according to well-defined structures like data models; and third, curating it with semantic analysis [153] for the ultimate purpose of describing a physical system. The modeling activity may need some iterations to achieve the needed level of precision and alignment to the descriptive representation requirements of a specific physical system. The behavior (and its related model) is embodied within the physical system, and a data-driven DT can capture and reveal the system's emergent state changes through the flow of data. Figure 3.1 provides an example of this paradigm. On the left, a simplified layered architecture depicts various functional blocks. The sensing aggregation layer handles data generation and aggregation, with sensors and actuators feeding data to an IoT gateway. Subsequently, the data management layer is responsible for collecting, transporting, and formatting the data, mapping it to a predefined data model. This layer also semantically enhances the data to accurately represent the physical system's status and stores it in a specialized data store (ContextBroker) for potential visualization and exploitation.

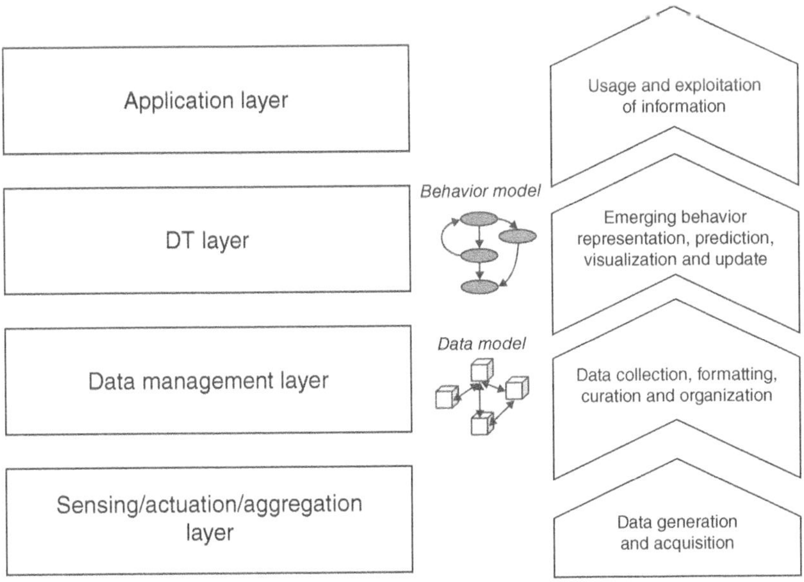

Figure 3.1 Descriptive modeling: from data acquisition to data exploitation.

The DT layer can then provide a limited set of functions, such as effectively mapping available information to the data required for visualization or other applications. Furthermore, it can facilitate the creation of new data, including predictions. The application layer encompasses the diverse range of applications made possible by the available data and the enhanced insights from the DT system. On the right, the diagram highlights some of the key functions performed by each of these layers.

This organizational structure is straightforward to implement, thanks to the wide availability of tools and systems for effective data management—a key asset in today's technological landscape. By leveraging existing data and digital threads, it becomes possible to maintain a continuous representation of the physical system's status.

Moreover, the ability to predict state changes through historical data manipulation contributes to establishing a robust framework for DT representation. Visualization and interface capabilities further enhance the DT, enabling its interpretation as either a "real-time" reflection of the physical system or a means to gather information via Application Programming Interfaces (APIs). This results in a general assumption that a DT is an accurate and timely visualization of the physical system.

3.2 Data-driven Architecture

Effective data organization is crucial for structuring and interpreting information, with the data model serving as a fundamental framework that defines relationships, attributes, and properties to ensure accurate representation and efficient management of real-world systems. A data model explicitly formalizes and dictates the structure of data and how different data entities relate to each other over time. For instance, ETSI is basing the formalization of information models and APIs on the usage of Next Generation Service Interface-Linked Data (NGSI-LD) [148].

Particularly aligned with this approach is the FIWARE initiative [149], for instance, Ref. [150] explicitly mentions that *a DT is an object universally identified by a URI (Universal Resource Identifier), associated with a well-known type (e.g., the Bus type or the Room type) also universally identified by a URI; and it is characterized by attributes classified as: properties associated with data (e.g., the "current speed" of a Bus, or "max temperature" in a Room); and relationships, i.e., the URI identifying a DT entity the given entity is linked to (e.g., the concrete building where a concrete Room is located).* Central to this effort is the specification and implementation of a **ContextBroker** [151], an entity capable of organizing data according to specific data models and making them available in a timely manner (e.g., by means of PubSub solutions). The smart data model initiative[1] [150] aims to design and use interoperable data models addressing different problem domains (particularly associated with IoT).

The ContextBroker is a central architectural element around which to define and build a data-driven architecture. Figure 3.2 depicts a DT software system based on FIWARE components. It can be seen as a detailed description in Figure 3.1 where the layers are transformed into partitions of functionalities and components represent more granular functionalities. This organization is able to capture data from sensors and actuators and to manipulate them to fit into specific data models.

Formatted data are then controlled, formatted, curated, and injected into the Context Broker. This phase, the injection chain, is particularly important for providing "reliable and timely data" to applications [152, 153].

A data-driven DT system is represented as a set of different parts, each one devoted to a set of complementary tasks. A brief description is provided:

- The *sensor network* comprises elements capable of collecting measures from the environment or able to execute actions and verify the results. These components collect data and send them for further control and checks.
- The *Edge* part comprises elements capable of communication with the sensor network elements (through commands or by messages). They collect and

1 Available at: https://smartdatamodels.org. Last checked on 15 April 2025.

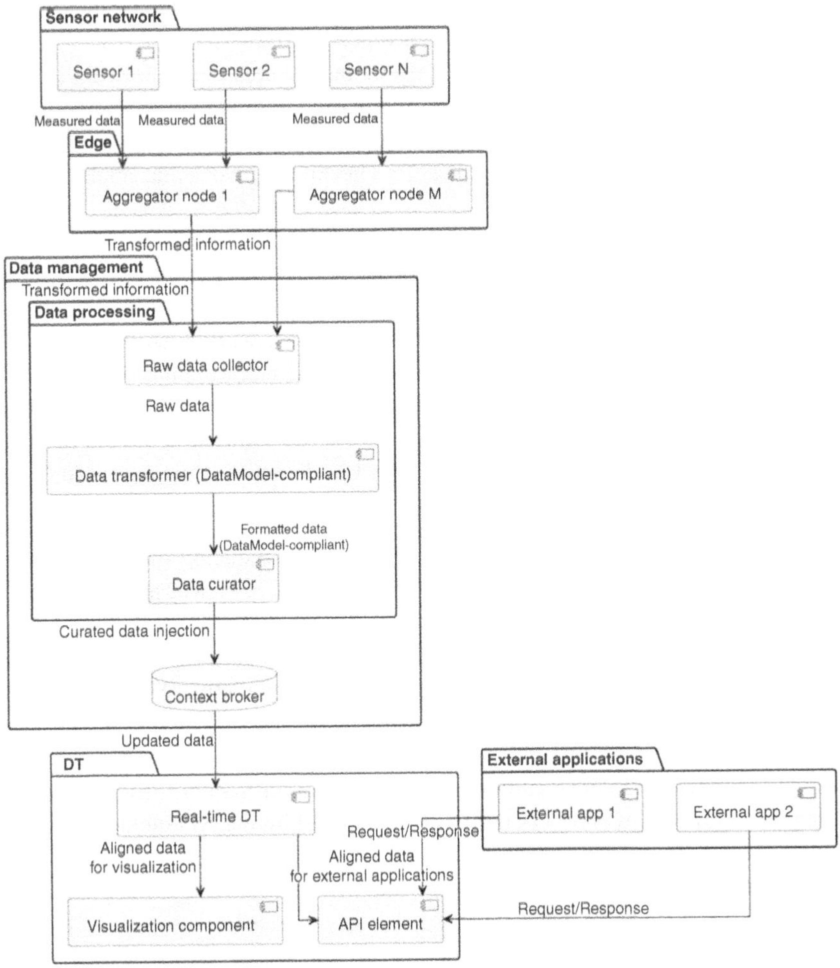

Figure 3.2 Data-driven modeling of a DT based on Fiware's ContextBroker.

partially manipulate the received data to avoid duplication and/or limit the transmission to controlling elements of duplicated data. They can be seen as screening functions that check the received data from the sensor network and forward the relevant information to the data management part. They can also receive commands or notifications of actions to be passed to actuators by the controlling infrastructure.

- *Data Management* is a function that collects all the relevant data for accurate and timely representation of the physical system's status. The data are transformed according to the data models used for the system representation and passed to a data curator that will check for errors, incompatibilities, need for interpolations, and the possibility to relate different kinds of data to each other to find new relations that better represent the system.

- The *Context Broker* ingests data, stores them, and creates a historical dataset. At the same time, it is capable of notifying the interested elements about the availability of fresh data. It can also be queried for the retrieval of data according to specific applications' needs or for checking for particular relationships or time sequences.
- The *DT* subsystem, in this organization, supports a simple real-time function for checking and organizing the received notifications and related data according to the specific needs of the applications. It can also serve the needs of the visualization component and can cooperate with the API element to restrict or help in the capture of information needed by applications.
- The *External Application's* subsystem represents the set of applications that needs to access the data and functions of the DT either as a stream of data (regulated, for instance, by the real-time DT element) or through visualization or specific samples of data.

This architecture prioritizes the flow of data while reducing the need for an extensive behavior model. The real-time DT element can be viewed as a standalone subsystem, adaptable to various functionalities required for defining a specific type of DT. For instance, a prediction component could be incorporated to anticipate future system states, transforming a passive DT into a predictive DT or a minimal behavior model can be implemented to move toward other types of DTs.

The use of data models provides another key advantage: enabling data formalization to support APIs and facilitate interactions between system entities. As illustrated in Figure 3.2, this functionality is represented by the API element, which exposes interfaces to external applications while ensuring their parameters and features align with the chosen data model that defines system representation.

3.3 Which Data to Include in a DT

Data encapsulate and convey the problem domain that the DT is designed to address. There is a strong relationship between the identification of relevant components, the structure, and the data they need to deal with. However, the *expressive power* offered by data is fundamental for characterizing the problem domain. An example can illustrate the intertwining of the two representation capabilities and their mutual complementarity. Figure 3.3 shows a high-level behavior model of a traffic light system.

The system is structured into two components: a controller, responsible for deciding actions to be executed and capable of controlling another element, and an actuator, which carries out externally determined commands and provides feedback on execution or potential issues. These two components communicate through the exchange of commands and events. This arrangement is typical of

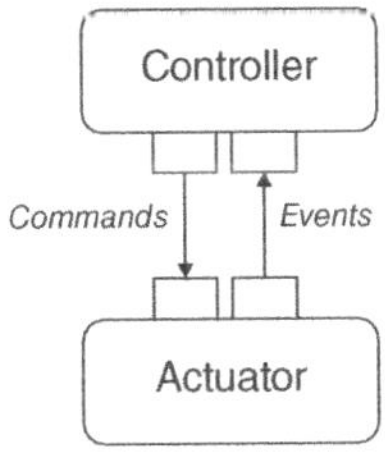

Figure 3.3 An initial representation of a controller–actuator system for a traffic light.

many systems, and it is an initial description of a physical system's structure. However, it is generic and needs additional details to be applied to actual cases.

This structure could be used to model a traffic light system. In this case, the traffic light controller determines the logic governing the actuator's behavior (the traffic light), i.e., when and how long to turn on and off a set of lights by means of the traffic light part. The traffic light actuator informs the controller via messages about the execution of commands.

However, the current system structure lacks a precise mapping of the actual problem to be represented. This problem can be seen as a combination of issues, namely a domain mapping and state representation gap:

- There is a lack of mapping between the abstract model elements and specific constructs of the target domain (i.e., the model is not yet contextualized for the application area in terms of data representation).
- There is no relationship or representation to capture the current status (at runtime) of the different parts of the system within the model.

A data model can greatly help in improving the DT representativeness with respect to the problem domain and the model embodiment with respect to the current status.

If the traffic light example is associated with a simple data model representing the actual problem domain data, the structure is immediately improved. Structure and interactions (the basic concepts of the behavior model) may exploit the capability of representing data by means of data structures. This ability can also be used for standardizing interfaces and APIs.

Figure 3.4 represents an initial model that describes possible commands between the controller and the traffic light. It also provides parameters and attributes for better characterizing the system properties.

The possible traffic light colors, timers, interactions between components, and confirmation options are all illustrated in Figure 3.4. For instance, the `allowedColors` attribute points to typical colors of a traffic light, and `command` points to the set of commands that the controller can send to the actuator. These commands also include timers for governing the transition from one state to

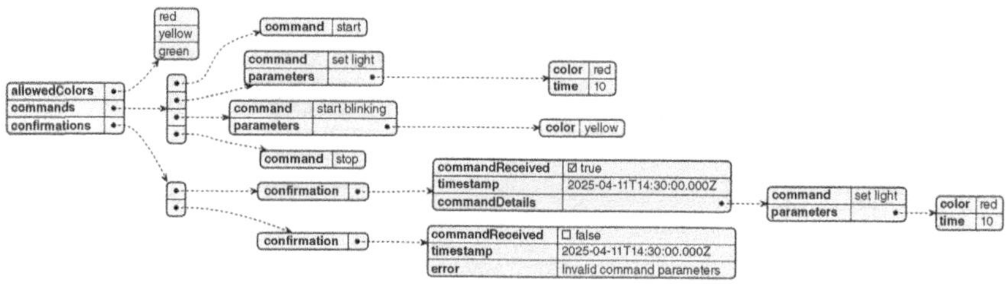

Figure 3.4 A JSON representation of data used in the traffic light example.

another. The `confirmation` provides information about the result of command execution.

The data model gives meaning to the structure and provides content for understanding the system and its current state. Having a stable and well-defined data model offers the possibility of providing a "granular" view of the system status. If the data model is extensible, then additional parameters and features can be added to increase the expressive power of the interface [154, 155].

3.4 Organizing Data into Data Models

The design of a DT is an iterative process that requires a high level of integration between the structuring of parts and elements of the architecture and data representation (see, for instance, Figure 2.7). As seen in previously discussed, e.g., Section 2.2.2, it is possible to design a passive DT that minimizes the need for a deep definition of the parts and elements of the physical system. These topics and their implications will be further discussed in the rest of this chapter.

3.4.1 Minimal DT Structure and Multiple Types of Data

The simple controller–actuator system can be extended a bit more to provide an example of how to build a DT by exploiting the data model capability of providing meaning.

The organization of Figure 3.3, can be functionally and structurally extended by adding sensing capabilities. The controller can now send commands to actuators and request measures from sensors. They can be used to get data about the physical system (or the environment in which it is operating) and actuators can be instructed to execute actions to change the PS status (or the environment that will affect the physical system's status). Figure 3.5 depicts this system. Ports represent the communication means between the involved parts.

Data will then characterize the architecture and the possible relationships between elements. Certain types of sensors must be specified, such as temperature, luminosity, humidity, and presence sensors. They help define the characteristics and requirements of the system to be developed. In addition to sensors, the system

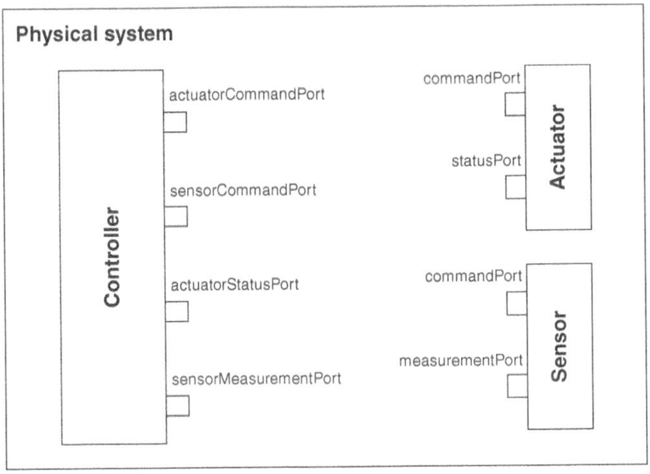

Figure 3.5 A step further in the description of a controller actuator–sensor system.

will integrate a set of actuators designed to control devices that influence environmental parameters, including temperature, lighting, humidity, and security (presence detection). The controller will supervise them and will orchestrate their capabilities according to users' decision and/or to a set of environmental rules. The controller sends requests to sensors, e.g., `getMeasure or setTrigger`, while it sends commands to actuators to perform actions such as `open, close,` .... All of these elements confirm each received command and add a timestamp.

An important aspect that characterizes this system is the target environment to control: a manufacturing plant control system requires a careful design and implementation, reaching extreme precision in measures and actions, while a home automation system poses more relaxed requirements. Requirements and constraints elicitation introduces a nuanced perspective in DT modeling. Some constraints and requirements relate to expected system behavior, making them closely tied to behavior modeling, while others focus on data relationships and structural aspects, aligning with descriptive modeling.

Behavioral requirements and constraints dictate how a system should act under conditions, what course of actions should occur, or how the system should react to specific events. These aspects are part of behavior modeling. Tools like use cases, activity diagrams, and state charts are used to capture dynamic aspects of a system. For example, a requirement stating *the system must lock the doors when no presence is detected* is associated with system functioning and is best modeled and validated through a behavior model.

Descriptive (data) requirements and constraints define the structure, relationships, and properties of the data managed by a system. Entity–relationship or class diagrams can represent these static aspects of the system. A constraint like *each sensor must be uniquely associated with a room* is a data relationship and is best captured in the data model.

This duality points to the need for requirements engineering to integrate behavior and descriptive perspectives. Requirements elicitation is an iterative activity and goes throughout the entire life cycle of a system. It makes explicit two types of needs: those that characterize system actions and those that drive the data structure definition. Effective modeling practices should therefore consider both aspects, ensuring that requirements and constraints are clearly defined and associated with appropriate model elements, whether behavior or descriptive.

The problem of requirement capture is also related to environmental aspects. Industrial and home automation systems have important differences, and so their requirements and constraints should capture and make explicit these differences.

Here is an example of a few descriptive requirements for a home automation system:

Descriptive Requirements for a Home Automation System:

- `Each device in the system shall have a unique identifier to ensure unambiguous identification.`
- `Each sensor shall be uniquely identified and associated with a specific room in the home.`
- `The system shall maintain an up-to-date registry of all connected actuators, including their type (e.g., light, lock, thermostat) and current state.`
- `All user-defined automation rules shall be stored with references to the relevant sensors and actuators they affect.`
- `The system shall record time-stamped logs of all sensor readings and actuator state changes for at least 30 days.`
- `Each user profile shall include a list of authorized devices and permitted control actions.`

Requirements such as, `Room temperature should not exceed` N °C are more related to a behavior definition, and they express the expected course of actions of a system.

3.4.2 Data Representations for the DT

The data representation for the extended system is shown in Figure 3.6.

On one hand, it provides a clear description of messages exchanged between different elements of the system. On the other hand, it does not provide hints about the rules for dealing with different measures and when to apply them.

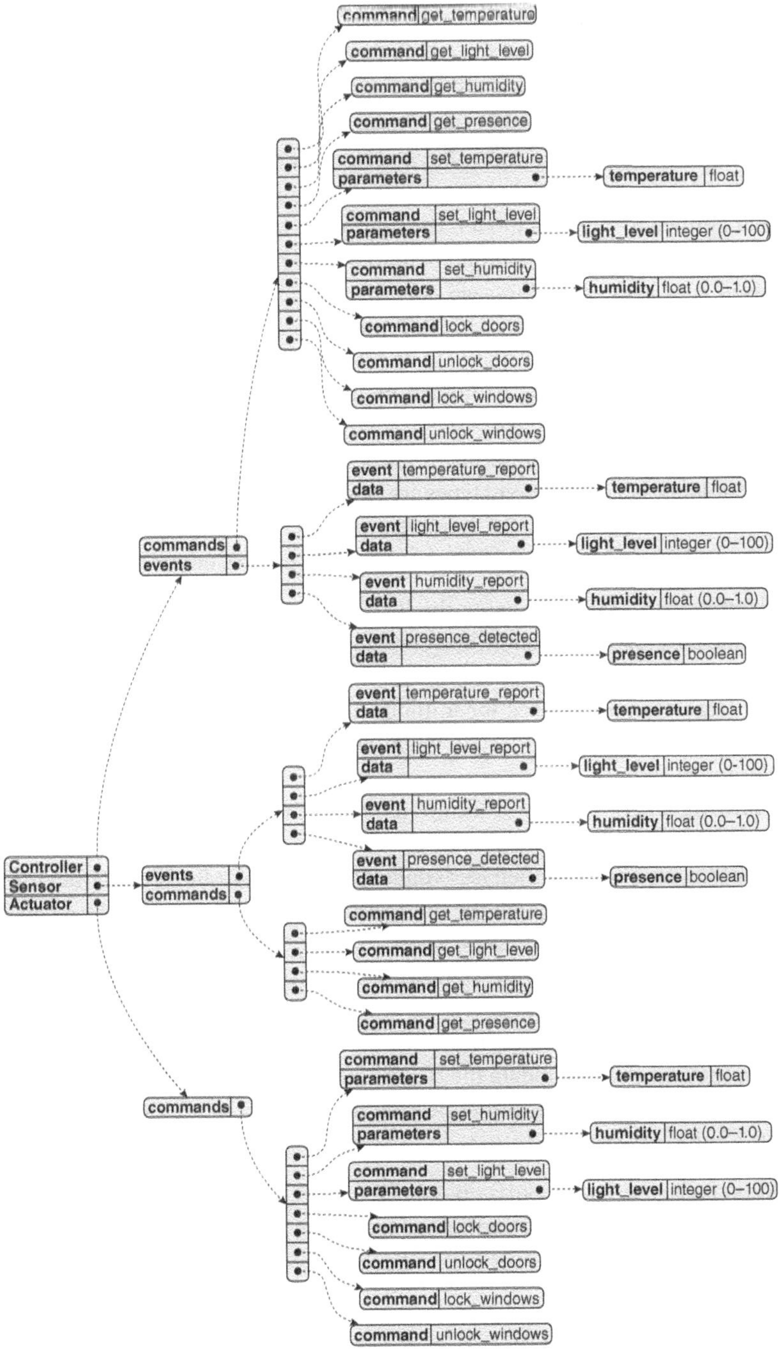

Figure 3.6 A JSON representation of a home automation system.

3.4.3 Data Models and APIs

A data model can be used to define the attributes of an API. A DT API leverages formats and structures as specified by the data model to ensure consistency and accurate representation within the system. Through the API, it is possible to query the current status of the controller and its associated sensors and actuators. Attributes and states of the DT system elements are aligned and constrained to the format defined by the data model. Data instances stored in the ContextBroker or other components of the DT implementation can be accessed or modified via `REST`-based messages, with message content structured according to the data model definition (see, for instance, [156]). Typical operations include `GET` requests to query status, `POST` or `PUT` requests to update or create new data, and `DELETE` requests to remove data. All these interactions are formatted according to the data model definition.

APIs can be differentiated in terms of goals, intent, and accessibility to better meet stakeholders' needs. Different types are listed in the following (a more refined list can be found in Appendix A.1.1, presenting also some examples of message types using REST and MQTT payloads, as well as access to ContextBroker API):

1. **Infrastructure API:** Managing the life-cycles of DTs or their components, allowing the creation, deletion, and configuration of instances of DT elements (controllers, sensors, and actuators) and their relationships.
2. **Data Ingestion API:** Used for initialization of components and elements, and for correction of a DT's state when needed or under the supervision of system managers.
3. **Streaming API:** To manage continuous or high-frequency data streams feeding into the twin. It includes data formatting and validation, ensuring data is usable by components. It then feeds data into the Context Broker by either formatting the message to match the ContextBroker's requirements or by receiving the streams as one of its subscribers.
4. **Event API:** Handling discrete, significant events that occur within the system or that are user-generated.
5. **Mediation API:** Collecting, transforming, enriching, and validating data before they are used to update the twin's state.
6. **Security API:** Managing authentication, authorization, and access control for the entire DT system.

These APIs can be used to support control of DT, as well as their management and access to data. Also, APIs can be partitioned according to the DT system functions.

3.4.3.1 Example of the Relationship Between a Data Model and an API

The DT embodies a smart home controller orchestrating various sensors and actuators. To simplify the examples, a reduced data model containing only the attributes relevant to the example scenarios is depicted:

Listing 3.1: JSON Data Model

```
{
        "controllerId": "controller001",
        "temperature": {
                "value": 23.5,
                "unit": "Celsius",
                "timestamp": "2025-04-27T13:00:00Z"
        },
        "heatingThreshold": 20.0,
        "actuators": [
        {
                "actuatorId": "thermostat001",
                "actuatorType": "thermostat",
                "targetTemperature": 22.0
        }
        ],
        "sensors": [
        {
                "sensorId": "tempSensor001",
                "sensorType": "temperature",
                "status": "active"
        }
        ]
}
```

An example, **Scenario 1: Temperature Threshold Exceeded**, is briefly presented with references to APIs described in this section and further illustrated in Appendix A.1.1. Another scenario is presented in A.1.1.1.

1. **Event Generation (Sensor):** The `tempSensor001` detects that the `temperature.value` has exceeded a predefined threshold (e.g., 28 °C).
2. **Event API (Publish):** The sensor publishes a `temperatureExceeded` event via the event API:

```
POST /events/temperatureExceeded
     {
     "controllerId": "controller001",
     "sensorId": "tempSensor001",
     "temperature": 28.5,
     "timestamp": "2025-04-27T15:00:00Z"
     }
```

3. **Controller Reaction (Event Handler):** The `controller001` receives the `temperatureExceeded` event.
4. **Action (Controller):** The controller uses the `actuator's` information (specifically, the `thermostat001`) from its data model to take action. It calls the Streaming API to lower the `targetTemperature` of the thermostat:

```
PUT /twins/thermostat001/properties/targetTemperature
      {
      "targetTemperature": 22.0
      }
```

The Context Broker is updated with a new value for `targetTemperature`.

This example (and the other presented in A.1.1.1) illustrates how the attributes defined in the data model (e.g., `temperature`, `targetTemperature`, `heatingThreshold`) are used to facilitate interactions between sensors, controllers, users, and the Context Broker through the defined APIs.

3.4.3.1.1 Role of the ContextBroker

The ContextBroker plays a central role in this Home Automation DT 9, and in general, in Data-driven DTs). Its main functionalities are briefly described here:

- **Data Storage:** It stores the current state of all entities (controllers, sensors, and actuators).
- **Data Abstraction:** Provides a uniform API to access and update entity data, regardless of the underlying data sources.
- **Real-Time Updates:** Publishes updates (context changes) to subscribed components, enabling real-time reactivity.
- **Complex Queries:** Supports complex queries across multiple entities.
- **Relationships with APIs:**
  - *Streaming API:* Feeds continuous sensor data to the ContextBroker.
  - *Event API:* Alerts the ContextBroker about important occurrences.
  - *Data Ingestion API:* Initializes or corrects the state of the twin within the ContextBroker.
  - *Mediation API:* Ensures data is properly formatted before being sent to the ContextBroker.

APIs may help in defining and organizing the functional aspects of a DT. For instance, a data ingestion API can facilitate the initialization and correction of DT component states. While the event API is more related to state changes of the physical system or important components.

More broadly, the availability of diverse APIs enables structured interactions with the DT, providing multiple ways to control the physical system and the DT itself. Specific attributes, such as thresholds, can be modified directly by users via

APIs supported by external applications. Additionally, events can be transmitted to these applications to aid decision-making.

In its simplest form, a DT can operate as a passive DT, where the data model is updated via the ContextBroker, while all essential logic pathways remain external to the DT system. This minimalist approach focuses on mirroring state and data changes, informing external elements which, via APIs, adjust thresholds and other key parameters to define the DT's basic behavior.

Ultimately, a minimal DT is fundamentally built on its supporting data model and an API framework for event exchange and behavior parameter adjustments.

3.5 Data Models for a DT

Data representation is a crucial aspect in the design and definition of DTs. Existing approaches and techniques for building them can be applied and reused [157]. A simplified methodology can be represented in the following steps:

- The first task is to represent entities from a data perspective. In this case, the evolved representation capabilities and methodologies developed for supporting object orientation, and in particular, UML [158], can help. Examples of entities/devices include: smart devices such as lights, thermostats, locks, and controllers, and are represented as objects/entities.
- Specific attributes or properties are, then, considered and specified, such as: state (on/off), level (brightness), temperature, etc.
- Next, the entities are studied and represented while considering their relationships. Devices can be grouped (e.g., all lights in the living room) or linked (e.g., a motion sensor triggers a light).
- The exchange of data and information between the entities is also relevant, for instance, to identify events/commands, i.e., actions that can be triggered (e.g., "turn on light," "set thermostat to 22 °C").
- The data representation and the collection of instances can lead to time-series data, for instance, sensor measures (temperature, humidity, and motion) can be stored as time-stamped records for subsequent statistical or Machine Learning/Deep Learning (ML/DL) analysis and automation.

3.5.1 Data Modeling Techniques and Semantic Enrichment in DTs

Data model definition for DTs leverage established data modeling techniques, such as the entity-relationship (ER) model and object-oriented modeling, to represent and structure virtual counterparts of physical entities [159–161]. These foundational approaches are often extended and specialized through the adoption of modern data representation formats, notably JSON and JSON-LD [162], which allow for more expressive power in modeling relationships between entities. For example, platforms like Azure DTs [163] define models in a manner similar to programming classes, including entities (e.g., `Room`, `TemperatureSensor`) and the explicit relationships between them [159].

The Digital Twin Definition Language (DTDL) [164, 165] uses JSON-LD to support explicit and navigable relationships within a DT graph. This approach eases the representation of complex interconnections and semantics in cyber-physical systems [159, 161].

Ontologies further enrich DT data models with semantic layers. By providing shared vocabularies and formally defined relationships, ontologies enhance the contextualization of data, enabling interoperability and deeper understanding across heterogeneous systems [160, 161]. This semantic enrichment is increasingly recognized as essential for advanced analytics, integration, and automation in complex DT environments [161].

Table 3.1 summarizes the main aspects of DT data modeling and their typical implementations and supporting techniques/tools.

In summary, DT data models build upon established modeling techniques and enhance data representation formats such as JSON-LD to better express complex relationships. Ontologies further enrich these models by adding semantic layers, supporting a deeper understanding and contextualization of data within DT environments. The management of data in real time or in batch, generated by sensors, is one of the most important features that data modeling should consider and ease. Data injection chains [153] are a means to transform and enrich raw data into usable and well-structured information as prescribed by data models. Data are collected and curated, then formatted according to the data model, so that data types can be linked in such a way as to find relationships between them. They enrich the data structure and can be stored in the ContextBroker. For instance, in Listing 3.2, two sensors (`sensor001` for temperature and `sensor002` for humidity) are tied together by means of a new relationship attribute (`relatedToHumidity`) in the temperature sensor entity, which references the humidity sensor entity. This relationship represents the logical or physical association between the two sensors, rather than a direct relationship between the temperature and humidity properties themselves. This approach is consistent with NGSI-LD modeling guidelines, where relationships are used to connect entities, not individual properties [148].

Table 3.1 A representation of aspects, approaches and tools for supporting data modeling.

Layer	Approach	Tools
Conceptual	ER, semantic graphs	UML, NGSI-LD
Data	Linked data	JSON-LD, RDF
Semantic	Ontologies	OWL, NGSI-LD Context

Listing 3.2: NGSI-LD Representation of Temperature and Humidity Relationship

```
{
        "id": "urn:ngsi-ld:Sensor:001",
        "type": "MultiSensor",
        "temperature": {
                "type": "Property",
                "value": 22.5,
                "unitCode": "CEL"
        },
        "humidity": {
                "type": "Property",
                "value": 45,
                "unitCode": "P1"
        },
        "relatedToHumidity": {
                "type": "Relationship",
                "object": "urn:ngsi-ld:Sensor:002"
        }
}
```

3.5.2 Existing Data Models for DTs

There are already a large number of data models that can be fruitfully exploited for designing a DT. Some of them are derived from activities related to IoT specifications, others are related to specific needs of newer problem domains, and others are designed with DT goals already in mind.[2,3] As the application of DTs expands to new problem domains, the number of these models is expected to increase to meet the growing demand.

Table 3.2 summarizes a few approaches and provides references to some especially promising data models.

Table 3.2 Various data models for DT.

Platform/data model	Description	References
FIWARE smart data models	Open, NGSI-LD-based models for many domains (cities, industry, energy, etc.), supporting interoperability and context management	[114]
NGSI-LD	JSON-LD-based standard for context information management, enabling linked data and knowledge graph representations for digital twins	[57]

(Continued)

2 https://smartdatamodels.org/
3 See Microsoft's Digital Twins Definition Language (DTDL): https://learn.microsoft.com/en-us/azure/digital-twins/concepts-models

Table 3.2 (Continued)

Platform/data model	Description	References
Azure DTDL	Microsoft's JSON-LD-based modeling language for defining DT entities, relationships, and telemetry in Azure DTs	[166]
BIM/IFC	Building Information Modeling (BIM) and Industry Foundation Classes (IFC) are standards for construction and facility DTs, supporting semantic and geometric modeling	[167]
ISO/IEC standards	Reference architectures and interoperability standards for DTs, including ISO 23247 (manufacturing), ISO 30146 (smart cities)	[168]
ITU standards	International Telecommunication Union standards addressing DT interoperability and data modeling frameworks for smart cities and IoT	[169]
W3C Web of Things (WoT) Thing Description 1.1	WoT Thing Description document outlines a JSON-based format for describing metadata, properties, actions, and events of a "thing" enabling interoperability between different IoT platforms and devices	[170]
Domain-specific (OPC UA, etc.)	Used in specific sectors (e.g., industrial automation, process control), often mapped to NGSI-LD or other open models for interoperability	[166]
Digital Twin Consortium (DTC) reference architecture	Industry-led reference architecture and taxonomy for DTs, promoting best practices and interoperability across sectors	[171]

The transformation of a JSON data model (see snippets described in Section 3.4 and noted in Listing A.1) into an NGSI-LD representation is discussed below. This example highlights NGSI-LD's ability to include richer semantics, relationships, and context-aware attributes compared to a simple JSON representation.

Listing 3.3: NGSI-LD Representation

```
{
        "id": "urn:ngsi-ld:Controller:controller001",
        "type": "Controller",
        "temperature": {
                "type": "Property",
                "value": 23.5,
                "unitCode": "CEL",
                "observedAt": "2025-04-27T13:00:00Z"
        },
        "heatingThreshold": {
                "type": "Property",
                "value": 20.0
        },
        "actuators": {
```

```
                "type": "Relationship",
                "object": [
                {
                        "id": "urn:ngsi-ld:Actuator:
                            thermostat001",
                        "type": "Thermostat",
                        "targetTemperature": {
                                "type": "Property",
                                "value": 22.0
                        }
                }
                ]
        },
        "sensors": {
                "type": "Relationship",
                "object": [
                {
                        "id": "urn:ngsi-ld:Sensor:
                            tempSensor001",
                        "type": "Sensor",
                        "sensorType": {
                                "type": "Property",
                                "value": "temperature"
                        },
                        "status": {
                                "type": "Property",
                                "value": "active"
                        }
                }
                ]
        }
}
```

There are several differences between Listings 3.3 and A.1, including:

- **Structure:** The JSON model is designed for specific applications, making it static and tightly coupled to the implementation. It lacks semantic interrelationships and extensibility. In contrast, the NGSI-LD model adopts a graph-based approach, allowing for semantic representation of entities, properties, and relationships with rich metadata.
- **Semantics:** The JSON model primarily handles raw data without explicit relationships or context definitions. NGSI-LD, however, introduces structured, typed data, where attributes are explicitly categorized as property, relationship, or geometry, following linked data principles to enhance interoperability and enable complex reasoning.
- **Relationships:** JSON models typically embed relationships within entity definitions, limiting flexibility. NGSI-LD employs explicit relationship types

to interconnect entities, making it well-suited for representing complex systems, such as IoT ecosystems.
- **Generalization:** JSON models are often application-specific, lacking adaptability for broader use cases.

NGSI-LD, by design, supports cross-domain interoperability and contextual data integration, making it applicable in smart environments like cities, manufacturing, and healthcare. It ensures seamless data exchange across IoT devices, systems, and platforms while avoiding traditional JSON-induced data silos.

Furthermore, NGSI-LD prioritizes scalability and extensibility, allowing modifications without altering its core structure. New relationships, properties, and systems can integrate seamlessly—a crucial factor in dynamic design phases where physical system structures evolve rapidly. This flexibility is essential, as a DT's definition expands throughout the system's life-cycle, incorporating new attributes and features.

3.6 Extending Data Models to Fit the Stakeholders' Needs

The simple model represented by Listing 3.3 is essentially focused on the needs and capabilities associated with a single user in a limited environment (the examples were focused on a single `Controller` operating in a single `Room`). In reality, the system should scale up to consider the entire apartment/home or even a building and to include different stakeholders. A requirement could be to extend the data model to encompass the existing system into a larger structure in which a building manager system needs to monitor, control, and govern the set of apartments under its responsibility. Another simple extension could offer users the option to adapt the system to their own preferences within limitations and ranges posed by the building manager. The building manager could implement and impose rules decided by regulators (e.g., the temperature in the home should not exceed 22° in winter). Additional stakeholders or actors could have specific requirements and/or impose constraints on the system. The flexibility and ability to capture and represent the data model's relationships are essential for scaling up and encompassing any new requirements. Some simple examples related to the building manager's and the users' perspectives are provided.

Considering the NGSI-LD model for `urn:ngsi-ld:Controller:controller001` as described in Listing 3.3 and the building manager and user stakeholders, it is possible to identify potential extensions in terms of **Requirements** and **Constraints** in a similar style as SYSML 2.0.

3.6.1 Stakeholder 1: Building Manager

This stakeholder is responsible for guaranteeing an efficient usage of the system with a particular focus on energy efficiency and system integrity. **Stakeholder**

Needs (Requirements): The building manager must monitor and optimize the energy consumption of the HVAC system as operated by a set of `Controllers`. In addition, the building manager also needs to track the operational status and maintenance history of each controller to fulfill its responsibility for proactive maintenance and fault detection.

Building Manager Requirements:

Extension to Requirements Set Considering Building Manager's Views:

- `REQ-ENG-001 (Energy Monitoring): The system shall provide data on the energy consumption for each controller and associated actuators (e.g., Thermostat).`
- `REQ-OPS-002 (Operational Status Reporting): The system shall report the current operational status of each controller (e.g., nominal, degraded, faulty).`
- `REQ-MAINT-001 (Maintenance Tracking): The system shall record and provide access to the maintenance history of each Controller, including the date of the last maintenance and personnel involved.`

To fulfill these requirements, the data model should be extended to encompass new properties and relations. Some **NGSI-LD Extensions (aligning with Requirements)** are listed below:

- `energyConsumption` (Property): Represents a quantifiable **Property** of the `Controller` related to `REQ-ENG-001`. Value: Numeric (e.g., 1.2), Unit: `unitCode`: "kWh", `observedAt`: Timestamp, Metadata (Context): `source`: "meter001."
- `operationalStatus` (Property): Represents a discrete **Property** of the `Controller` indicating its state, fulfilling `REQ-OPS-002`. Value: Enumeration (e.g., "nominal", "degraded", "faulty"), `observedAt`: Timestamp.
- `lastMaintenance` (Property): Represents a temporal **Property** associated with the `Controller`, addressing `REQ-MAINT-001`. Value: Date ("2024-12-15"), Metadata (Context): `performedBy`: "MaintenanceCrewAlpha."

These extensions can be easily introduced in the NGSI-LD data model to allow for new capabilities of the entire system (obviously, the physical devices or some mediators should be able to provide these measures). For instance, the `lastMaintenance` property is not necessarily implemented or offered by the single `Controller`. It could be supported directly by the DT (augmentation property of the DT) that will record the date of last intervention of the management team. These data could be injected into the system by means of data ingestion APIs with explicit reference to the identifier of the device that has been maintained.

Another stakeholder example (requirement mapping and NGSI-LD model extension)is considered in A.1.2. This case represents the possibility to accommodate tenant/user personalized comfort and control. Likewise, the DT can augment a few capabilities of the system. For instance, the `comfortLevel` property is not necessarily supported by all the `Controllers`. The DT implementation can extend the system capabilities that will be passed by the users to the DT by means of APIs (e.g., event APIs).

By framing the extensions in terms of stakeholder needs and aligning them with requirements and constraints, an exemplification of a structured and engineering-focused approach to data model evolution is provided. This allows for better mapping between stakeholder needs, system requirements, and the actual data model design. The extensibility and flexibility of the data model are extremely useful for system evolution. The physical system's capabilities have an important role. If, for instance, the system is not capable of measuring the room temperature, the envisaged solution makes no sense. However, the DT offers a degree of flexibility that can be used to functionally extend the entire system at the software level without necessarily impacting the physical system. It is up to the designers to flexibly and intelligently exploit the capability of the DT software as well as the possibility to change the supporting data model.

3.7 Relationships Between Descriptive and Behavior Models

Descriptive and behavior models each offer distinct insights. A well-formed descriptive model organizes and presents data to end users, providing a structured view of the physical system's status (passive DT). In contrast, the behavior model defines the system's components, their interactions, and governing conditions. While it helps explain outcomes, a behavior model without a continuous flow of real-world data remains theoretical rather than a true DT. A structured framework, composed of laws, rules, and established relationships, enhances the ability to interpret system behavior and its resulting data patterns.

In an ideal DT, the data model serves as the foundation for structuring and feeding data into the behavior model, enabling reasoned analysis of system dynamics and predictive insights. The two representational approaches are most effective when seamlessly integrated.

A critical first step is ensuring that the data model adequately represents all necessary data for the behavior model to function. System entities must consistently reflect their states through data model properties, and interactions between components should be fully supported by the expressive power of the data model.

Another key representational aspect is the ability to componentize the system, associating states and interfaces with each component. Rules govern events and determine state transitions, making flexibility important in structuring representations. The Modular Open System Approach (MOSA) [172–174], developed by the U.S. Department of Defense, advocates for open, modular architectures built from "gray" components, units offering well-defined functionality through standardized interfaces while allowing variations in implementation.

This approach aligns closely with integrated behavior and descriptive modeling, where system components represent distinct functions while offering structured interfaces and state definitions via a standardized data model. The foundation of an effective DT lies in defining both component behavior and the data structures necessary to represent state transitions and interactions.

3.7.1 Data Exploitation Chain: From Passive to Prescriptive DT

This section highlights how a data-driven paradigm supports various types of DTs while reducing the reliance on extensive behavior models.

3.7.1.1 Predictive DT

The NGSI-LD model can be utilized for storing historical temperature data. This is a prerequisite for predicting future room temperatures. This can be achieved by recording multiple instances of the `temperature` property with their corresponding `observedAt` timestamps for the `urn:ngsi-ld:Controller:controller001` entity or by creating linked `TemperatureObservation` entities associated with the `urn:ngsi-ld:Sensor:tempSensor001`.

The collection of historical data at different observation times allows for a well-structured and organized set of measures that represents the evolution of the controlled temperature as represented in Listing 3.4.

Listing 3.4: Historical Temperature Data as Linked Entities

```
{
        "id": "urn:ngsi-ld:TemperatureObservation:obs001",
        "type": "TemperatureObservation",
        "observedBy": {
                "type": "Relationship",
                "object": "urn:ngsi-ld:Sensor:tempSensor001"
        },
        "temperature": {
                "type": "Property",
                "value": 23.5,
                "unitCode": "CEL",
                "observedAt": "2025-04-27T13:00:00Z"
```

```
            }
        },
        {
            "id": "urn:ngsi-ld:TemperatureObservation:obs002",
            "type": "TemperatureObservation",
            "observedBy": {
                "type": "Relationship",
                "object": "urn:ngsi-ld:Sensor:tempSensor001"
            },
            "temperature": {
                "type": "Property",
                "value": 23.7,
                "unitCode": "CEL",
                "observedAt": "2025-04-27T13:05:00Z"
            }
        },
        // ... more observations
```

The `observedAt` property provides the temporal context for time series analysis. The `observedBy` relationship explicitly links the readings to a specific sensor. This historical data can then be used to train various forecasting models to predict future temperature trends.

The model can be extended with additional contextual information (extensibility) representing other factors that might influence room temperature, such as:

- External Temperature: Readings from an external weather sensor (as another linked entity).
- Heating/Cooling System Status: The status of the thermostat or other actuators (using the actuators relationship and their properties).
- Occupancy: Data from occupancy sensors (as another linked entity).
- Time of Day/Day of Week: These can be derived from the `observedAt` timestamp but could also be explicitly added as properties if needed for specific prediction models.

The historical data stored according to the NGSI-LD model can be retrieved and used as input for various forecasting models, including: statistical methods such as Autoregressive Integrated Moving Average (ARIMA), exponential smoothing, etc.; ML/DL models [27, 175]: Recurrent Neural Networks (RNNs) like Long Short-term Memory networks (LSTMs) or Gated Recurrent Units (GRUs), time series transformers, etc. The choice of model depends on the complexity of temperature patterns and the availability of other relevant data.

Eventually, the NGSI-LD model could be extended to represent predictions (potential extensions), e.g., a `predictedTemperature` property can be used to store and provide a predicted temperature for a room to the building manager or the user.

These capabilities, built on top of the passive DT, constitute the basis for building a predictive DT capable of forecasting about the future evolution of the system.

3.7.1.2 Inferring the Behavior

The home automation example can help in understanding how to extract some behavior information from the data and how to transform it into a set of rules that can be used to describe the system behavior. If a sequence of data expressed in a form compatible with the chosen data model is available, it can be used to analyze the behavior of the home automation system over time. For instance, if JSON or even better, NGSI-LD descriptions of historical data are available, they can be used to verify the system behavior.

Listing 3.5: Sample JSON Record

```
{
        "timestamp": "2025-04-26T20:00:00Z",
        "roomId": "living_room",
        "temperature": 6.5,
        "luminosity": 0.1,
        "humidity": 0.8,
        "presence": false,
        "timeOfDay": "night",
        "action": [
        "lock doors and windows",
        "set temperature to 15",
        "keep luminosity as is"
        ]
}
```

Some attributes of a room and the actions taken by the system in that situation are represented in Listing 3.5. In this case, the home automation system decided that, in accordance with the "time of the day," the presence of people, the temperature, luminosity, and humidity of the room, a set of actions should be executed, namely to `lock doors and windows`, `set the temperature to 15°C`, and `keep the temperature as it is`. Having a historical set of records of physical system actions in relation to situations and commands gives an indication of how the physical system reacts to different conditions and situations. As shown in Figure 3.7, the sensor data records the temperature, humidity, and actions in each room.

By using ML techniques and tools (e.g., decision tree algorithms or their derivatives [176, 177]) and tools (e.g., Weka [178] an initial behavior of the physical system can be inferred and successively used and improved to incrementally approximate the physical system's behavior. Figure 3.8 represents a possible decision tree generated by analyzing the available records.

Timestamp	Room	Temp (°C)	Luminosity	Humidity	Presence	Time of Day	Actions
2025-04-26T10:00:00	office	16	0.1	0.6	No	daylight	lock doors, set temp, ask luminosity
2025-04-26T14:00:00	bedroom	22	0.6	0.25	Yes	daylight	generate alarm
2025-04-26T19:00:00	living_room	8	0.3	0.7	Yes	night	(none)
2025-04-26T20:00:00	living_room	6.5	0.1	0.8	No	night	lock doors, set temp, lower temp, keep luminosity
2025-04-26T23:00:00	kitchen	5	0.15	0.5	Yes	night	set temp, increase luminosity

Figure 3.7 An example of records generated by a home automation system with room sensors and related actions taken.

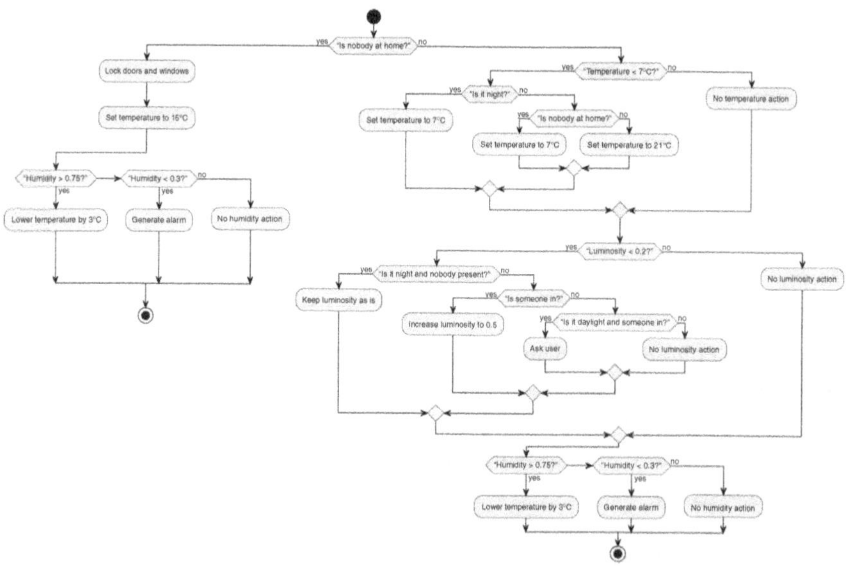

Figure 3.8 A decision tree supporting the home automation behavior.

3.7.1.3 Towards a Prescriptive DT

Being able to predict events and infer behavior can be a basis for the aggregation of additional functions in a DT. A **Prescriptive DT** can be defined by leveraging the predictive capabilities offered by availability of NGSI-LD labeled records and integrating data-driven insights from approaches like decision trees or random forests.

3.7.1.3.1 Understanding Prescriptive DTs

Prescriptive DTs are a type of DT that combines predictive, inferring, and recommendation capabilities. They can detect the current status of the associated physical system, infer the possible future actions, and recommend the best course of action to optimize the behavior of the system. The prescriptive capability can be limited to suggestions given to external applications or humans. The ability to actually decide the actions to perform benefits from the availability of a behavior model. Prescriptive DTs are used to pursue specific goals and objectives. For the time being, the analysis focuses on a minimization of the behavior description and on the maximization of data usage. In this perspective, a data-driven prescriptive DT does not simply mirror the current and past states of a physical asset (descriptive) or forecast its future behavior (predictive). It actively recommends actions and interventions to optimize the asset's performance, prevent failures, and/or achieve specific goals.

3.7.1.3.2 How NGSI-LD and Decision Tree/Forest Techniques Enable Prescriptive Capabilities

The prediction and decision capabilities of DTs have been discussed as part of the possibilities offered by the availability of well-formed data and historical time series. The use of structured data models and ontologies helps to pursue the definition of data-driven prescriptive DT.

1. **Rich Contextual Data (NGSI-LD):** The NGSI-LD model supports a semantically rich and context-aware representation of a physical asset (e.g., the `Controller` and its associated sensors and actuators in a specific environment [a room]). It allows the integration of various relevant data, such as:
   - Current and historical sensor readings (e.g., `temperature`).
   - Actuator states (e.g., `targetTemperature` of the `Thermostat`).
   - Environmental conditions (if integrated, e.g., external temperature).
   - Operational parameters (`operationalStatus`).
   - Maintenance history (`lastMaintenance`).
2. **Behavior Modeling by Data (Decision Tree/Forest):** Decision trees and random forests are powerful ML techniques for learning complex relationships and deriving rules from data. By training these models on the historical data stored in the NGSI-LD model, it is possible to:
   - **Identify patterns:** Discover correlations between different data points and the resulting system behavior (e.g., how temperature changes based on the heating threshold and external temperature);
   - **Predict outcomes:** Forecast future states of a system (as discussed previously); and

- **Derive actionable rules:** Extract clear "if-then-else" rules (from a decision tree) or probabilistic insights (from a random forest) that link specific conditions to desired or undesired outcomes.

Other ML/DL technologies can be used; for instance, LSTM provides insights about past behavior and suggestions about what to do next. The choice of decision trees made here is to highlight the possibilities offered by different AI techniques in conjunction with data models.

3.7.1.3.3 Defining a Prescriptive DT with This Approach

By combining these elements, a DT can provide prescriptive functions based on data in the following ways:

1. **Identifying Suboptimal Conditions:** The decision tree/forest model, trained on historical data that includes instances of inefficiency or deviations from desired states, can identify current or predicted conditions that are likely to lead to these suboptimal outcomes (e.g., high energy consumption, temperature fluctuations).
2. **Recommending Actions:** Based on the learned rules or patterns, the DT can suggest specific actions to take. For example:
   - **If** the `predictedTemperature` in the next hour is below the tenant's preferred range **and** the `heatingThreshold` is high, **then** recommend lowering the `heatingThreshold`.
   - **If** the `operationalStatus` is "degraded" **and** `predictedEnergy-Consumption` is significantly higher than the usual quantity for similar conditions, **then** recommend scheduling maintenance.
   - **If** `predictedEternalTemperature` is predicted to rise significantly **and** `currentRoomTemperature` is approaching the upper comfort limit, **then** recommend proactively adjusting the `targetTemperature` of the `Thermostat` downwards.
3. **Evaluating Potential Actions:** The predictive capabilities of the model can also be used to simulate the potential impact of different recommended actions before they are implemented in the physical system. This allows for evaluating the effectiveness and potential side effects of the prescriptions.

3.7.1.3.4 Example Scenario

Imagine a hypothetical scenario in which the Decision Tree model has learned that when the external temperature drops below 5 °C and the `heatingThreshold` is set to 22 °C, the room temperature fluctuates significantly, leading to tenant discomfort and increased energy consumption.

The prescriptive DT, observing the current low external temperature and the high `heatingThreshold` in the NGSI-LD model, could:

1. **Predict:** Forecast potential temperature fluctuations and high energy use in the near future.
2. **Prescribe:** Recommend lowering the `heatingThreshold` to 20 °C based on learned rules.
3. **Explain:** Provide a justification for the recommendation based on historical data and model's insights (e.g., "Historical data shows that lowering the heating threshold in these conditions stabilizes room temperature and reduces energy consumption").

3.7.1.3.5 Considerations for a Data-driven Prescriptive DT

An initial set of insights/considerations can be drawn based on the hypothetical scenarios considered in this section:

- **Data Quality and Completeness:** The accuracy and effectiveness of prescriptive recommendations heavily rely on the quality and completeness of the historical data stored in the NGSI-LD model. Creating a large historical dataset can provide a significant amount of insights, but, at the same time, may require a large data management system that may not fit with the class of service (e.g., a home automation system).
- **Model Accuracy and Interpretability:** The decision tree or random forest model must be accurate and, ideally, interpretable enough to make it possible to understand the reasoning behind recommendations. Decision trees excel in interpretability, making their decision process easy to follow. Random forests usually provide higher accuracy but at the cost of reduced transparency. Other ML techniques, such as LSTM networks, can offer even higher accuracy but often sacrifice interpretability, introducing additional complexity and making the decision process less understandable.
- **Integration with Actuation Systems:** To fully realize the prescriptive potential, the DT needs to be integrated with the systems that control the physical asset (e.g., the building management system that controls the thermostats) to allow the recommended actions for stakeholders (users or managers) to be implemented.
- **Continuous Learning and Adaptation:** The prescriptive model should be designed to continuously learn from new data and adapt its recommendations over time to optimize performance and respond to changing conditions.

The prescriptive DT, like many recommendation systems, requires access to data and efforts to maintain consistency and update the data sets. For simple services, this may result in an expensive and overrated system with respect to the envisaged potential market. An evaluation of the functions and potential of services is fundamental for deciding the level of functions and complexity that would be affordable and appropriate for the chosen type of users [179].

In conclusion, by combining the rich contextual data provided by the NGSI-LD model with the behavior insights and rule-derivation capabilities of artificial intelligence (ML/DL), a powerful data-driven prescriptive DT can be created. This would not only understand and predict the behavior of physical assets, but it could also recommend actions to achieve desired outcomes.

4

Digital Twin as a Behavior Model of a Physical System

After reading this chapter, you should be able to:

- Define and design a behavior model for a physical system.
- Explain the difference between different behavior model representations and constructions.
- Justify and exemplify the benefits to represent the operating environment in the definition of a digital twin.
- Interpret the difference and relationships between context and situation.
- Understand how different artificial intelligence techniques can be applied to help define or embody the behavior of a DT.
- Understand the relationships between a behavior model and simulation.

4.1 Behavior Modeling

A physical system (PS) is characterized by its behavior, i.e., the actions put in place by the system in response to stimuli from other systems and its environment. Modeling the system behavior means creating representations that explain how and under what conditions a system responds to stimuli and how its parts interact to accomplish tasks. A behavior model provides indications about when, how, and why a system carries out a certain course of actions as responses to stimuli or during a period of time. Behavior modeling is an incremental (and sometimes iterative) activity that aims at defining and structuring a system in terms of its relevant entities, their relationships, the logic behind interactions, and the identification of requirements and constraints that characterize its functioning. This modeling activity can span design, specification, development, and testing/validation phases.

One important aspect is the identification, design, and implementation of the relevant components characterizing the system. The componentization process identifies parts and their expected behavior in terms of rules, laws, prescriptions, and habits that regulate the performance of actions and interactions between them. In essence, the behavior model represents and describes the reactions in terms of actions to be performed by a system after its exposure to (external or internal) events. When events and actions occur, they cause changes of state in the PS or in some of its parts. A descriptive model (actually the current data) captures these changes. The behavior model describes under what conditions, why, when, and how these actions are executed. The two descriptions complement each other to fully expose the dynamics behind the PS functioning and how the corresponding Digital Twin (DT) should be designed and implemented.

Figure 3.3 presented a simple model consisting of two components: a traffic light controller (the controller) and a traffic light (the actuator). The controller issues commands to the actuator, which in turn returns events, such as execution notifications or malfunction alerts.

However, this basic setup does not fully capture the behavior of the PS. Additional elements and features must be incorporated for a more complete representation. As paraphrased from Ref. [88], "structure defines a system and its components at various levels of abstraction, describing their interconnections via interfaces. Behavior, in contrast, explains how the system evolves over time in response to different stimuli."

These stimuli and interactions emerge from the continuous flow of PS data toward the DT, reinforcing the dynamic nature of its representation.

4.1.1 An Example: The Traffic Light System Behavior

The representation of Figure 3.3 is not detailed enough to grasp the actual behavior of the traffic light system. A more informative representation of the behavior is needed. In the following, sequence messages [180], state machine [181], and activity [182] diagrams illustrate a baseline description of a more detailed behavior.

Figure 4.1 represents the case in which, after an initialization phase, the "parts"[1] (controller and actuator) exchange messages, actually commands and replies, aiming at changing the attribute "color" of the traffic light according to the logic determined by the controller. The response is OK, if the command is well received and executed; otherwise, an error message is returned (the attribute could also be used for determining the status of the traffic light part). A first consideration that differentiates the behavior from descriptive modeling is also terminological: the term logic indicates that the system's behavior is determined by a set of rules and

1 Following SYSML 2.0 jargon, a part in this section represents a modular unit of a system's structure.

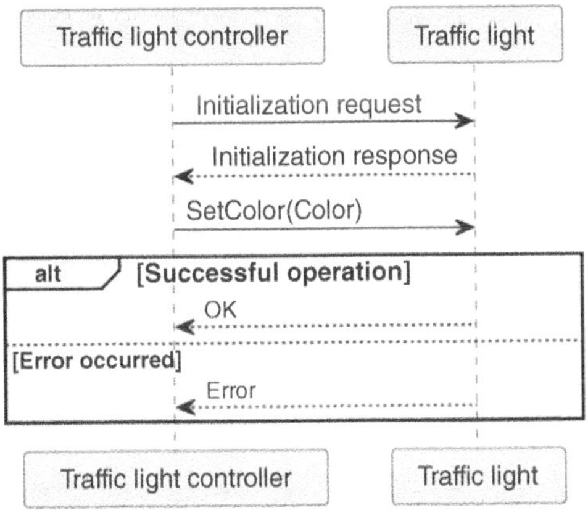

Figure 4.1 Message sequences between parts of the traffic light control.

choices that determine the traffic light system's behavior as a whole, and its components, according to different conditions and situations, and several events, and corresponding actions.

The example offers initial insight into the system's behavior, however, the information and the descriptions are not enough to understand the logic (the functioning model) of the traffic light. The state machine diagram shown in Figure 4.2 is more informative. It describes a finite state machine of the system, showing the different states and the possible transitions from one state to another.

For instance, it illustrates state transitions in relation to expiring timers.[2] It also shows that during the night, the traffic light is programmed to blink with color set to yellow. So far, the system's behavior can be summarized as a controller implementing a state machine model. When a status change is required, the controller sends commands to the traffic light. Appropriate behavior rules are defined to handle specific cases (e.g., night activity). The possibility of setting different timers could offer additional logic personalization: the switching from green to red and back to green can be regulated in a way that considers the variations of traffic during the day (not represented in Figure 4.2). To better specify the simplified expected behavior, activity diagrams can also be used. A simple one is represented in Figure 4.3.

An activity diagram clarifies the system's expected functioning. The system's different phases are easier to understand when the behavior and descriptive models are interrelated. Defining rules and expected behaviors alongside resulting state or attribute changes offers deeper insights into how the system operates. In other

2 Errors or synchronization with the TrafficLight system governing the crossroad are disregarded in order to keep the example simple to illustrate the concepts.

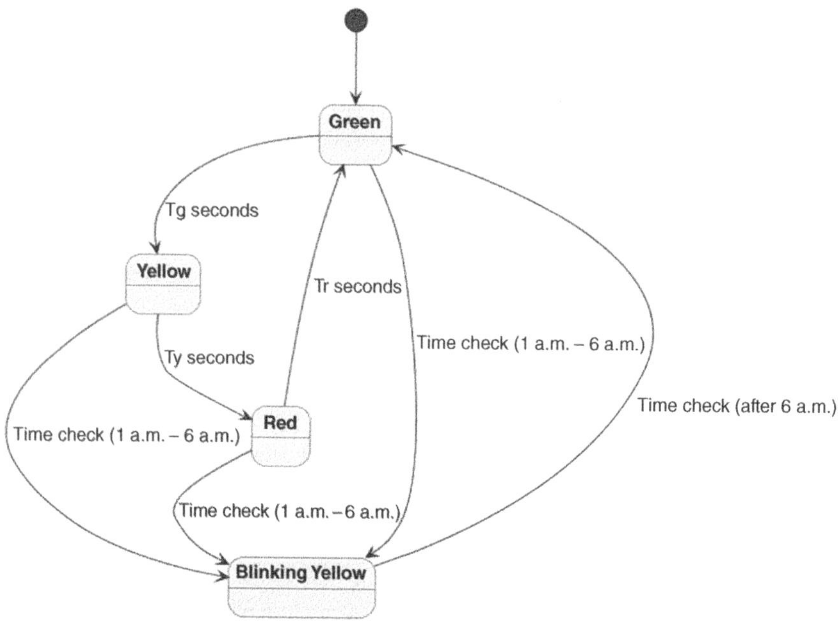

Figure 4.2 A simple traffic light's state model.

words, the interplay between triggered actions and their effects highlights system progression and provides explanations for its evolution.

4.1.2 Behavior Modeling Challenges and Needs

The previous examples minimized complexity, making it easier to understand and maintain relationships between parts and to represent a simple behavior. With an increase in the number of components, and in the complexity of the system, it will become more difficult to maintain the consistency between the different parts and to comprehend the behavior at various levels of abstraction (and nesting) of parts. This complexity is even more evident when the PS and the DT are composed of aggregate parts that need to be consistent in themselves and must contribute to the global coherence of the entire system [183, 184]. Consistency of **aggregation** and **abstraction** are two important features that can create issues when representing a PS and its digital counterpart. The designer should carefully identify all the discrepancies or inaccurate definitions to avoid misfunction of the system and its software representation.

Figure 4.4 represents the issues of maintaining consistency inside componentized systems (physical and DT) and between the two systems. Even for a simple PS with only a few components, maintaining consistency in its DT may require

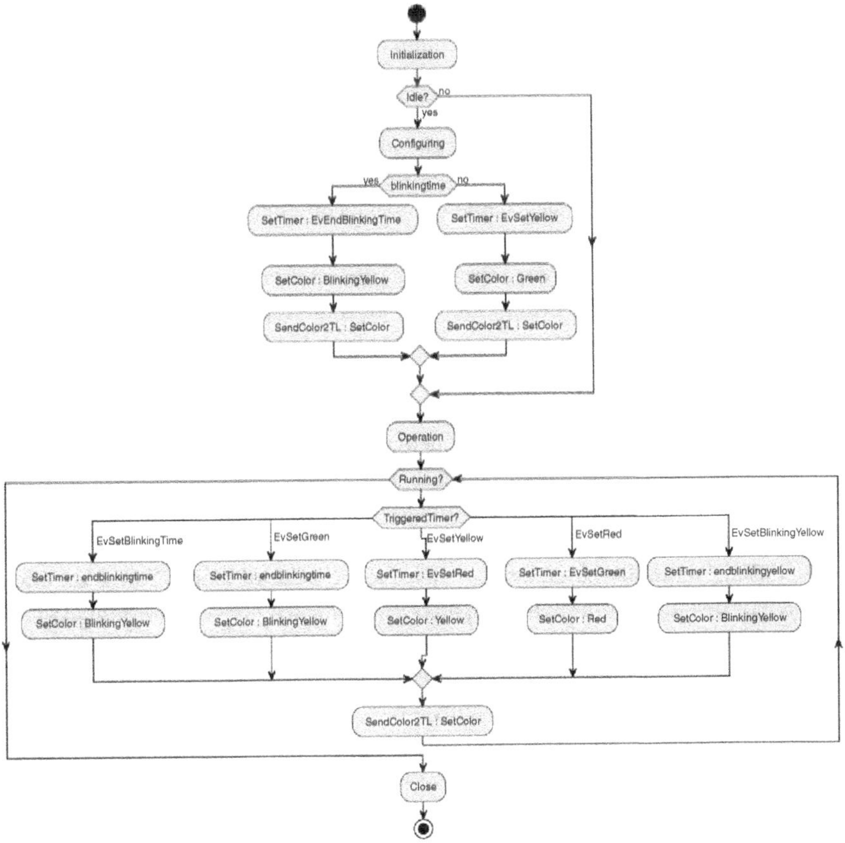

Figure 4.3 An activity diagram for illustrating the working of the traffic light.

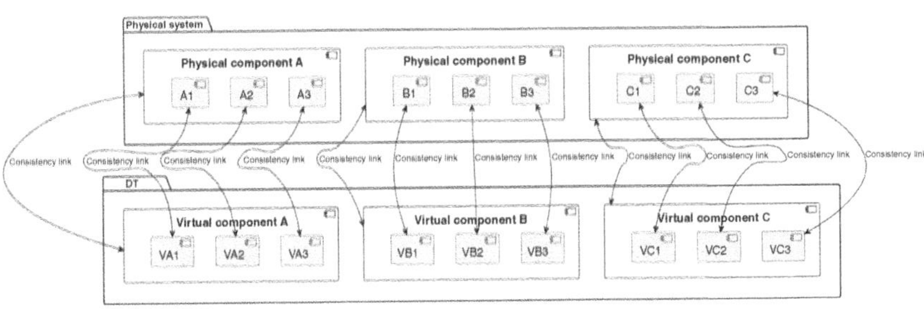

Figure 4.4 Maintaining consistency between parts and abstraction levels in a physical system–digital twin relation.

considerable effort. The more componentized the PS is, the more crucial it becomes for the DT components to remain consistent and updated—adhering to representativeness, reflection, and entanglement properties—to provide an accurate representation of the PS.

Componentization and abstraction must be used carefully [154]. Overabstraction, where components or parts of the PS are not fully represented, may lead to a loss of representativeness, while excessive componentization can introduce significant complexity in representing the PS. In any case, extreme componentization can later be mitigated by representing aggregated components, if the smaller components are not relevant for the overall representation of the PS (composability property). However, an overly high level of abstraction can make later modifications difficult and hinder achieving effective representativeness.

Another key aspect of behavior modeling is the identification of requirements and constraints that influence the system dynamics and responses. With reference to Figures 4.2 and 4.3, the model's purpose is to support the change of traffic light signals during a large part of the day and to set the traffic light to a blinking state during a period of the night. If a new requirement is introduced, the system behavior could substantially change as a consequence of fulfillment of new requirements. For instance, a traffic light in a poorly trafficked area during Sundays can be set to a blinking state in those periods. This option is expressed by Figure 4.5.

This simple change propagates in several modifications of traffic light system behavior description as shown in Figure 4.6.

New requirements and constraints affecting the PS's functioning may necessitate significant modifications to the behavior model, increasing its complexity in both specification and implementation. Aggregation, abstraction, and the introduction of new requirements or constraints are among the key challenges in designing the behavior model. These factors add complexity to the overall description, making specification difficult and implementation even more challenging.

These examples are intended to demonstrate a step-by-step construction of viable behavior models. Embedding such models within a DT, however, offers significant additional benefits beyond what a simple program can provide. These

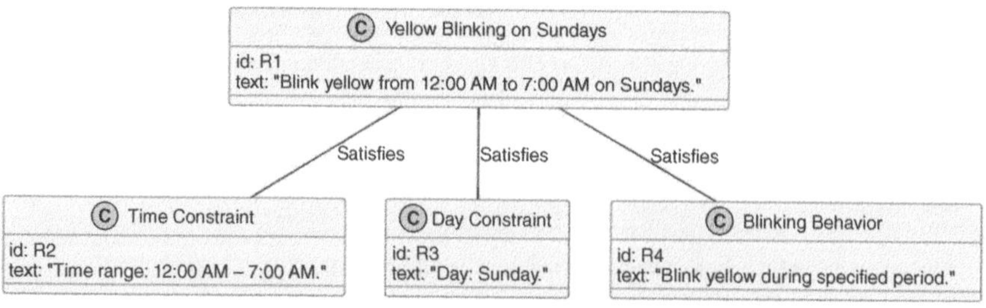

Figure 4.5 A new requirement about setting a traffic light to blinking yellow on Sundays.

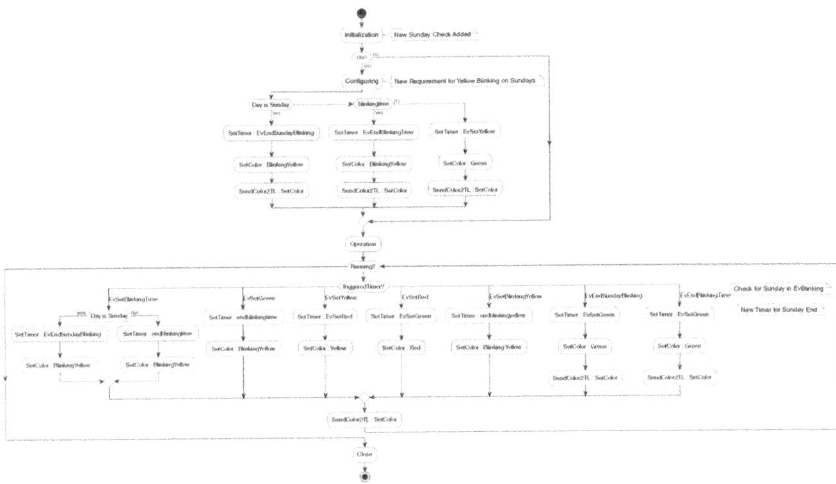

Figure 4.6 Impact of the Sunday requirement on the behavior description.

include the ability to simulate complex what-if scenarios, real-time control of the PS, and the flexibility to allocate specialized replicas for different customers or functional needs. Together, these capabilities enable more dynamic, adaptive, and context-aware representations that support advanced monitoring, optimization, and decision-making.

4.2 Foundational Behavior Models

Computationally, behavior models represent how a DT's corresponding physical entity responds to various conditions and stimuli [185]. Beyond capturing the system's status through data-driven representations, they define dynamic responses and interactions, allowing for the understanding of the state changes, predictive analysis of future behaviors, and simulation under different scenarios.

Their purpose and complexity vary depending on the physical asset, the DT's intended function, and available data [52, 183]. Behavior models play a crucial role in diverse applications. The integration of data model languages, system structure specifications, and behavior representations enriches DT descriptions, allowing them to better represent the PS. This integration is best achieved by leveraging Model-based Systems Engineering (MBSE). Two distinct patterns—or perspectives on how to build the DT—emerge from this approach (e.g., [77]):

- Closed Behavior Model Pattern: *Defines a system where all model elements are predetermined at design time, structured as a schema for specific object types.*
- Open Behavior Model Pattern: *Describes systems where behavior evolves at runtime, allowing dynamic modifications.*

The former can be applied to simple and stable systems (e.g., the traffic light example), the latter considers larger and more complex systems that show adaptive capabilities to change (e.g., large ecosystems).

4.2.1 Types of Behavior Models

In the literature, different approaches are possible for relating the behavior description to well-established modeling techniques, for instance:

- **Physics-based Models Also Called First Principles:** Represent behavior using fundamental physical laws (e.g., thermodynamics, fluid dynamics) often involving differential equations [18, 142].
- **Data-driven Models (Empirical Models):** Built from historical data using statistical or machine learning (ML) techniques (e.g., decision trees, neural networks) to learn input-output relationships (see Chapter 3).
- **Hybrid Models:** Combine physics-based and data-driven approaches, leveraging the strengths of both [186].
- **State-based Models:** Describe behavior through discrete states and transitions, such as Finite State Machines (FSMs) [187, 188].
- **Agent-based Models:** Simulate complex systems by modeling individual interacting components (agents) [189–191].

The behavior model's alignment with an open or closed pattern depends on its implementation within the DT architecture. A closed pattern, which relies on predefined behavior, is well-suited for physics-based models or state-based models. In this approach, the DT simply mirrors the PS's laws or fixed transitions, e.g., in the deterministic cycles of a traffic light. Conversely, an open pattern leverages models that can learn and adapt from evolving interactions of individual components or from continuous data capture. For example, an open DT for a city's traffic network may use a data-driven model to capture emergent behaviors and proactively adjust traffic light timing to optimize flow, showcasing its ability to evolve beyond a fixed set of rules.

4.2.2 Functions of Behavior Models in a DT

In addition to providing a clear description of the PS, the behavior models ease different tasks of the DT, for example:

- **Real-time Data Integration:** Sensors and IoT devices continuously provide operational data (e.g., temperature, humidity, presence) to the digital twin, ensuring synchronization between physical and virtual states corroborating the behavior model.

- **Simulation and What-if Analysis:** Allow a DT to simulate an asset's response to various scenarios without any physical impact. For a traffic light, this could involve determining the optimal behavior to implement during adverse weather conditions, such as icing.
- **Performance Prediction:** Forecast future performance metrics (e.g., remaining useful life, energy consumption). For example, determining when to replace a component in a traffic light to prevent system failure.
- **Anomaly Detection:** Identify deviations between predicted and actual behavior, indicating potential faults.
- **Control and Optimization:** Enable prescriptive DTs to recommend optimal control strategies.
- **Virtual Testing and Training:** Create virtual environments for testing and training.

A possible run-time operation cycle comprises the following activities:

- Data Acquisition: the system collects sensor data and contextual metadata (e.g., environmental conditions).
- Model Calibration: the DT aligns virtual parameters with physical measurements using digital thread methodologies [166].
- Execution: the DT allows the execution of simulations in sync with actual operations (the DT performs actions as dictated by the behavior model, but it allows for running predictions or simulation in parallel to the main thread of execution).
- Feedback Loop: the DT updates/instructs the PS with insights (e.g., adjusting the HVAC settings for energy efficiency).

4.2.3 Supporting Behavior Models with NGSI-LD

An NGSI-LD data model provides a structured representation of the traffic light system's state and behavior, enabling situation-aware management and smart city integration. A simplified version of the state machine from Figure 4.2 is detailed in Section A.2.1, offering a more comprehensive depiction for interested readers.

4.2.4 In the Context of Traffic Light Controller Example

The synchronization between behavior and data model enhances various functionalities within the DT, supporting its ability to achieve key objectives. For instance:

- A data-driven model could predict future temperature fluctuations based on historical data and actuator settings.

- A state-based model could represent the controller's operational modes (heating, cooling, idle).
- A hybrid model could combine heat transfer principles with historical data for more accurate temperature predictions. A hybrid model for the controller could use equations based on heat transfer principles to determine how the room's temperature should change based on the heater's output and the room's thermal properties, while the use of historical data about temperature, heater usage, and external weather could help to learn patterns and correct the physics-based model's predictions. For example, the model might learn that the room loses heat faster than the physics model predicts due to drafts around windows, and it can adjust its future temperature forecasts accordingly.

4.3 Developing a Behavior Model

In Section 2.1 and in Figure 2.3, the advantage of an integrated design of the PS and its DT was discussed and illustrated. If a DT is designed and developed alongside its physical counterpart, designers are more inclined to carefully consider key aspects of how the two parts are coupled. For this reason, it is preferable to keep freedom in the relationship in order to reuse the DT for controlling/monitoring other similar PSs or be ready to meet the needs of moving to another phase of the PS's life cycle. Specifying the behavior model, communication channels, control relationships, and implementation mechanisms—whether through message exchanges such as commands, events, and responses, or via structured APIs like publish-subscribe—enables a more precise and comprehensive description of the DT. A clear specification not only accurately captures the intended behavior but also serves as a foundation for reusing and adapting the DT's behavior and control logic across different systems, enhancing interoperability, coordination, and fidelity of the representation. Figure 4.7 depicts the case in which a traffic light twin is introduced. The twin will be notified of changes in the color of the traffic light directly by the controller. In this case, the traffic light twin will have a timely representation of the status of the traffic light system. In case of disruption

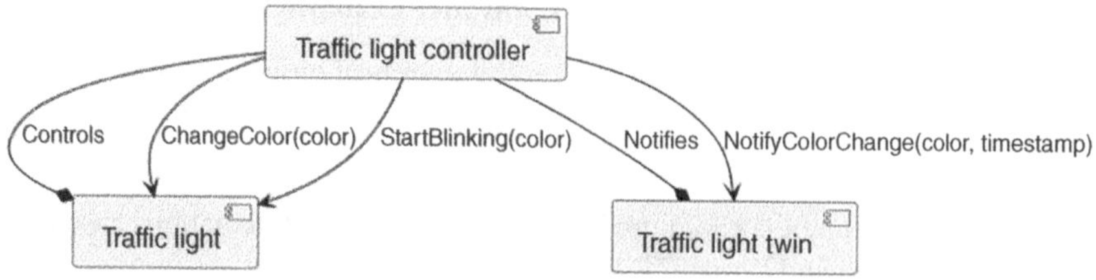

Figure 4.7 Adding a DT representation to the traffic light example.

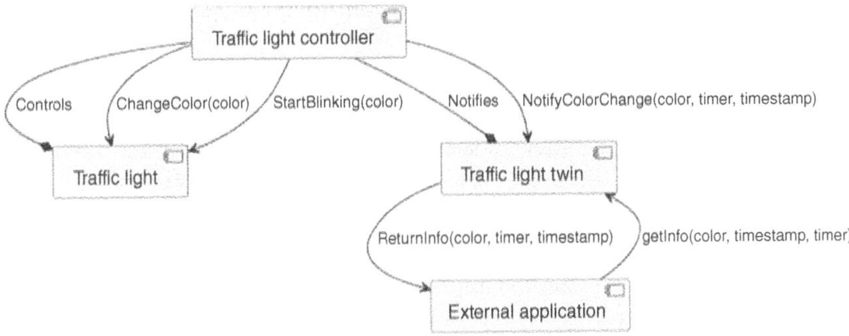

Figure 4.8 An external application interacting with traffic light twin with APIs.

of the communication between the controller and the twin, the twin can use the common behavior representation, for instance, the state machine diagram of Figure 4.2, to mimic the envisaged status of the actual PS.

This representation goes a bit beyond the capabilities of a passive DT because the sharing of a common behavior allows a simulation capability to the twin. If the DT actually "executes" the same behavior model in parallel, the expressive power and the capabilities associated with this twin increase.

The DT could offer an API to external applications to share with them relevant information about the whole system.

This case is shown in Figure 4.8. The traffic light twin decouples and mediates external applications from the actual system. This may result in increased capabilities to serve many external applications or in additional security protection. A Distributed Denial of Service (DDOS) attack could shut down the twin, leaving the traffic light system operating. The traffic light twin could also be replicated to better serve many different applications.

4.3.1 Implementing the Twin as a State Management Component

A state management application tracks and regulates system behavior, ensuring consistency and predictability. In a state machine diagram specified system (and its underlying finite state machines), it governs state transitions by storing relevant data, determining changes based on inputs, and enforcing transition rules to maintain integrity. It also communicates updates to other components, allowing synchronized operations. By providing structured state control, it enhances efficiency, debugging, and scalability, making it an essential part of system architecture. In the context of the traffic light: a twin could be implemented as or encompass a state management component that:

- Stores the Current State of the Virtual Traffic Light: This would include properties like the current color (`Green`, `Yellow`, `Red`, `BlinkingYellow`), the remaining time in the current state (`cycleTimer`), and potentially the current time context (`Day, Night, Sunday`).

- Handles Transitions Between States: Based on the behavior model (e.g., the state machine), the component would determine when to change the `currentState` (e.g., after `Tg` seconds in "Green," transition to "Yellow"). It would also manage transitions based on the `timeContext`.
- Notifies Other Parts of the Twin: If the twin has other modules (e.g., other traffic light components for controlling a complex crossroad and synchronize them, an API for external applications, a visualization component), the state management component would inform them whenever the traffic light's `currentState` changes so they can update their information accordingly.
- Implements the logic of the state machine: It would contain the rules defining the valid transitions between the different light states and the conditions that trigger these transitions (e.g., timer expiry, change in `timeContext`).

The traffic light control loop (to be replicated in the traffic light twin) could be implemented as represented in Figure 4.9.

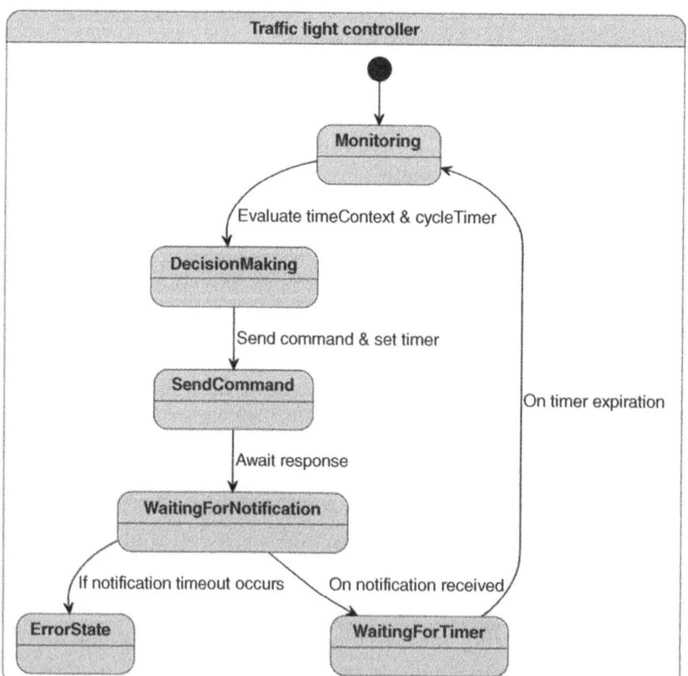

Figure 4.9 A control loop for the traffic light example.

4.3.2 Environment and DT Structure

A DT may also be designed to keep track of the environment's changes and the influence on the working and functions of the PS. In fact, the definitions of "system" in Section 1.1.1.1 and in particular the formal one explicitly refer to the environment. The system is influenced by the environment in which it operates, and hence, the DT should reflect and represent the actual aspects of the environment that influence the behavior of the system.

In the case of the traffic light system, information about events, conditions, and other contextualized information can be useful to better regulate its functioning. Traffic could be intense in opposite directions during the day depending on commuters' destinations, or schools and other public buildings nearby may need special treatment at specific times, etc. These cases can be complemented by others that can have a larger geographical impact, including gatherings, groupings, or other large events that have a high impact on the traffic in the area around the traffic light, meteorological conditions that create issues in the zone, a congestion in other nearby locations, or a natural event that needs special consideration. Each of these situations could be eased with a modified regulation of the traffic light under consideration.

Figure 4.10 shows a traffic light twin that can collect and process external information about the environment and then elaborate a plan to mitigate the effects of several situations.

In the case of traffic light system, there is the possibility of choosing among several behavior models. The right choice depends on the specific project and the purposes/requirements of the development. Some considerations can be outlined to suggest potential approaches for achieving an informed selection. One primary consideration is related to the importance of the "environment" with respect to the expected behavior of the DT.

4.3.2.1 Closed Behavior Model

If the environment has a minor impact (e.g., in conditions where the change of state of the environment does not impact or perturb the PS functioning), a

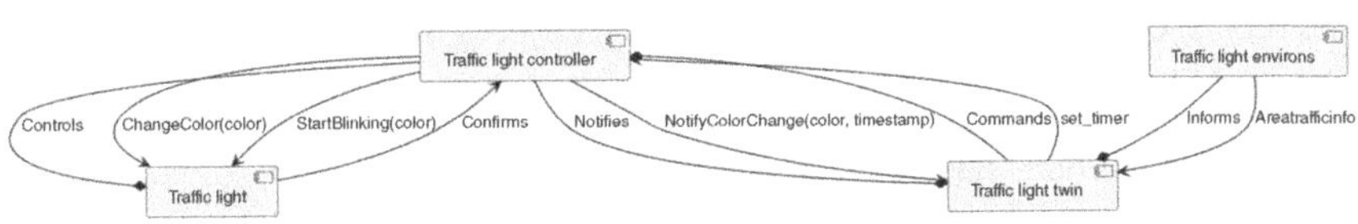

Figure 4.10 A DT and its relations with the environment.

closed behavior model can be considered. In the example of Figure 4.7, the behavior model of the PS and the corresponding DT could be fully decided "a priori" and implemented in a strict way. The DT could reflect the status of the physical entity and support the requests from external applications to provide them the current status of the entire system. A data-driven approach plus a set of finite state machines could fully satisfy the representation requirements. In addition, some level of redundancy is guaranteed by the presence of the DT.

4.3.2.2 Open Behavior Model

If the environment's impact is significant, then an open behavior model must be selected. From this perspective and considering Figure 4.10 as an example, there are multiple choices that can illustrate the potential of designing the PS with its DT. A behavior model can be allocated to a part of the system (e.g., the controller), while another part, such as the DT, replicates this model and can incorporate additional features to support software services. Depending on the structure of the PS or the DT itself, more complex configurations can be considered. For instance, the controller can implement a simple state machine model with the most common states and related transitions to ensure that the PS will work correctly. This model could also consider the possibility that the DT could control the transition to other states under its direct control. The DT could, for instance, implement a more complex behavior model for considering traffic patterns, meteorological conditions, and information related to gatherings in the nearby area. This model could be implemented as a hybrid solution (combining a more capable state-based model with data-driven behavior corroborated by predictive capabilities). If the complexity of the behavior to model increases, then it is very likely that a more complex structuring of elements, components, and their relations within the behavior model will be needed. Using the agent-based model, it could be possible to identify different actors impacting on the possible behavior of the system and to use them to understand the situation and to choose the most appropriate representation and, consequently, the actions to perform. The different actors could be agents of the meteorological situation, area traffic patterns, local gatherings, and other events, or disaster recovery agents. The supervising behavior model (allocated in the DT) can recompose the proposed guidelines into a sequence of actions and related commands to the controller(s) that governs the current local situation. Several AI techniques could be useful to achieve this combination.

4.3.2.3 Distribution and Complexity of the Behavior Model

The behavior model could be distributed over different parts and elements of the whole DT implementation. A pure distributed approach is possible, but it is likely that some of these elements (e.g., the traffic light twin) will act as a leader. This leads to another consideration: the behavior model of the PS (represented by the controller) and the DT should be integrated, but they may be different. The suggested approach is to keep the state-based model of the PS simpler but open to receive commands and indications from a more complex behavior model of the DT. There are several reasons for this:

- The DT is a software that could be more easily updated and improved than software instantiated in running physical devices;
- The cost of DT software development could be lower and more generalized than that needed to implement a complex behavior model in a hardware-limited device as a product;
- The DT can be deployed in powerful and well-connected machines, allowing for a more efficient execution of the logic;
- The same DT software can be reused for several PSs, either as a leader of a large system (e.g., the twin orchestrating different controllers) or as instances of it;
- The DT software can scale up to support different external applications by exploiting the replication property.

The PS and DT will most likely be distributed systems [192]. Since the DT does not typically operate within the same computing environment as the PS, their coordination relies on fundamental techniques from distributed computing, such as leader election [193] and consensus algorithms [194]. These mechanisms are essential for ensuring synchronization and maintaining system stability.

An essential architectural decision concerns the allocation of leadership and consensus management between the DT and PS. Depending on where these functions are placed, the system's behavior may be significantly affected. If decision-making is centralized within the DT, the PS will function as a subordinate entity, executing instructions rather than actively shaping decisions. Conversely, if governance resides on the PS side, the DT will primarily act as an analytical tool, supporting operations but not directing them.

Designers must carefully *define and structure governance*, as the chosen configuration directly influences system responsiveness and adaptability. The allocation of responsibilities should be explicit, avoiding unintended imbalances between the two subsystems. If a master-slave dynamic is intended, where the DT orchestrates the PS or vice versa, this must be a deliberate design choice rather than an emergent consequence. Clear architectural decisions ensure predictable interactions and operational consistency within the integrated system.

4.3.2.4 Structure of the DT

The Traffic Light System can be structured in different subsystems, parts, and components. This structuring tries to keep subsystems independent but with strong coordination capabilities. The state machine/behavior module in the controller and the corresponding one (behavior model/simulation engine) in the twin are the major components of a traffic light system. However, other components, as depicted in Figure 4.11, are needed to fully represent the system's capabilities. In the controller part, a communication module governs the external communication, the timer/scheduler is responsible for setting and updating the timers as received by the state machine, and an interface toward sensors and actuators is defined. The twin needs to have more modules beside the behavior module, e.g., a notification and event module for sending and receiving events to/from external entities, a state representation for collecting the data about the current state of the PS and an environment situation module for representing the current state of the environment. These modules contribute to the understanding of the whole situation and enable the behavior module to make the best decisions on the optimum measures and to communicate them to the controller.

Figure 4.11 shows one of the many possible arrangements of functions' disposition. For instance, a situation aware module could be implemented in the traffic Light Environs Module for higher-level representation (and integration into larger areas). The commands/recommendations sent to the traffic light twin will be checked with respect to the status of the local environment, and the received

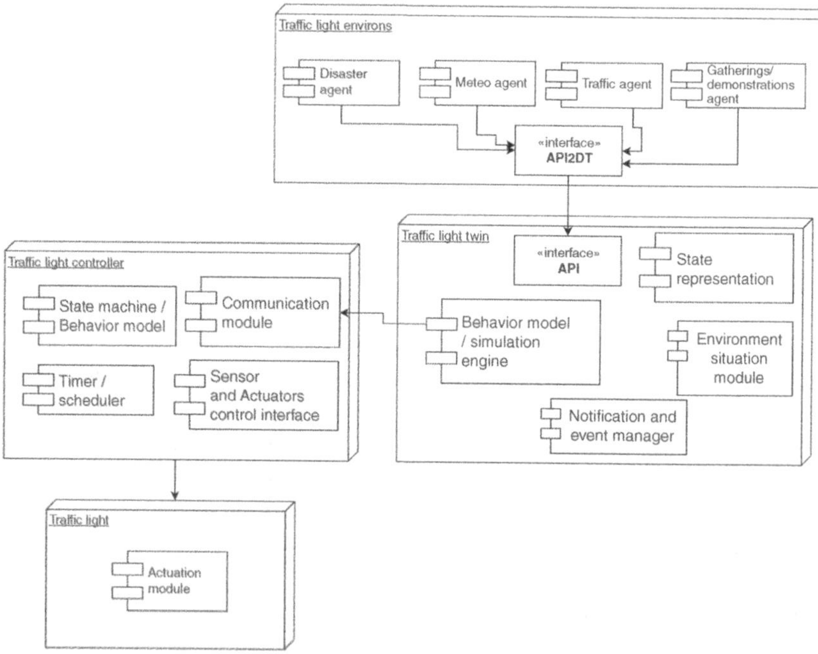

Figure 4.11 A DT and its components.

suggestion adapted to this situation, considering the local context. As this figure makes clear, the descriptions and variety of behavior model' concerns are many and as soon as the system increases in complexity, the choices multiply. The scope and goal of the DT implementation should also keep into consideration the future needs for scaling the solutions or the extension of control features to other physical objects/systems. In addition, the policies related to governance and coordination in distributed PS-DT systems are not shown here because it pertains to the system engine of Figure 1.3. This demonstrates the complexity of the DT organization and its representation (models) and its modeling.

4.4 AI and Digital Twins

DTs generate and process vast amounts of data, creating both opportunities and challenges in understanding and controlling complex cyber-physical systems. Artificial Intelligence (AI) empowers DTs not only to process this data but to extract actionable intelligence, enabling smarter, more autonomous, and adaptive digital counterparts.

At a high level, AI contributes to DTs through:

- **Data-driven Intelligence:** Transforming massive sensor and operational data into predictive and prescriptive insights.
- **Reasoning and Decision-making:** Leveraging approaches such as reinforcement learning, rule-based systems, fuzzy logic, and Bayesian networks for context-aware, interpretable reasoning and decisions.
- **Autonomy and Coordination:** Incorporating agentic AI to produce autonomic DTs, capable of proactive, distributed decision-making across edge and cloud environments.

Other advanced AI techniques such as symbolic AI, neuro-symbolic models, multi-agent systems, causal inference, and knowledge graphs further empower DTs for complex scenarios, supporting explainability, interoperability, and dynamic adaptation.

The application of AI technologies to DTs is vast and merits dedicated, detailed treatment to provide an exhaustive overview. In the remainder of this section, we present examples of AI tools and techniques to illustrate some of the possibilities offered by this integration. AI techniques play a pivotal role in enhancing DTs capabilities, enabling them to go beyond mere data mirroring and provide insights, predictions, and control strategies. In previous sections, ML techniques as decision trees and random forests or Deep Learning (DL) ones such as neural networks (and especially LSTM) were mentioned. There are several additional techniques that can be useful and applicable to DTs.

Supervised and unsupervised ML algorithms can be decisive for the functioning of DTs. For instance, **Regression techniques** can be used for predicting continuous values like the remaining useful life (RUL) of equipment, energy consumption, temperature fluctuations, or product quality. Several regression algorithms are available in Ref. [195]. **Classification** [196] can predict discrete categories like failure types, anomaly detection (normal vs. abnormal operation), or product defect classification. **Clustering** [197] identifies patterns and groupings in data without labeled outcomes, such as segmenting the different operational modes of a machine, identifying anomalies as outliers, or grouping similar user behaviors. **Dimensionality reduction** [198] simplifies complex datasets while preserving essential information. It can be useful for visualization, feature selection, and reducing computational costs for other AI models. **Reinforcement Learning (RL)** [199] for policy optimization. It is useful for training agents (the DT or its components) to make optimal decisions in dynamic environments to achieve specific goals, such as optimizing control parameters for a machine, scheduling maintenance, or managing energy consumption.

DL can greatly contribute to the development of DTs thanks to its ability to learn complex patterns from large amounts of data. Particularly useful DL techniques are: **Time series forecasting** [200] using Recurrent Neural Networks (RNNs), including LSTMs and GRUs, for predicting the future behavior of time-dependent data from sensors and systems as well as for context or situation evolution. **Image and video analysis** [201] using Convolutional Neural Networks (CNNs) for tasks like visual analysis of assets, defect detection in manufacturing, or understanding environmental conditions from camera feeds [202, 203]. **Natural Language Processing (NLP)** [204] for analyzing textual data like maintenance logs, user manuals, and customer feedback to extract insights, identify issues, or improve communication. **Generative models** [205] for data augmentation, simulating potential failure scenarios, or generating synthetic data for training other AI models.

Less commonly used technologies such as **expert systems** [206], rule-based systems [207] and case-based reasoning [208] can support the DT's needs for determining and enhancing an adaptive behavior to the current situation. These solutions leverage human expertise represented as rules to make decisions or provide recommendations. They can be valuable in DTs for: **fault diagnosis**: if-then rules based on expert knowledge to identify potential causes of malfunctions based on sensor readings. **Operational guidelines**: encoding best practices and standard operating procedures for controlling and maintaining the physical asset. **Case-based Reasoning (CBR)**: offering DTs the advantage of leveraging past experiences for problem-solving. By retrieving, reusing, revising, and retaining solutions from similar historical cases, CBR enhances DTs' capabilities in fault diagnosis, predictive maintenance, process optimization, and operator assistance. Its key benefits include exploiting existing knowledge, enabling transparent reasoning, providing continuous learning, and adapting to novel situations, making it a valuable AI technique for intelligent DT applications.

Other techniques like fuzzy logic, which enable approximate reasoning, or Bayesian Networks, which offer probabilistic models that represent conditional dependencies between variables, can also be used to augment DT applications.

In general, AI augments the capabilities of DTs beyond passive digital replicas by integrating predictive analytics, autonomous decision-making, and advanced reasoning. This integration enables DTs to forecast future states, dynamically infer optimal actions, and adapt their behaviors in response to evolving operational conditions. The specific AI techniques employed in a DT strongly depend on the nature of the PS, the goals of the digital representation, and the available data. A combination of different AI techniques may be the best way for setting up a comprehensive and intelligent DT solution. This integration can support several important functionalities related to the DT and its life cycle. Some examples of likely functionalities that can benefit from AI are discussed in the following: **Predictive maintenance** includes the ability to predict when equipment is likely to fail, enabling proactive maintenance by scheduling interventions in advance and reducing downtime. **Anomaly detection** identifies unusual patterns in operational data may indicate faults, inefficiencies, or security breaches in which the DT can intervene or suggest intervention measures. **Performance optimization** supports the analysis of operational data. This yields to the identification of areas for improvement in efficiency, throughput, and/or quality. The (iterative) modeling of the system can benefit from such optimization. **Control and automation**, especially related to the identification of situations, can help in developing intelligent control strategies that adapt to changing conditions and optimize the operation of the PS in due time. **Simulation and scenario planning** are essential parts of the definition of the DT, AI helps in creating more realistic and dynamic simulations by identifying and integrating learned behaviors and predicting outcomes under different scenarios. **Personalization and customization** helps in representing the current situation and in tuning up the behavior and recommendations of the DT based on specific user needs or operational contexts. **Knowledge extraction** makes it possible to derive insights and knowledge from large data sets generated by the PS and its environment.

The choice and combination of AI techniques depend on the needs, purposes, and constraints/limitations of each DT implementation. Large Language Models (LLMs), for instance, can help designers to better express requirements and constraints and, in general, to increase the modeling capabilities of descriptive up to prescriptive DTs [209]. However, in addition to their major advantages and putting aside, for the moment, the simulation (see Section 4.5), a few topics are dealt with in the next subsections with particular reference to modeling capabilities.

4.4.1 Iterative Refinement of DT Behavior Models Using Generative AI

Generative AI (GenAI) enhances a DT behavior model by iteratively generating rare real-life scenarios with limited data availability, including critical situations. It can synthesize realistic scenarios, potentially incorporating physical laws, to help designers refine the DT's response to mitigate these challenges. The generated data incrementally shapes the behavior model, addressing both the initial scenario and its evolution.

This iterative process is crucial because DT's responses actively influence the PS's state, altering subsequent scenarios. For instance, if a critical scenario unfolds across **N phases**, the DT's intervention at any phase modifies its progression. Thus, GenAI should generate an initial scenario and iteratively update possible evolutions based on the DT's responses. Designers can leverage this approach to model expected system behavior and anticipate real-world outcomes [123].

Figure 4.12 illustrates behavior modelers using GenAI to study critical scenarios. GenAI generates an initial scenario culminating in a disaster, prompting the

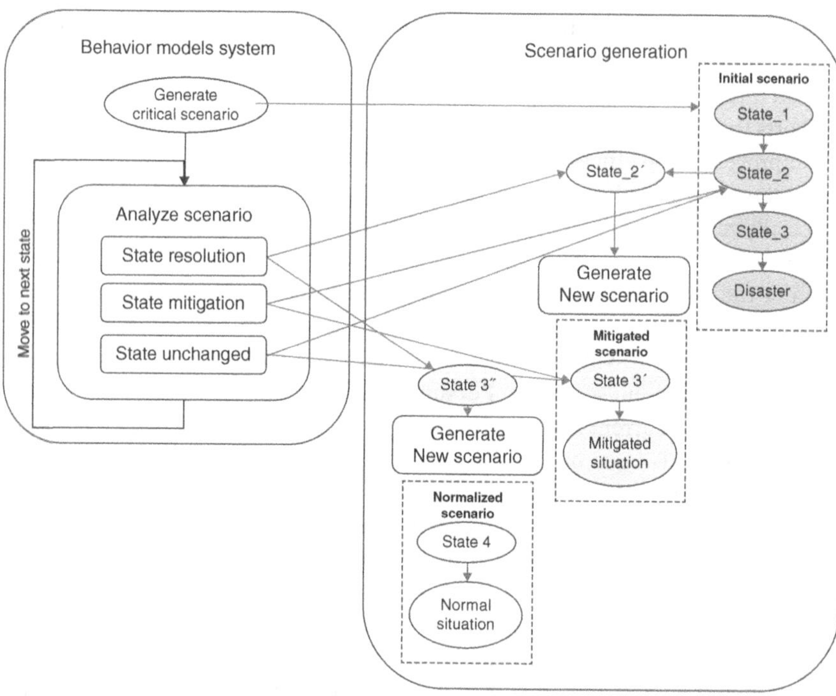

Figure 4.12 Iterative improvement of critical scenarios with GenAI.

behavior modeler to modify the DT's responses to counteract `state_1`. If successful, they transition the system to a revised state, `state_2'`, different from the AI-generated trajectory. Otherwise, they attempt mitigation, moving to `state_2`.

If the system successfully shifts to `state_2'`, a new scenario incorporating this updated state is AI generated. Otherwise, the initial scenario is revisited for improvements. Ultimately, the refined DT behavior either restores normality after a series of states or mitigates the scenario's impact. In the worst case, it at least identifies the scenario and warns humans of potential consequences.

In the context of the traffic light system (see Figure 4.7), GenAI can synthesize complex, rare scenarios such as simultaneous sensor failures, unexpected pedestrian surges, or severe weather events. These scenarios challenge the system's behavior model, and if untreated, could cause errors or lowered performance. The DT's behavior model is then iteratively updated and refined to better handle these situations. This process is dynamic: as the DT mitigates the initial scenario's effects, the scenario itself evolves in response, requiring further adaptation of the behavior model [210].

The iterative process can be summarized as follows:

1. **Initial Scenario Generation:** GenAI creates a critical or rare scenario (e.g., sensor malfunction, pedestrian surge, or adverse weather).
2. **Behavior Model Design/Refinement:** The DT behavior model is (re)designed or tuned to address and mitigate the early phases of the scenario.
3. **Scenario Evolution:** GenAI updates the scenario in response to the DT's mitigation actions (e.g., increased vehicle congestion due to extended pedestrian surge phases).
4. **Iterative Adaptation:** The DT behavior model is further refined to cope with the new scenario state, and GenAI continues to evolve the scenario based on these responses.
5. **Convergence:** This cycle continues until the DT demonstrates robust mitigation across a range of scenario evolutions.

This closed-loop, scenario-driven evolution ensures the DT is not only prepared for the initial critical scenario but also for cascading consequences of its own actions, a key requirement for robust, real-world deployment [211].

4.4.1.1 Iterative Scenario Generation and Behavior Model Refinement Using GenAI

The following pseudocode (Listing 4.1) illustrates how GenAI can be used to generate critical scenarios and iteratively refine the behavior model of a DT to mitigate such scenarios. This approach is particularly relevant for complex systems, like the traffic light example shown in Figure 4.7.

Listing 4.1: Iterative GenAI Refinement of Traffic Light Twin Behavior Model

```
// Step 1: Generate initial critical scenario
scenario = GenAI.generateScenario({
        sensorFailure: true,
        pedestrianSurge: high,
        weather: heavyRain
});
// The scenario combines rare events difficult to observe in real life

// Step 2: Design/refine DT behavior model to mitigate initial scenario phases
DT.behaviorModel.update({
        activateBackupSensors: true,
        extendPedestrianGreenTime: true,
        alertVehiclesToSlowDown: true
});
// The behavior model is tuned to respond proactively

// Step 3: Simulate scenario evolution based on DT mitigation actions
scenario = GenAI.evolveScenario(
previousScenario = scenario,
DTactions = DT.behaviorModel.currentActions()
);
// For example, increased vehicle congestion due to longer pedestrian phases

// Step 4: Refine DT behavior model to handle evolved scenario
DT.behaviorModel.refine({
        implementDynamicLaneReversals: true,
        coordinateWithNeighboringIntersections: true
});
// The model adapts to new challenges created by prior mitigation

// Step 5: Repeat iterative adaptation until convergence
while (!DT.behaviorModel.isRobustAgainst(scenario)) {
        scenario = GenAI.evolveScenario(
        previousScenario = scenario,
        DTactions = DT.behaviorModel.currentActions()
        );
        DT.behaviorModel.refineBasedOn(scenario);
}
// Iteration continues until the DT reliably mitigates scenario effects

// Outcome: DT behavior model robustly manages rare critical scenarios,
// improving system resilience and safety.
```

This iterative closed-loop process enables DT designers to progressively identify and adapt the behavior model to complex, evolving situations, thereby enhancing the DT's capability to maintain safe and efficient operation under rare or extreme conditions.

This methodology effectively augments limited real-world data, supports adaptive learning, and enables safe exploration of high-risk situations. For the traffic light example, it means the DT can be engineered to respond to highly unusual but potentially catastrophic events, improving both safety and system robustness [38, 123, 210].

4.4.2 Extraction of Behavior Rules from Data

The design of a DT is typically integrated with the PS's specifications. However, some PSs, especially complex ones like cities, evolve in ways that make integrated planning and design difficult. In such cases, a bottom-up approach can be valuable, identifying the governing rules and laws through incremental data-driven modeling. This method derives the system's behavior by observing real-world data, progressively formulating explicit and interpretable rules [38, 119, 131, 212].

While decision trees and random forests are widely used for behavior modeling (see Subsection 3.7.1.2), other techniques can also be used. Neural networks, though powerful, generally lack interpretability, making them unsuitable for extracting transparent rules that can be modified by human experts [213].

Various methodologies enable the extraction of explicit and interpretable rules from data, allowing designers to model the behavior of complex PSs effectively.

When deriving explicit, interpretable rules or models from data to represent a PS's behavior, alternative modeling techniques should be considered if decision trees or random forests do not yield satisfactory results. The following approaches support bottom-up, data-driven behavior modeling:

- Rule Induction Algorithms [213, 214]: These algorithms learn explicit if-then rules from data, producing human-readable logic. Popular methods are RIPPER (Repeated Incremental Pruning to Produce Error Reduction), CN2 [215], PART (Partial Decision Trees). The main advantage is that these techniques produce a set of clear, incremental rules that can be reviewed, edited, and extended.
- Association Rule Mining [216]: These techniques discover relationships between variables in large datasets, typically in the form of `If [conditions], THEN [outcome]`. Two popular algorithms are Apriori and FP-Growth, which are useful for finding frequent patterns or correlations that can be translated into behavior rules. Other association rule mining methods are kTail [217] and Evidence-driven State Merging (EDSM) [218]. They produce explicit state-transition diagrams, which are interpretable and directly usable for control logic.

- Fuzzy Rule Learning [219, 220]: These methods are based on fuzzy IF-THEN rules that handle uncertainty and vagueness, often using data clustering and rule extraction. Some solutions in this area are the Wang–Mendel algorithm, and fuzzy decision trees. Both of them detect rules that are explicit and can handle imprecise data, useful for systems with noisy measurements.

4.4.2.1 Explicit Rule Induction for Traffic Light Behavior

For the traffic light system of Figure 4.7, a rule induction algorithm could be applied to derive the behavior model from operational data if a historical dataset about the traffic light system existed, including time of day, detected vehicle count, pedestrian button presses, and the signal phase should be available. Using a rule induction algorithm (e.g., RIPPER), it would be possible to derive rules such as:

Extracting Rules from Data:

- `IF time_of_day in [07:00, 09:00] AND vehicle_count > 10 THEN phase = 'Green for Main Road'`
- `IF pedestrian_button_pressed = TRUE AND vehicle_count < 5 THEN phase = 'Pedestrian Green'`
- `IF vehicle_count = 0 AND time_of_day in [00:00, 05:00] THEN phase = 'Blinking Yellow'`

The set of rules is built incrementally, and the algorithms also capture rules about rare events over the long period (if they occur). As new data is collected (e.g., new traffic patterns, special events), the rule induction process can be rerun or updated to refine or add rules so that the behavior model evolves with the system's real-world operation [214]. The derived rules can be directly implemented in the traffic light twin, allowing it to predict the behavior of the PS even when communication with the controller is disrupted, as mentioned in Section 4.7. Furthermore, these rules can be reviewed, edited, and extended by domain experts, combining data-driven insights with human expertise.

Table 4.1 summarizes the possibilities offered by these AI techniques and relates them to the traffic light example.

Table 4.1 AI techniques to derive rules for DT behavior.

Technique	Output type	Example of use in traffic light system
Rule Induction (RIPPER, CN2)	IF-THEN rules	Phase selection logic
Association rule mining	Association rules	Detecting pattern anomalies
FSM inference	State diagrams	Modeling phase transitions
Fuzzy rule learning	Fuzzy IF-THEN rules	Handling sensor uncertainty

The possibility of creating and understanding rules that govern a PS that has not been designed to work in parallel with a DT is important. Complex systems such as cities, large transport systems, and the like can benefit from the incremental identification of underlying rules governing their behavior.

4.4.3 Enhancing AI Explainability in DTs Through Behavior Models

Research seems to converge toward the fact that if multiple AI algorithms achieve comparable accuracy, then explainability becomes a key factor, making white-box algorithms with explainability properties preferable [221]. This is particularly important in critical systems, where understanding the logic and functioning behind system's decisions is essential.

DTs integrate real-time data with behavior models to monitor, simulate, and predict the future states of PSs. While DL models, such as artificial neural networks (ANNs), provide powerful predictive capabilities, their black-box nature often limits the transparency and **explainability** of these models [222]. Incorporating behavior models, e.g., rules-based systems, laws, or state machines, can significantly improve explainability by providing interpretable data and a related set of rules that corroborate AI predictions [18].

Explainable AI (XAI) techniques aim to make AI decisions transparent and understandable [223]. Behavior models are inherently white-box approaches that define explicit state transitions and rules. When combined with ANN predictions, they create a hybrid modeling approach that leverages the predictive power of AI while maintaining interpretability [224].

4.4.3.1 Theoretical Foundation

The integration of XAI [221] with DTs [37] is thus a key research area. XAI techniques [225] aim to make AI systems more transparent and understandable to human operators. By incorporating behavior models alongside AI components, DTs may offer higher levels of explainability through several mechanisms:

- **Complementary Explanation Frameworks**: Behavior models provide a structured framework that can validate and explain AI predictions. When an AI component makes a prediction, the behavior model can offer rules-based reasoning that supports or challenges that prediction. The two parts are complementary, providing an accurate predictions associated with a set of rules that explain the expected behavior. For example, an ANN predicts a system's change of state; the behavior model verifies whether this change complies with established rules and provides an explanation of the rationale behind the decision. *AI makes a prediction, and the behavior model explains or challenges it.*

- **White-box Validation**: While DL models are often considered "black boxes," behavior models like state machines and rules-based systems are inherently more interpretable "white-box" approaches. These can be used to verify that AI predictions align with established domain knowledge. This knowledge could be represented by rules or laws related to the operational context. For example, if an AI suggests a certain action, the white-box model can verify if this action is consistent with established rules or domain knowledge considering the actual initial conditions. *AI makes a prediction, this approach ensures there is alignment with real-world constraints and domain knowledge.*
- **Hybrid Modeling Approach**: Combining the predictive power of AI with the explainability of behavior models creates a hybrid approach that leverages the strengths of both paradigms: a traffic light system where the AI predicts optimal timing, but the behavior model enforces safety constraints, and together they decide the final action. *AI predicts an action, behavior model enforces structural rules before execution.*

Some simple examples can illustrate the usefulness of this integration of behavior and AI modeling.

4.4.3.2 Traffic Light Control Example

In a traffic light DT, an ANN predicts congestion and suggests timing adjustments [226]. The behavior model includes states `Red`, `Yellow`, and `Green`, with rules such as:

Applying Rules to Predictions

- IF an emergency vehicle is detected, THEN transition to green in its direction.
- IF north–south traffic volume exceeds threshold T and east–west volume is below T_2, THEN prioritize north–south flow.

This logic combines AI prediction with explicit rules and state transitions, improving transparency and trust.

4.4.3.3 Home Automation Example

In a smart home DT, an ANN predicts occupancy and optimal temperature settings. The behavior model defines states such as `Occupied`, `Away`, and `Night Mode`, with rules like:

Adapting the Optimal Temperature to the Actual State

- WHEN transitioning to `Night Mode`, set temperature to the user-preferred sleeping temperature.

If the system lowers the temperature at 8:30 PM, it can explain:

Extracting Rules from Data
"Temperature is set to 68 °F because the ANN predicted a transition to Night Mode based on historical occupancy. Rule H12 prescribes setting the temperature to the preferred sleeping value upon entering Night Mode, consistent with user preferences."

This hybrid explanation enhances interpretability and user satisfaction [227].

4.4.3.4 Benefits of XAI-DT Integration

The integration of behavior models with AI in DTs offers several key benefits [18, 222, 224]:

- **Improved Trust:** Providing clear explanations for decisions helps users and operators develop greater trust.
- **Debugging Capability:** Behavior models help identify incorrect predictions generated by AI or rule inconsistencies.
- **Regulatory Compliance:** Explainability is often required in critical infrastructure, healthcare, and transportation sectors.

However, there are still many challenges to solve in the XAI and DT integration:

- **Complexity Management:** Maintaining comprehensive and consistent rule sets becomes difficult as systems scale.
- **Consistency:** Ensuring alignment between AI predictions and behavior models requires careful design and validation.
- **Performance Trade-offs:** The most accurate AI models are sometimes the least explainable, necessitating a balance between performance and transparency [224].

The emerging field of Explainable AI Digital Twins (XAI-DT) may address these challenges by developing solutions and frameworks that integrate XAI techniques with DTs, aiming to maintain high accuracy while providing the transparency required for critical applications [228].

By combining the predictive power of DL with the explanatory capabilities of behavior models, DTs can achieve a high level of explainability that supports better decision-making, increased user trust, and improved system reliability.

4.4.4 Autonomic DTs and Agentic AI

An autonomic digital twin is a DT capable of representing the conditions within its environment and taking actions to optimize the behavior of the corresponding

PS. Due to the distributed nature of the large systems they represent, autonomic DTs must capture events, situations, and courses of action occurring at multiple locations. This requires a distributed software organization capable of making local decisions while coordinating with a centralized logic. Local decision-making is essential for responsiveness and scalability, but it must also cooperate with other local decision makers and a global coordinator to ensure system-wide optimization and consistency. To achieve this, autonomic DTs leverage the extrinsic properties of the system and dynamically adapt to changing environmental conditions.

The growing interest in agentic AI [229] provides a viable framework for supporting such autonomic DTs. Agentic AI entails autonomous agents that can perceive, reason, learn, and act independently toward objectives. This approach facilitates capturing emergent behaviors and supports distributed deployment spanning the entire computational continuum—from edge-based sensor data capture and processing to cloud-based orchestration [230].

Recent applications highlight agentic DTs' potential in domains such as telecom network optimization, manufacturing predictive maintenance, and autonomous energy management [231, 232]. These systems exploit the edge-cloud continuum to balance real-time local actions with scalable data aggregation and learning, enabling continuous adaptation and optimization throughout their life cycle.

4.5 Simulation Models, Behavior Validation, and GenAI Integration in DTs

Simulation capabilities offered by a DT are an important aspect of the increasing success of the concept [36]. DTs apply several simulation paradigms to mirror PSs. The field of DT is rapidly improving by integrating AI, simulation, and largely distributed computing technologies. It is important to understand how major simulation approaches can interact with AI-supported behavior models. In addition, the ability to create behavior MetaModels, i.e., behavior representations that can be executed and simulated, should be further analyzed to lead to a more unified execution and simulation. Changes to the behavior model stemming from simulations or improvements in behavior definition (e.g., because of corrections induced by GenAI defined scenarios) should be kept aligned (as discussed in Section 2.7.1 with a particular reference to Figure 2.17).

4.5.1 Applicable Simulation Models

There are major simulation models for DTs; they vary in goals, complexity, and applicability with respect to the DT and its life cycle. In this section, the run-time execution of the DT will mainly be considered. Some major simulation techniques applicable to DTs are:

- **Discrete Event Simulation (DES):** Models system behavior as sequences of events over time. Widely used for process optimization in manufacturing and logistics [233]. Example: Simulating traffic light state changes triggered by sensor inputs.
- **Physics-based Simulation:** Uses mathematical models of physical laws (e.g., fluid dynamics, mechanical stress). Critical for aerospace and energy DTs [234]. Some open modeling frameworks and related tools (e.g., Open Modelica and Modelio [235]) or others are available and can be integrated with DTs.
- **State-based Simulation:** Represents system behavior through finite state machines. Ideal for rule-driven systems like smart homes [236].
- **Hybrid Simulation:** Combines multiple paradigms (e.g., Discrete Event Simulation (DES) + physics) for complex systems [237].

4.5.1.1 Behavior Models and Simulation Synergy

Behavior models—whether based on rules, state machines, or precise descriptions of a PS's behavior—are closely interconnected with simulations. Simulations serve as a validation tool, testing the consistency of rules and behaviors under both standard and edge-case scenarios. For the traffic light example, DES can verify that pedestrian and connected vehicle prioritization rules do not cause problems in the environment [238]. On the other hand, behavior models pose constraints on simulations. Rules prevent states that are not allowed or impossible. In the home automation example, law limits the maximum and minimum temperatures allowed in the home in winter time. Simulations need to respect valid constraints. In addition, homes are very strongly characterized by the behavior of people and their habits. These can be seen as constraints and requirements when building applications [239, 240].

4.5.2 MetaModel for Unified Execution and Simulation

The ability to use GenAI technologies (as discussed in subsection 4.4.1) can be exploited for supporting and improving the simulation capabilities of a DT. Behavior models and GenAI play complementary roles in enhancing completeness and adaptability to the DT definition. This can be extremely beneficial for simulations because GenAI enhances capabilities through:

- **Rare Scenario Generation:** Creates synthetic training data [241]. This can be applied to generate datasets for analyzing low-probability events (e.g., earthquake impacts on traffic systems).

- **MetaModel Refinement:** Uses simulation outcomes to improve GenAI's physical consistency via constrained generation [210].
- **Predictive State Integration:** Combines ANN-predicted states with simulated trajectories for robust decision-making [242].

A MetaModel architecture integrating GenAI capabilities with behavior model execution and simulation can be explored (Figure 4.13). It enables stakeholders to switch between execution and simulation modes while maintaining alignment in improvement and verification of behavior model functionalities and responses. It is based on maintaining the possibility to execute and keep aligned the same model for execution and simulation purposes. The behavior MetaModeling is a trend in modeling of complex systems (e.g., human or production systems [243, 244]). The AI/GenAI module is composed of functionalities that can predict (AIPredictor) future states of the system and/or generate iterative scenarios for testing the behavior model under different conditions. These data flows are injected into a behavior engine that comprises two major modules: one for simulation and one for execution. They are respectively devoted to the execution of simulations using scenarios or predicted data, and to the implementation of the expected and stable behavior of the DT. They can run in parallel, allowing the simulations of past or future scenarios, while the current DT executes its designated performance. The two modules have a simulation and an execution engine that run different

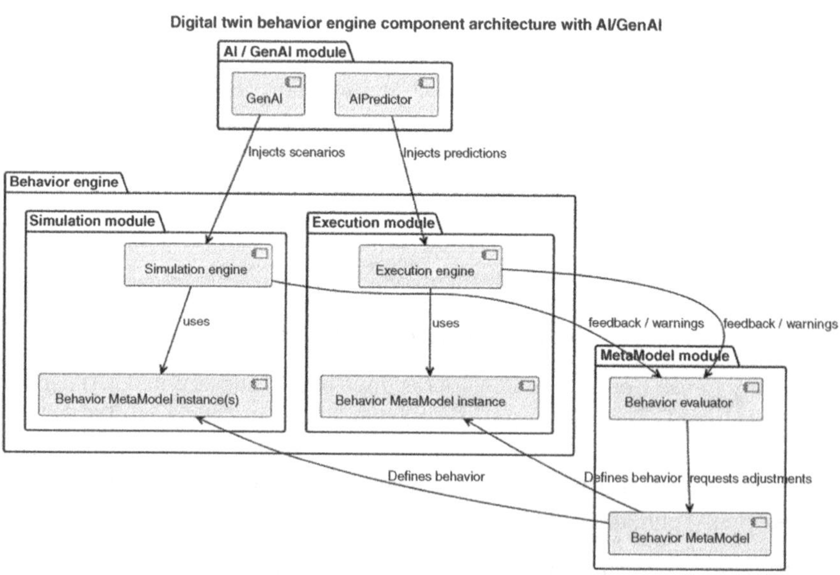

Figure 4.13 A behavior MetaModel serving simulation and execution.

instances of the behavior model. In the simulations, several instances can be executed to cover different scenarios and needs. They instantiate the general behavior MetaModel that is stored, checked, validated, consolidated, and improved by the MetaModel module. This consists of two components: the Behavior MetaModel that represents the current version of the behavior model for execution and simulation and a behavior evaluator that seeks to identify the needed changes of the model as a consequence of learning new rules (automatic update) or designer changes or decisions. The behavior evaluator keeps the behavior MetaModel consistent and usable for simulations and execution.

Key properties of this approach are:

- The MetaModel module is the point of convergence and integration of behavior modeling. It keeps the behavior model unique and consistent for execution and simulation; and it evaluates and ensures the consistency of new or modified states/rules. It can be considered as a behavior convergence hub.
- Modifications to the behavior model due to simulations or changes in the baseline behavior propagate bidirectionally: changing rules because of simulation needs updates to execution logic, and vice versa.
- GenAI generates synthetic scenarios to detect new behavior rules that adhere to MetaModel constraints [210].
- The behavior MetaModel enables the incremental definition, integration, and improvement while ensuring consistent execution and simulation. While the model evolves, it increases in complexity gradually—one step at a time—reducing the need for a fully fledged specification from the outset.

4.5.3 Evolving the Traffic Light DT with Situation-aware Behavior Modeling

The modular MetaModel architecture for DTs enables the continuous refinement of system behavior in response to evolving requirements and operational contexts. This can be illustrated by an extended traffic light scenario, where the initial simple behavior model is improved as a consequence of the need to prioritize ambulance trips to a nearby hospital.

4.5.3.1 Initial Behavior Model

The baseline behavior model for the traffic light is defined as a state machine with states (`Red`, `Yellow`, `Green`) and transitions governed by standard traffic rules and congestion levels, as described in Section 4.3.2. The model ensures safe and efficient traffic flow under typical conditions.

4.5.3.2 Contextual Extension: Hospital Proximity and Ambulance Priority

When a new requirement arises, e.g., a hospital is located near the intersection, and the traffic light must give priority to ambulances, the MetaModel needs changes. To address this, the behavior MetaModel is extended with new rules:

A New Behavior Scenario: Some Requirements

- `IF an ambulance is detected approaching the intersection, AND the current state is not already Green in the ambulance's direction, THEN transition to Green as soon as safely possible.`
- `IF multiple emergency vehicles are detected, THEN prioritize based on proximity and direction relative to the hospital.`

These rules are integrated into the MetaModel, ensuring both simulation and execution modules are updated consistently.

4.5.3.3 Scenario Generation with GenAI

To validate and optimize the new behavior, GenAI is employed to synthesize diverse scenarios, including:

- Ambulance arrivals at different times of day (rush hour, night, etc.).
- Varying background traffic conditions, learned from historical traffic databases [222].
- Edge cases such as simultaneous arrival of multiple emergency vehicles or conflicting traffic demands.

GenAI, thus, supports the iterative tuning of a behavior model for rare and complex situations that may not be well-represented in historical data [245].

4.5.3.4 Simulation-based Evaluation and Optimization

When updating the behavior MetaModel instance, the simulation module executes both GenAI-generated and historical scenarios evaluating different attributes (Key performance indicators [KPIs]) such as:

- Average and maximum ambulance waiting times at the intersection.
- Impact on overall traffic flow and congestion.
- Safety and compliance with traffic regulations.

Simulation results are analyzed and if the behavior is evaluated as acceptable, then the *behavior evaluation* component commits to the changes, ensuring that they do not impact on other previously considered scenarios. If suboptimal outcomes are detected (e.g., excessive delays for ambulances or negative side effects on general traffic), the evaluation component can recommend further refinements to the

MetaModel. These refinements can be enacted automatically or with human oversight.

4.5.3.5 Continuous Alignment and Deployment

Once the updated behavior model demonstrates satisfactory performance in simulations across all relevant scenarios, it is approved and "committed" by the behavior evaluation, and it is stored as the new version of the behavior MetaModel. It can be uploaded and run by the execution module. The behavior evaluation component continues to monitor additional modifications of the behavior MetaModel, enabling further adaptation as needed.

This example shows how the MetaModel architecture, combined with GenAI and simulation, enables the DT to:

- Rapidly adapt to new operational requirements (e.g., ambulance priority near a hospital).
- Validate and optimize behavior using both synthetic and historical scenarios.
- Maintain consistent, explainable, and robust behavior across simulation and execution.

Similar critical scenarios could be identified for the home automation system in which simulations and the related behavior can be defined to preserve or mitigate the effects on specific stakeholders.

The convergence of behavior models, multi-paradigm simulation, and constrained GenAI enables DTs to adapt to both common and rare operational scenarios while preserving explainability. MetaModels establish the foundational framework for aligning virtual and PSs throughout their life cycle. They also facilitate incremental complexity management, starting with baseline behavior and progressively enhancing the PSs capabilities (via its DT) to address emerging environmental challenges.

4.6 Behavior Models for Prognosis and Prescriptive DTs

This section presents some of the approaches and sketched solutions for modeling the behavior and structuring the components of prognosis and prescriptive DTs.

4.6.1 Behavior Models for Prognostic DTs

Prognostic capabilities are a key advantage of DTs, enabling the anticipation of future issues, assessment of their potential impact, and implementation of proactive mitigation strategies. By integrating behavior models with predictive analytics and simulation, prognostic DTs evolve beyond reactive responses, adopting preventive and prescriptive approaches [27, 37, 246].

4.6.1.1 Forecasting and Mitigation Through Integrated Components

The integration of prediction capabilities with historical data, behavior engines, and simulation engines creates a powerful framework for prognostic analysis:

- **Predictive Analytics:** AI models trained on historical operational data identify patterns that precede system issues or suboptimal performance (e.g., by an AIPredictor component).
- **Behavior Engine:** The formalized behavior MetaModel provides logic for predictions, ensuring they align with system constraints and operational rules.
- **Simulation Engine:** It enables testing of predicted scenarios and proposed mitigation strategies before implementation.
- **GenAI Component:** It generates diverse potential scenarios and evaluates their impact, including rare edge cases that may not be well-represented in historical data.

This integrated approach enables the DT to not only predict potential issues but also to develop and validate mitigation strategies through simulation before they are needed in the real system [245].

4.6.1.1.1 Case-based Reasoning for Prognostic DTs

A possible enabler for prognostic capabilities is case-based reasoning (CBR). It is a technique that preserves knowledge about predicted scenarios, their impacts, and successful mitigation strategies. This approach addresses a fundamental challenge in prognostic systems: the *paradox of successful prediction and intervention*. When a prognostic DT successfully predicts and mitigates an issue before it occurs [247], that issue gradually disappears from the historical data. This creates a paradoxical situation where the system becomes less likely to predict an issue precisely because it has been effective at preventing it, i.e., a form of "proactive prediction decay." To address this paradox, the prognostic DT may:

- Store predicted scenarios and their mitigation strategies in a case library, even if they were successfully prevented.
- Maintain these cases with appropriate metadata about the situation in the context of the PS, predicted impact, and mitigation effectiveness.
- Periodically review and validate these cases through simulation to ensure mitigation strategies remain effective as the system evolves.

This approach ensures that even if the successful mitigation significantly reduces the frequency of issues in operational data, the system retains the ability to recognize and respond to similar situations when they arise again.

Figure 4.14 represents a few functionalities and related components that can integrate the ability of the MetaModel (executed in the behavior engine) to predict and mitigate issues. The prognosis module contains components such as situation model, able to represent the current and future situation in the context of the PS operations, a case library containing the representation of past cases that have been successfully mitigated, and a mitigation recommender that can suggest to the behavior engine what to do in an upcoming situation that needs intervention. This approach can lead to modifications of current behavior, ensuring that mitigation capabilities are enclosed for future occurrences of the issue. Additionally, it updates the case library, providing guidance on prevention and effective strategies for mitigating similar challenges in the future. The mitigation recommender is a specialized module capable of suggesting actions to humans.

4.6.1.2 Coping with Weather Impact on Traffic Light Bulb Lifetime

In addition to behavior adaptations for traffic management, prognostic capabilities in DTs can anticipate hardware degradation influenced by environmental factors. Consider a traffic light system where the expected end-of-life of bulbs is predicted based on usage patterns. External conditions such as weather and nonstandard operating environments can significantly affect bulb longevity.

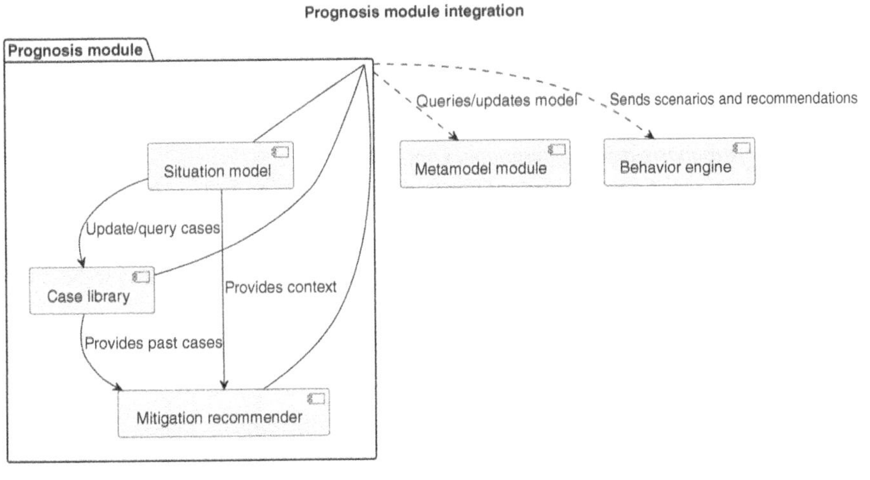

Figure 4.14 Componentization of the prognosis module.

4.6.1.2.1 Predictive Analysis of Bulb Lifetime

The DT integrates historical data on bulb usage with predictive models to estimate the remaining useful life (RUL) of each traffic light bulb. Factors influencing the prognosis include:

- **Usage Intensity:** Frequency and duration of bulb illumination.
- **Weather Conditions:** Temperature extremes, humidity, and precipitation can accelerate deterioration.
- **Lamp Variants:** Different lamp models or manufacturers may have varying durability.

4.6.1.2.2 Adaptive Mitigation via a Behavior Engine

A behavior engine, informed by the prognosis module, can adjust operational parameters to extend bulb life. For example:

- Modulating light intensity during low-traffic periods.
- Adjusting blinking patterns or duty cycles to reduce stress.
- Prioritizing maintenance scheduling based on predicted failure risk.

4.6.1.2.3 Situation Awareness and Case-based Reasoning

The Prognosis Module incorporates a *Situation Model* that contextualizes environmental data (e.g., recent or future weather events) and operational status. It references a *Case Library* containing past failure cases and successful mitigation strategies. This enables the system to:

- Detect deviations from expected bulb lifetime due to unusual conditions.
- Recommend preemptive maintenance before failures occur.
- Adapt mitigation strategies based on historical effectiveness.

4.6.1.2.4 Prognosis-driven Operational Continuity

If a bulb shows signs of imminent failure, the prognosis module collaborates with the behavior engine to:

- Exploit remaining bulb capabilities by reducing load or switching to backup lighting modes.
- Schedule maintenance activities proactively, minimizing traffic disruption.
- Inform operators with explainable recommendations, enhancing trust, and decision-making.

This scenario illustrates how prognostic DTs leverage predictive analytics, behavior modeling, and case-based reasoning to maintain system reliability under varying environmental and usage conditions. By anticipating hardware degradation influenced by weather and operational factors, the system can proactively mitigate risks, optimize maintenance, and ensure continuous safe operation of traffic infrastructure.

This approach to prognostic DTs offers several advantages:

- **Proactive Risk Management:** Issues are addressed before they severely impact system performance or safety.
- **Explainable Predictions:** The behavior model provides context and reasoning for predictions and mitigation strategies.
- **Knowledge Retention:** Successful prevention avoids the unmanaged information decay of potential awareness of issues.
- **Continuous Improvement:** Each predicted scenario enriches the case library, improving future prognostic capabilities.

By combining AI prediction with behavior modeling, simulation, and case-based reasoning, prognostic DTs can maintain awareness of potential issues even as their successful prevention makes them increasingly rare in operational data [225, 245].

4.6.2 Prescriptive Model and Integration with Prognosis Capabilities

Prescriptive representation (model) in DTs extends beyond prediction, prognosis, and simulation by actively recommending and executing actions to optimize system performance, safety, and efficiency. Behavior models enable prescriptive capabilities by effectively embodying domain knowledge, operational constraints, and decision logic to guide actionable recommendations. Integrating them with prognosis functions further enhances prescription, allowing for the prediction of future states and the execution of preemptive actions. Different types of behavior models exist for prescriptive DTs:

1. **Rule-based Systems:** These models use explicit if-then rules to prescribe actions based on system states or measurements. Their interpretability and ease of updating make them suitable for well-understood domains with clear policies.
2. **State Machines and Automata:** These represent system behavior as discrete states and transitions. They enable prescriptive control by defining allowable actions and sequences.
3. **Optimization Models:** These models use mathematical programming or heuristics to determine optimal control actions under constraints. Integrated with behavior models, they prescribe actions to maximize performance metrics (e.g., to minimize traffic congestion).
4. **Hybrid Models:** Combining AI predictions with behavior models leverages the predictive power of ML and the interpretability of rule/state-based systems for actionable prescriptions.

4.6.3 Recommendation Systems in DTs

Recommendation systems extend prescriptive models and enhance DT capabilities by providing tailored suggestions to users or autonomic agents. Based on current status, historical data, and predictive insights, these agents actively interact with the PS to implement the decided policy. They significantly improve DTs by enabling:

- **Augmentation of DT Capabilities:** These systems suggest maintenance strategies, operational adjustments, and user behaviors to optimize performance.
- **Integration with Behavior Models:** These recommendations incorporate AI predictions while ensuring adherence to behavior models that encode domain rules and constraints.
- **Explainability:** By linking recommendations to behavior models and historical cases, DTs provide transparent explanations, enhancing user trust and supporting informed decision-making.

4.6.3.1 Prognosis Functions and Prescriptive Recommendations

Integrating prognosis functions with behavior models and recommendation systems enables proactive and adaptive decision-making. Prognosis functions (e.g., the Prognosis Module) use predictive analytics to anticipate potential future issues and their impacts. By incorporating these predictions into the recommendation process, prescriptive DTs can suggest actions that prevent problems before they occur. General functions that can benefit from Prescriptive DT include:

- **Predictive Maintenance:** Prognosis functions can forecast when a component is likely to fail, and the prescriptive functions can recommend preemptive maintenance to avoid downtime.
- **Adaptive Control:** Based on predicted future conditions, the behavior model can dynamically adjust operating parameters to optimize performance and extend system life.
- **Risk Mitigation:** The prescriptive DT can recommend actions to mitigate potential risks identified by the prognosis functions, such as adjusting traffic light timing to reduce congestion during predicted bad weather.

4.6.4 The Role of Autonomics in Prescriptive DTs

Autonomics amplifies the capabilities of prescriptive DTs [248] by enabling self-management features that transform passive recommendation systems into proactive, self-optimizing entities. In prescriptive DTs, autonomic computing principles of self-*, i.e., self-configuration, self-healing, self-optimization, and self-protection, allow the prescriptive functions to not only recommend actions but also actuate them with minimal human intervention. When integrated with behavior models and prognosis systems, autonomic capabilities enable DTs to detect anomalies, predict potential issues, and automatically adjust system parameters within predefined constraints. For example, a traffic light DT with autonomic features could independently modify signal timing in response to predicted congestion patterns while adhering to safety rules encoded in its behavior model. This self-governance is particularly valuable in time-critical scenarios where human response might be too slow, or in complex systems where the interrelationships between components are difficult for operators to manage manually. By incorporating autonomics, prescriptive DTs evolve from advisory systems to trusted autonomic agents that continuously optimize performance while maintaining explainability through their underlying behavior models.

In this case as well, GenAI could play a decisive role in the incremental implementation of autonomics capabilities. Scenarios tested through GenAI and refined via iterative behavior optimization, once approved under human supervision, can be delegated to the autonomic functions of the DT. Meanwhile, new or uncertain scenarios will still require human oversight. Figure 4.15 represents a Prescriptive Module added to the set of components for the DT's functioning. This module interacts with the Behavior and the Prognosis Modules and can use the available predictions and historical data as well the scenario generation capability as supported by the AI/GenAI Module. The prescriptive module role is essentially a leader one; it coordinates different capabilities offered by the DT system to determine a viable policy to be actuated. The goal is to determine the current situation

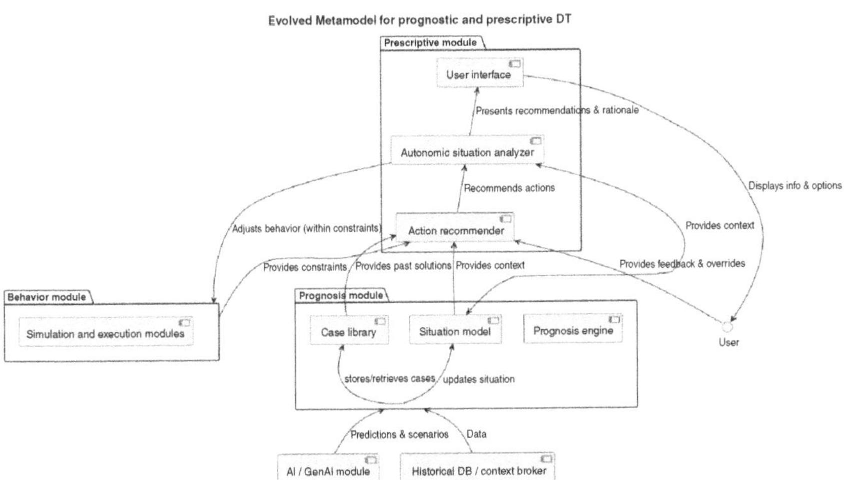

Figure 4.15 Prescriptive module and its relationships with other modules.

and then, by cooperating with the other modules, to determine the best actions to execute. If these are within the "autonomics" capabilities granted to the DT, the prescriptive module will use the autonomic situation analyzer and the ActionRecommendation component to instruct the other modules to execute actions under its supervision. If the scenario is not committed (i.e., not yet human-approved), the prescriptive module will recommend mitigation actions to humans and then execute them according to user decisions.

4.6.5 Benefits of Behavior Models in Prescriptive DTs

There are several advantages associated with the integration of Prescriptive models into a DT system:

- **Consistency and Safety:** Behavior models enforce operational constraints, preventing unsafe or unfeasible recommendations.
- **Explainability:** Rule-based and state machine models provide a transparent basis for recommendations.
- **Adaptability:** Hybrid models allow DTs to adapt prescriptions as system conditions evolve.
- **User Trust:** Clear explanations and actionable recommendations improve operator confidence and acceptance.
- **Autonomics:** Self-capabilities enable a DT to recommend and actuate decisions. This reduces the time required to optimize the behavior with respect to the situation. However, some limitations may be imposed, especially for newer situations that are to be supervised by humans.

4.6.5.1 Example: Traffic Light DT Enhanced with Prescription

The adoption of a prescriptive model could provide benefits in the case of a traffic light for example:

- **Prognosis Module:** Predicts that weather conditions (e.g., heavy rain) will reduce visibility and increase traffic accidents.
- **Recommendation:** Based on this prognosis, the prescriptive module prescribes adjusting traffic light timing to slow traffic flow and increase safety during the predicted period.

The prescriptive module can provide **justification** by explaining its recommendation with reference to the behavior model, prognosis data, and relevant safety guidelines. This integration ensures prescriptions are data-driven, rule-compliant, and forward-looking, enabling safe and efficient traffic management.

4.7 Behavior Modeling Recap

This chapter introduces **behavior models and modeling** in the context of **DTs**, outlining key approaches for representing behavior, exploring significant behavior models, and detailing the process of behavior model development. Additionally, it examines how **AI technologies** enhance behavior definition and modeling, while **simulation** plays an essential role in refining and improving behavior representation.

The chapter then analyzes various types of **behavior models** applied to critical DT functions such as **prognosis and prescription**. Functional extensions to a **baseline model**, along with the introduction of **supporting modules and components**, progressively enhance the DT's ability to **lead and govern** the operation of the PS, especially when system limitations require DT intervention.

The evolution of **behavior modeling** moves from simple representations toward **more advanced and autonomous modeling capabilities**, significantly increasing the DT's capacity for independent decision-making. These advancements are **empowered by the synergy between AI and behavior models**, allowing DTs to:

- **Predict future events and state changes**.
- **Generate alternative scenarios that challenge expected system behavior**.
- **Progress toward autonomous decision-making with minimal human intervention**.

Ultimately, the integration of **behavior models with prescriptive and prognosis functions** enables advanced, capable **autonomic DTs** that are not just **predictive and diagnostic** but also **proactive and adaptive**. By delivering actionable recommendations rooted in domain knowledge and predictive insights, these DTs optimize system performance, enhance safety, and support informed decision-making in complex environments.

5

Architecting and Implementing Digital Twin Systems: Approaches, Guidelines, and Best Practices

After reading this chapter, you should be able to:

- Understand the complexity and requirements of Digital Twin architectures.
- Identify the main functional domains and core features of a Digital Twin platform.
- Learn software interaction and componentization paradigms for Digital Twin implementation.
- Apply emerging best practices, including standards adherence, componentization, and life cycle management.
- Understand the Digital Twin life cycle and the importance of model and software validation.

5.1 Requirements, Structural Concepts, and Terminology for a Digital Twin Architecture

The rise of Digital Twins (DTs) has sparked significant interest, leading to numerous implementations and platform developments. These advancements have influenced industry standards and shaped practical use cases across various sectors ([4–7, 13, 17, 57, 249, 250] and others as reported in Section 6.5.2). In spite of this interest, the support for the design and implementation of DTs is confined to a few platforms and architectures [146, 171] supported by definition languages (e.g., [164]) or data models [141]. Meanwhile, the development of Model-based System Engineering (MBSE) is moving toward the definition of tools and architectures for exploiting the power of DT [65]. However, the software part is not yet completely defined and requires further improvements.

Existing solutions have yet to converge into a consolidated, widely accepted approach. This chapter seeks to systematize key requirements and propose a structured organization for a DT architecture, incorporating a behavior model as a fundamental component.

5.1.1 Requirements and Properties of DTs

DTs represent a paradigm shift in how physical systems are designed, monitored, and optimized. According to the paper [7] and as discussed in Section 1.3, DTs are defined by essential properties, which must be supported and facilitated by enabling platforms. They are not just complementary but are fundamental to ensuring that DTs can fully embody and leverage their key characteristics. Furthermore, as explored in the modeling sections, modern DT platforms and implementations must provide:

- **Explainability:** The ability to explain decisions and predictions to users.
- **Adaptability:** The ability to evolve as the physical system changes.
- **Scalability:** The support for multiple, potentially interacting DTs.
- **Autonomy:** The support for decision-making and the ability to actually implement decisions.

The combination of two facets, the ability to represent the behavior and data of the physical system and the enforcement of foundational DT properties, characterizes a proper DT software architecture.

5.1.2 State of the Art in DT Architectures

Current DT architectural approaches can be categorized into different trends, each with distinct strengths and limitations. MBSE approaches [20, 251] provide comprehensive frameworks for system modeling but often disregard the DT and treat it as a byproduct of the physical system design rather than a co-designed entity [252]. This practice creates a gap between the physical system design and the DT specification and implementation.

IoT-driven platforms like FIWARE [149] are based on robust data management and interoperability through standardized interfaces and context brokers. However, these platforms typically emphasize dataflow and information management [253], while providing limited support for complex behavior modeling and simulation. The chain passive, predictive DT, and up to prognostic and prescriptive is a typical result of this trend [123].

Cloud-based architectures are solutions offered by the big players of this sector (Amazon, Microsoft, Alibaba) and are based on their consolidated cloud platforms and extensions for IoT (e.g., AWS IoT TwinMaker,[1] Microsoft Azure

---

1 https://aws.amazon.com/iot-twinmaker/ last visited 02 May 2025

Digital Twins,[2] Alibaba's Industrial Brain[3]); or specialized big players of automation like Siemens[4] or PTC[5] or communications enterprises such as Huawei[6] [78]. They offer scalability and computational resources, but often lack a tight integration with physical systems required for true digital twinning. These approaches frequently treat behavior models as black-box components rather than first-class architectural elements.

The limitations in existing approaches highlight an important gap: the need for architectures that support concurrent physical-digital design, development, and testing while providing robust behavior modeling capabilities and the possibility to exploit distributed computing resources (e.g., edge computing for optimizing the DT implementation and responsiveness).

5.1.3 Reimagining a Versatile DT Architecture

An initial architecture has been drafted and is shown in Figure 1.3. To address the limitations in current approaches, the previously introduced behavior MetaModel (Section 4.5.2) and the initial architecture serve as foundational components of a DT architecture. It also leverages the powerfulness provided by descriptive model and related data management as supported by a ContextBroker.

This approach seems promising and offers several advantages:

- **Data-driven:** Leveraging the data contextualization and management, it can encompass the data-driven development of DTs as emerging in industry and academia.
- **Behavior-oriented Design:** By elevating behavior models to first-class architectural elements, the system behavior is explicitly designed rather than emergent.
- **Concurrent Development:** The MetaModel supports simultaneous development of physical and digital components.
- **Explainability by Design:** The behavior model and the organization of functions provide a basis for explaining system decisions and actions.
- **Simulation-execution Consistency:** Using the same behavior model for simulation and execution ensures consistency across development and operation.

2 https://azure.microsoft.com/en-us/products/digital-twins/ last visited 02 May 2025
3 https://www.alibabacloud.com/blog/598949 last visited 01 October 2025
4 https://plm.sw.siemens.com/en-US/insights-hub/ last visited 02 May 2025
5 https://www.ptc.com/en/products/thingworx last visited 02 May 2025
6 https://e.huawei.com/en/news/2024/industries/government/twin-next-gen-city-solution last visited 02 May 2025

- **AI-driven:** A flexible framework designed to harness AI technologies, enabling seamless data and behavior modeling while optimizing the platform for efficient DT execution.
- **Incremental Behavior Constructions:** Leveraging the integration of GenAI, simulation, and behavioral modeling, incremental development, and functional augmentation of the system is made possible. The DT system can grow over time to cover new requirements or new scenarios.
- **Autonomics:** Exploiting the possible integration of prognostic, predictive, simulation, and incremental behavior modeling, the architecture can support the development of increasingly autonomic behavior under the supervision of humans.

As a methodological note, a simplified terminology is introduced to facilitate reader comprehension. The following sections progressively define architectural components using terminology partially aligned with SYSML 2.0, naming components according to their goals, characteristics, and capabilities. Key entities include:

- **Module:** A structural *Block* aggregating related functions to implement a coherent set of responsibilities, encapsulating constituent *Parts* for modular design.
- **Engine:** A specialized module optimized for efficient execution of specific, often computationally intensive tasks within the system architecture.
- **Agent:** An autonomous *Block* exhibiting proactive, goal-driven behavior and capable of interaction and adaptation within the system environment.
- **Manager, Analyzer, Optimizer:** Specialized modules emphasizing particular functional roles, responsible for coordinating, organizing, or optimizing task execution by managing workflows, applying analytical methods, or enhancing decision-making.

These terms provide a foundation for discussing system architecture components with clarity and consistency.

In this architecture, shown in Figure 5.1, a DT System is represented by its internal subsystems (i.e., DT engine, data management, and system engine) and their major interactions with external systems. Internal subsystems are further decomposed into modules, which aggregate smaller components dedicated to executing specific functions and achieving specific goals. The behavior module works alongside the predictive module and ContextBroker to form the foundation of the DT. The ContextBroker manages dataflow between the physical and digital components, while the behavior module provides the behavior logic that drives both simulation and execution, while the predictive module processes data to provide predictions of the different states for future changes of the physical system.

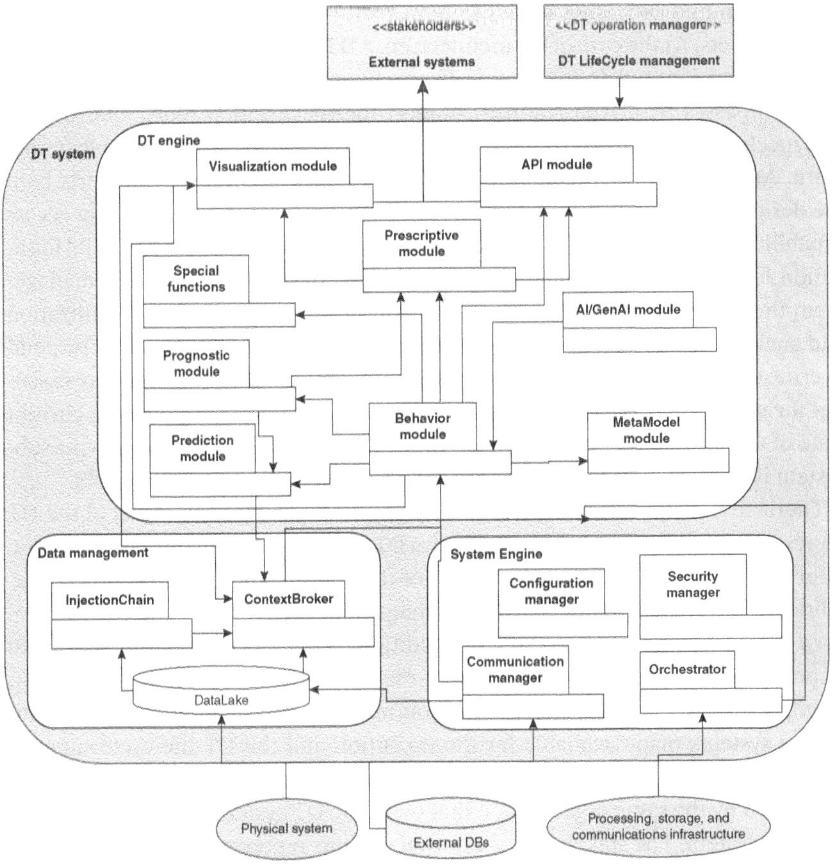

Figure 5.1 The context DT architecture.

For simplicity, the picture does not depict all components and their connections; some will be introduced in later sections. This architecture serves as a flexible framework, allowing designers and implementers to incorporate additional modules and components as needed. The grouping of functions emphasizes their common objectives in supporting a set of functionalities, but in implementation and deployment, components can be aggregated based on the solution's specific requirements. The DT system consists of three major components. The **System Engine** is responsible for allocating processing, storage, and communication resources essential for DT implementation and execution, particularly in large edge/cloud deployments. It also facilitates communication by means of mechanisms, such as MQTT and HTTPS/REST. **Data Management** handles data acquisition, aggregation, and curation, transforming raw data into contextualized information and providing access to both real-time data streams and historical batch datasets. At the core of the architecture, a **DT Engine** supports both descriptive and behavior models, integrating diverse functions to enhance DT capabilities. It encompasses AI-driven features, support for visualization tools, and interaction mechanisms with external systems, ensuring a dynamic and adaptable framework. Another key subsystem is **DT LifeCycle Management**. It supports both the design and implementation phases by leveraging simulation and data access capabilities to refine and define an accurate behavior model, ensuring a solid foundation for DT development. It also facilitates seamless operations and management throughout the DT life cycle, optimizing system engine resource utilization and enabling critical event management, allowing humans to effectively respond to critical situations requiring new policies. While these functionalities are essential for operational DT development, further advancements beyond the current state of the art remain necessary (e.g., [63]). The DT LifeCycle management subsystem is fundamental to the successful deployment and utilization of DTs.

There are several external systems. The physical system is the object of the DT representation. It is connected to the entire DT system and sends and receives data, information, and instructions by means of the combined communications capabilities of the system engine and data management (in particular the ContextBroker). External DataBases represent the additional data and information needed to improve the functioning of the DT (e.g., meteorological data for the traffic light example). The processing, storage, and communications capabilities are the computing systems made available for the execution and the DT life-cycle support. The physical system and the processing capabilities are usually "owned" or at least controlled by the same organization that owns the DT system, and most likely the physical system. The stakeholders' external systems represent external customers (or different departments of the owner organization) that actually use the services and functions offered by the DT.

This approach addresses the limitations in current architectures by providing explicit support for behavior modeling and the needed incremental construction capabilities while maintaining the data management features required for DT implementation. A more detailed description of these software functions is provided in the next sections.

5.2 Software Interaction Paradigms for DT Implementation

The implementation of DT systems can leverage a range of software paradigms, each offering distinct architectural and operational benefits. Here, the focus is on four paradigms highly relevant to DTs: client-server, event-driven, agent-based, and data-sharing architectures, and their roles are discussed in the context of a home automation DT.

5.2.1 Client-server Paradigm

The client-server model is a classic distributed computing architecture in which clients (such as external applications) request services or data from centralized servers, which process these requests and return results. This paradigm is widely used for its clear separation of concerns and centralized management of data and logic, facilitating maintainability and scalability in DT implementations [254].

5.2.2 Event-driven Paradigm

Event-driven Architecture (EDA) is centered around the production, detection, and reaction to events. In this model, components communicate by emitting and responding to events, enabling real-time updates and decoupled interactions. EDA is particularly suitable for DTs that must reflect the state of the physical system dynamically and support asynchronous, scalable operations [255].

5.2.3 Agent-based Paradigm

Agent-based architectures employ autonomous software agents that interact with each other and the environment to achieve individual or collective goals. In DTs, this allows for decentralized decision-making, adaptability, and the modeling of complex interactions, making the system more resilient and flexible [256].

5.2.4 Data-sharing Paradigm

The data-sharing paradigm enables multiple processes or components to read from and write to a shared data space, often referred to as a "whiteboard" pattern. The OMG Data Distribution Service (DDS) standard exemplifies this approach by providing a global data space where DT components can publish and subscribe to topics without direct coupling [257]. This facilitates modularity and real-time synchronization across the DT system.

5.2.4.1 Advantages for DT Implementation

Each paradigm brings advantages and possibilities to DT development:

- **Client-server:** Simplifies centralized management of DT logic and data, eases access control, and supports multiple client interfaces [254].
- **Event-driven:** Enables real-time updates, decouples system components, supports scalability, and facilitates asynchronous processing-essential for responsive DTs [258].
- **Agent-based:** Provides flexibility and autonomy, supports emergent behaviors, and is well-suited for complex, adaptive DT environments [256].

- **Data-sharing:** Promotes modularity, simplifies integration, and allows for real-time, decoupled data exchange among DT modules, as standardized by DDS and whiteboard patterns [257].

5.2.4.2 Home Automation Example

To illustrate the application of these paradigms, consider a home automation DT:

- **Client-server:** A central DT server maintains the home's digital state, while multiple clients (mobile apps, voice assistants) interact with it to retrieve information or issue commands (e.g., turning on lights or adjusting the thermostat).
- **Event-driven:** Sensors (motion, temperature) generate events when changes occur (e.g., motion detected in the living room). The DT Engine processes these events to update the digital state and trigger actions, such as activating lights or sending alerts [258].
- **Agent-based:** Each smart device (e.g., thermostat, light controller) is represented by an agent that autonomously manages its behavior and coordinates with other agents (e.g., the thermostat agent collaborates with window agents to optimize energy use) [256].
- **Data-sharing:** All devices and DT modules read and write to a shared data space (as per DDS or whiteboard pattern), so when a sensor updates its status, other components (e.g., the Visualization Module or Behavior Module) can instantly access the new data and react accordingly [259].

5.2.4.2.1 Modularity, Granularity, and Composability

Microservices are complementary to the paradigms discussed above and can be extensively employed throughout a DT architecture. Their fine granularity and composability enable the independent development, deployment, and scaling of DT components, supporting a wide range of interaction and coordination models.

A key aspect of DT architecture is the ability to componentize functions into fine-grained, reusable modules. These components can be composed, either as chains of client-server calls, orchestrated by a central server or leader, or choreographed through message exchanges, to deliver the required functionalities. Microservices can be implemented within any of the discussed paradigms, making them a natural target for further refinement of DT architectures.

The DT platform should inherently support these and other mechanisms, granting designers the flexibility to select the most appropriate paradigm for each problem domain. However, each paradigm requires specific support to be effectively implemented and offered. While the system engine is primarily responsible for enabling these interaction paradigms, many other modules and components in the architecture may also be affected by the paradigm choice. Designers should carefully evaluate the advantages and disadvantages of each approach and, where beneficial, consider adopting hybrid paradigms to best meet system requirements.

5.3 Componentization of DT Architecture

A DT can be seen as a large distributed application that requires substantial interactions with external sources or sinks of data and information. In addition, the composability and replication properties of a DT allow for a large distribution and componentization of DT parts. The DT software framework is, thus, complex and must be supported by a distributed processing environment capable of providing processing, storage, and communications capabilities to large distributed applications as well as extensive capabilities to communicate with external systems. In addition, the data-driven nature of many DT developments and implementations requires an effective and powerful data management framework. Finally, the functions needed to support the development and real-time behavior modeling and execution of a DT require a careful design and implementation in terms of components. The DT system provides these capabilities, in which the system engine functions are ancillary to the ability to execute a DT, the data management functions are enablers for achieving data-driven DTs, and the DT engine is instrumental to the execution of the DT itself. Service development functions (in the DT LifeCycle Management Module) are now introduced because they have a role in the incremental construction, tuning, and, possibly, change of phase in the DT life cycle.

5.3.1 System Engine

This subsystem can be seen as a general infrastructure on top of which the DT (as well as other applications) can be executed. It controls a physical infrastructure composed of resources such as processing and storage nodes interconnected to support the exchange of data. On top of this infrastructure, there is a set of virtualization functions useful to orchestrate resources, allocate components to appropriate virtual nodes, and management, security, and optimization functions. This system engine could itself make use of a network DT [137, 138] representation for managing and optimizing the infrastructure. Figure 5.2 represents the high-level components of the system engine.

The central points of this subsystem are two:

- The **Communication Manager**, that governs the information exchange between the components of the architecture through well-consolidated mechanisms (e.g., PubSub) and related protocols. Whenever needed, the communication can be direct between the components through their internal APIs (internal to the DT system).

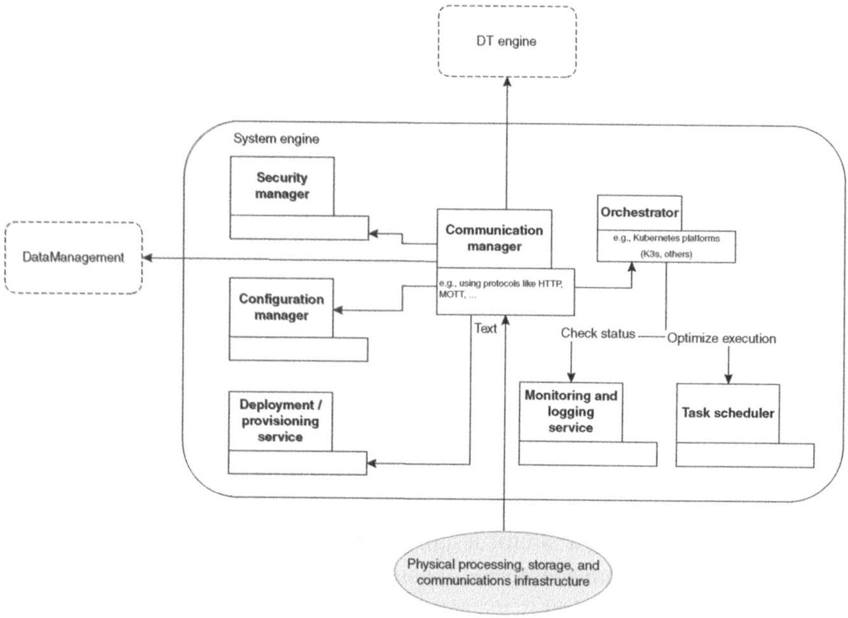

Figure 5.2 The system engine componentization.

- The **Orchestrator** which is in charge of correctly allocating virtual resources to the requesting functionalities and microservices.

The other components cooperate to monitor and report the effectiveness of the decisions taken by the orchestrator (monitoring and logging service, task scheduler); or they cooperate to determine the best configuration and deployment according to constraints and rules imposed by the application (e.g., the configuration manager, the deployment/provisioning Service). The security manager provides secure mechanisms to ensure that the platform is safe and can effectively provide its promised services. This can be seen as a state-of-the-art virtual platform management [260] infrastructure that can further evolve toward the specific needs of DTs [261, 262].

5.3.2 Data Management

This subsystem is largely based on the evolution of FIWARE platforms and architecture (e.g., [114]). The ability of data management to capture and curate the different data streams needed for the functioning of a DT in all of its facets deserves special attention. The injections chain module and its components are particularly relevant in this framework [153]. Figure 5.3 provides an initial description of

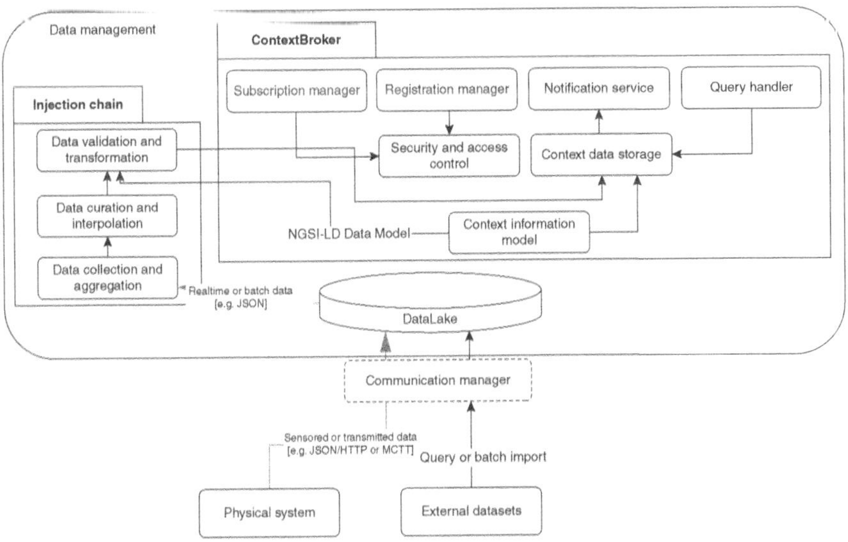

Figure 5.3 Data management organization.

modules and components that can provide the expected services. Data are collected and aggregated either by means of the support of the Communication Manager (e.g., by means of PubSub mechanisms, to which the Data Management subscribes to get updates to specific topics offered by external systems) or directly through crawling mechanisms (or others). The data are collected and, through the usage of the DataLake component [263, 264], are progressively examined, curated (or even integrated), and finally formatted according to specific data models used by the DT and validated. These data are injected into the ContextBroker, which notifies and makes them available to subscribers (notably components of the DT engine). The ContextBroker makes other functions available for semantically organized data query. It also supports registration for and subscription to specific updates of the DT system components, and uses security mechanisms to ensure the proper usage of the information. The DT engine components are able to access real-time data streams and historical data when they are needed or available.

5.3.3 DT Engine

The DT engine supports a set of functions useful for the execution and evolution of the DT representation. It is characterized by the ability to integrate different model capabilities and by its access to and usage of data as provided by the ContextBroker. Figure 5.4 offers a general view of the major components and a few of the relationships between them.

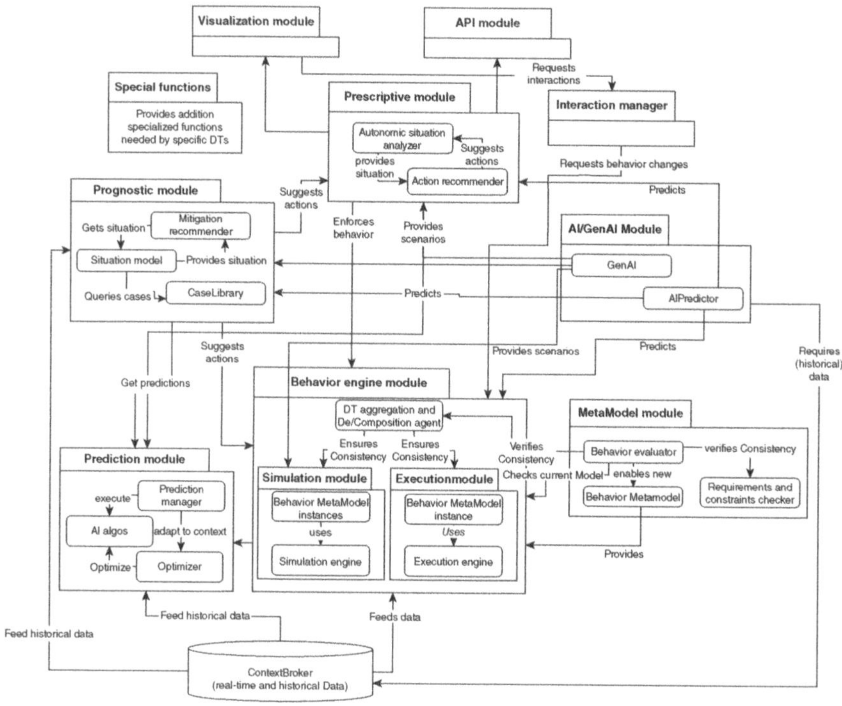

Figure 5.4 DT engine componentization.

The modules and their components are briefly described below:

- The **Behavior Engine Module** ensures that the behavior model, represented by the behavior MetaModel, is correctly executed for the specific physical system and has access to all required data streams (via integration with data management components such as the InjectionChain and ContextBroker). It interacts with other modules (e.g., AI/GenAI, prescriptive, and prognostic modules) to provide extended capabilities as the DT is upgraded or evolves. Additionally, it supports interaction with the DT development agent (not shown in Figure 5.4) to allow the incremental tuning and refinement of the behavior model. The behavior engine module is composed of the following parts (with their respective components) and a core execution component:
  - An ExecutionModule devoted to the execution of the current version of the computational representation of the expected behavior of the physical system(i.e., behavior MetaModel). It can request access to data as needed. It is composed of the following components:
    - An execution engine that executes the current model considering all the requirements and constraints as defined in the MetaModel and

ensures timely access to the data streams needed to be elaborated by the module.

    - A behavior Metamodel Instance, the executable description of the behavior MetaModel, which uses the execution engine for coordinating, interacting, and actuating the functions, actions and interactions required to represent the behavior of the physical system. It could be considered as a sort of image to be executed by the execution engine.
  - A simulation module, which is similar in terms of internal components to the execution module; however, it can run more than one instance of the behavior MetaModel for simulation purposes.
  - A DT aggregation and De/Composition agent; this component ensures that the representation of aggregated objects and their decomposition into several elements is consistent and aligned with the current execution of the behavior MetaModel. It communicates with the MetaModel Module to ensure consistency.
- A **Prediction Module** provides all the predictive capabilities needed to forecast possible states of the physical system. This module cooperates with the behavior engine module to synchronize the data with the expected behavior states and with other modules providing predictions useful to determine the need for intervention due to malfunction or other occurrences. It is structured in different sub-modules:
  - A prediction manager supervises all the requests and interactions with other modules that require forecasting capabilities. According to the requests (or the normal working in the case of specific types of DT that require continuous prediction), it selects the requested or needed AI algorithms and engages with the needed problem domain specialization by interacting with specific functions. This manager acts as a high-level orchestrator, deciding which algorithm to use or optimizing their parameters (in cooperation with others) to achieve the best possible forecast. This moves beyond a simple "one-size-fits-all" approach.
  - Domain knowledge optimizer is in charge of adapting the existing algorithms and their capabilities to the specific problem domain. For instance, domain-specific rules, constraints, or expertise can be used to refine and improve the predictive models, making the results more relevant and trustworthy.
  - AI Algos sub-module offers algorithmic diversity: the inclusion of different algorithm types, like time-series analysis and TreeBasedOnes, recognizes that no single model is best for all tasks. This allows the system to choose and execute the most suitable algorithm for a given dataset or prediction task. The cooperation with the optimizer guarantees that these algorithms can be specialized to reflect properties of the problem domain.

The addition of newly needed AI functions is carried out in conjunction between the prediction manager and the AI Algos sub-module.

- A **MetaModel Module** that ensures that the current version of the behavior model is correct and executable. It consists of the following components:
  - A behavior Metamodel that represents and preserves the behavior models, current and past ones for versioning. These could be considered as images that can be executed by the behavior engine model.
  - A behavior evaluator that cooperates with the behavior engine components to ensure consistency and executability of the instances of the behavior MetaModel. In addition, this evaluator helps in maintaining the consistency of complex aggregations of components by interacting with DT aggregation. It ensures the validity of the models.
  - A requirements and constraints checker, which consistently verifies that the model respects the requirements and constraints imposed on the physical system. These limitations could be functional or incur at real time: they are imposed in such a way to ensure their fulfillment or, in the case of problems, to warn the DT of issues.
- The **AI/GenAI Module** provides the AI functions required to support the DT. Predictions and the generation of synthetic data/scenarios may be requested internally by the DT system or externally (e.g., for tuning the behavior model's purposes from the DT development functions). This module accesses the ContextBroker data and uses them to predict or generate scenarios. It consists of two major components:
  - An AIPredictor that uses the historical data to predict future states of the physical system or of some part of it. AIPredictor can use different AI tools according to the requirements and technological evolution.
  - A GenAI component, which is used for creating meaningful scenarios that can support other modules or the DT development to determine how to adapt the behavior to the envisaged scenario.
- A **Prognostic Module** is devoted to the preventive identification and resolution of the physical system's issues. It monitors the physical system data (accessing streams of real-time data) and identifies differences from the expected behavior, or it uses AI/GenAI functions to predict malfunctions or issues. A prognosis module comprises the following components:
  - A situation model for collecting the available information and building a situation's representation mapped to existing or already considered cases.
  - A CaseLibrary, which is a sort of repository of current or past cases and the adopted successful mitigation strategies. It provides the relevant cases that the situation model will actually map to the current situation.
  - A mitigation recommender, which uses the representation of the situation and the mapped successful cases to elaborate the optimal strategy and

suggests it to the behavior engine module. The actual execution of the strategy will typically depend on the authorization provided by humans.

- The **Prescriptive Module** extends the functionalities of the prognostic module and elaborates long-term and complex strategies for optimizing the behavior of the physical system while also considering the environment's evolution and other relevant parameters. This module interacts with AI/GenAI for predictive or scenario generation insights. If the scenario mitigation policies are committed to by humans, it will instruct the behavior engine module to execute them. An autonomic behavior for already committed policies can be implemented. This module consists of two components:
  - An autonomic situation analyzer, which identifies a complex situation and determines the important issues to cope with first. It cooperates with the action recommender to determine the optimized policy to propose.
  - An action recommender, which cooperates with the autonomic situation analyzer and with the AI/GenAI module to identify the short- and long-term actions that best fit with the current situation. It proposes these actions to the analyzer; they may be submitted for humans' decisions or directly committed.
- The **Special Function** represents the capability of this architecture to add additional functions as needed to cope with specific issues of a problem domain (e.g., e-health with more rigorous checks on the actions to be executed). These can be seen as a growing repository of the current DT with complementary solutions.

This DT engine's organization is to be considered as a flexible framework that needs to be incrementally extended according to successful implementations; amended in case of evident failures in satisfying requirements, and according to its ability to support the compelling DT design and implementation requirements.

5.3.4 DT Life-cycle Management

This subsystem provides enabling functionalities, primarily the ability to incrementally construct and improve the DT, as well as operational functions for optimizing the resource allocation and exploitation to support the execution of a DT and the management (with user intervention) of critical situations that may require a change of DT behavior. This subsystem contains four components, as shown in Figure 5.5.

Their functions are briefly sketched out:

- The **DT Development Agent** supports the creation, development, and consolidation/update/tuning of the DT with respect to the requirements and objective of the representation. It uses templates of basic DT models for

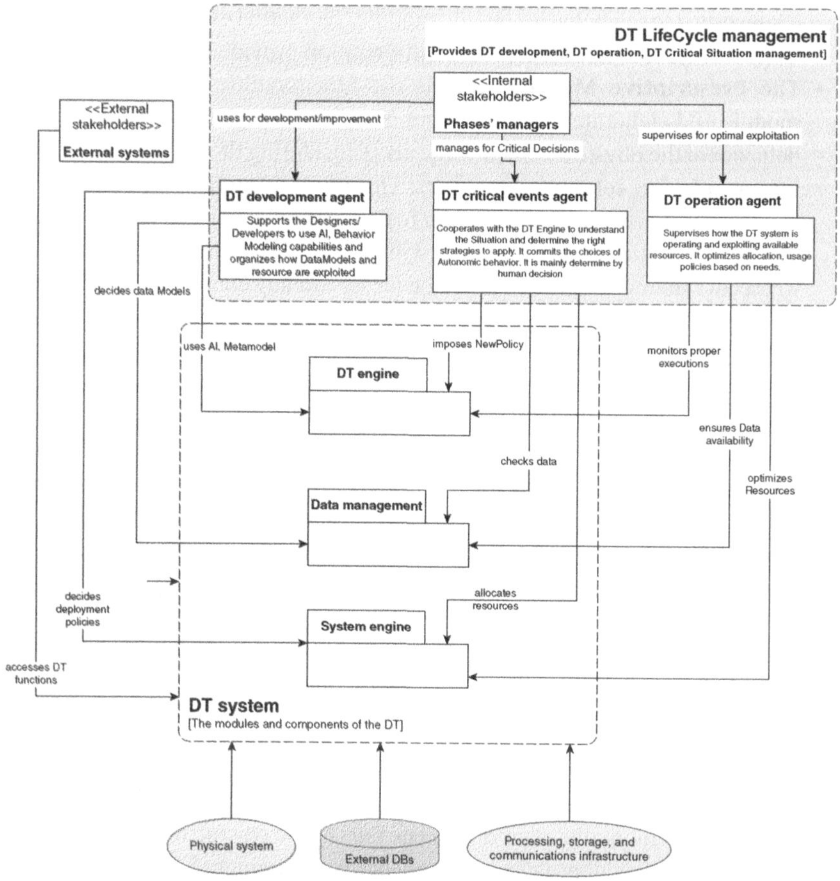

Figure 5.5 DT life-cycle management componentization.

bootstrapping the definition of the actual behavior model, and it uses simulation, and AI capabilities offered by the DT Engine to improve the basic expected behavior. It also allows us to select and setup the data models required for the desired representation in cooperation with the data management part. It creates and integrates functions and components, and determines initial deployment of the software by interacting with the system engine.

- The **DT Operation Agent** supervises the execution of the DT system and ensures that the resources made available by the system engine and the data management modules are sufficient for the expected responses and performance of the DT engine. It also ensures that the external systems are available and can interact with the DT system, so that acceptable levels of service can be guaranteed.

- The **DT Critical Event Management Agent** enables the cooperation between dedicated human operators and the DT System. In critical situations, the DT system recommends actions and proposes solution strategies. This Agent will support the interaction with humans to determine the best course of actions "approved" and committed by the operators. They will also be able to monitor the evolution of the situation and to decide additional mitigation actions imposed on the DT system.
- The **Phases's Managers** indicate the different groups involved in the implementation/improvement, operation, and solution of critical behavior of the DT. This component largely depends on the internal structure of the organization managing the DT.

An important aspect of DT development that has not yet been fully investigated is the definition and reuse of Behavior Templates [38, 67, 77]. The DT development agent can be seen as a sort of integrated development environment for DT, and it should encompass different methodologies and tools to facilitate the development of solutions. One important contribution in this field is the identification and preparation of behavior templates that represent typical cases of DT usage that can be tailored to specific needs. A few patterns in DT behavior for supporting applications can be identified, for instance:

- Large aggregation of cooperating objects with complementary goals in a single system. This requires a template in which different elements can cooperate for achieving the physical system's goals. An example could be a vessel (a tank or container) used for separating oil from gases, water, and residual material (e.g., sand). The shape and design of the vessel ensure the effective separation of gas, oil, water, and residual solids. However, sensors and actuators are needed to control and manage the process. They must be coordinated to optimize the process and reduce waste or risks. The impact of the operational environment is minimal, and it can be taken into consideration by monitoring temperature and pressure levels of the vessel. A well-defined and generalized behavior model of this example can become a template for other applications (e.g., water purification, but also separation of different elements).
- Goals-based independent objects operating on the same "environment": This pattern could be applied to different objects with specific goals but that need to operate in the same environment. There are two specializations of this template: cooperating objects (e.g., in a factory different objects will contribute to the execution of an optimized process) or competing objects attempting to use limited environment's resources (e.g., cars in a city seeking to reduce their traveling times). These two sub-patterns could be represented in well-formed behavior models (templates of logic) that can be tailored to specific problem domains.

- Large open system monitoring and optimization: This template corresponds to the general need to monitor how different entities and stakeholders allocate and use shared resources. Optimization policies associated with priorities assigned to entities or stakeholders could be represented in a behavior model and then specialized in specific problem domains. For instance, a network DT can be seen as an example of an optimization pattern. Depending on stakeholders, available processing, storage, and communication virtualized resources could be allocated and assigned. The allocation should reflect and fulfill Service Level Agreements (SLAs) to be satisfied even when the resource usage changes.

The specialization of templates should go hand in hand with the choice of applicable data models, as this would facilitate the developers' task, reducing the development and implementation times. These templates should be collected and made available within the DT development agent as starting points for beginning the development process. This could bring several advantages:

- Development teams should not necessarily start from scratch (developing a DT takes a considerable amount of time). The availability of well-structured behavior templates could drastically reduce the initial development time.
- Templates can lead to homogeneity in the software development of the different teams of an organization. This would allow the efficient exploitation of components and approaches to solve problems.
- Templates also have an important role in fostering interoperability across different development teams and even between organizations. By maintaining a comprehensive library of templates, particularly for behavior models tailored to various problem types, developers can significantly accelerate the DT development process. This approach not only reduces development time but also lowers the barrier to entry, making advanced DT technologies accessible to a broader community of developers and stakeholders. Standardized templates ensure greater consistency, reusability, and compatibility, thereby supporting the creation of interoperable and scalable DT solutions.

Another important aspect of this subsystem is the need to develop tools and best practices for managing the shift of a DT from one phase to another of a product's life cycle. These topics have an increasing importance [265].

5.4 Model First

The modeling strategy adopted for a DT fundamentally impacts its architecture, capabilities, and integration with physical systems. The *Model-First* principle highlights that the initial choice for modeling a physical system strongly influences the DT's structure, the types of questions it can answer, the value it provides, and the effort required for its development and maintenance. Two essential modeling paradigms are recognized: top-down and bottom-up. Each approach offers distinct advantages and aligns with different engineering and data management philosophies. They are also associated with the actual capability and interests of an organization in building a DT representation.

5.4.1 Alignment with the Reference Architecture

The architecture proposed in this section (see Figure 5.1) embodies the *Model-First* principle by positioning the **MetaModel Module** and **Behavior Engine Module** at the core of the DT engine. These modules serve as the foundation for the DT's behavior and reasoning capabilities, ensuring that both the structural and dynamic aspects of the system are explicitly modeled and centrally managed. Furthermore, the architecture supports continuous feedback and adaptation through components such as the ContextBroker, DataLake, and prognostic module, facilitating the ongoing refinement and synchronization of both digital and physical models. The architecture also integrates advanced modules such as the AI/GenAI module, and prescriptive module, which enable the DT to evolve beyond a mere data representation and simulation, supporting predictive, prescriptive, and autonomous decision-making.

5.4.1.1 Top-down Digital Twins

The top-down approach is closely aligned with MBSE methodologies [65, 185, 266, 267]. It begins with a high-level abstraction of the system, capturing business goals, requirements, and functional specifications. The system is then progressively decomposed into subsystems and components, with each element inheriting constraints and objectives from higher abstraction levels. This approach often leverages formal modeling languages, enabling unambiguous representation and supporting automated reasoning and model-based analyses such as simulation and verification. The important point to stress out here is the need to design the DT as an integral part of the physical system for exploiting the convergence of modeling for the physical system and its software counterpart.

In the presented architecture, the **MetaModel Module** and the **DT Life-Cycle Management** are the primary enablers for top-down modeling. They support the definition of system-wide models and behaviors (even from well-established templates), which are then instantiated and managed by the **Behavior Engine Module**. This ensures consistency, traceability, and alignment with organizational objectives throughout the DT life cycle.

The key characteristics of this approach are:

- **Requirements-driven:** Design begins with organizational goals and system requirements, ensuring alignment with strategic objectives [39].
- **Structured Decomposition:** Complex systems are hierarchically broken down into manageable subsystems and components.
- **Formal Models:** Employs formal modeling languages and frameworks (e.g., SYSML, UML) to represent system structure and behavior, facilitating consistency and integration.
- **Integration:** Promotes consistency and interoperability across business units and technical domains, often via shared data models defined at higher levels.
- **Traceability:** Provides clear traceability from requirements to implementation, supporting rigorous verification and validation.

The advantages of the top-down approach can be summarized in the capabilities of ensuring a comprehensive coverage of requirements and business needs; support for organizational consistency and integration; and its exploitation of rigorous verification and validation. On the other hand, some drawbacks can be identified: the approach can be time-consuming and resource-intensive during the initial phases. There is a risk of disconnect between high-level models and real-world operational data if there is no process to ensure continuous updating via robust feedback loops and empirical validation [39, 252].

5.4.1.2 Bottom-up Digital Twins

The bottom-up approach aligns more closely with descriptive, data-driven modeling paradigms [38, 39, 131, 185, 250]. It starts with existing data sources, such as sensor streams, control systems, maintenance logs, and environmental data, building the DT incrementally by integrating and modeling these concrete elements. This approach focuses on what is directly and actually measurable and observable in the physical system.

In the reference architecture, the **AI/GenAI Module** and the **Data Management** part (including the ContextBroker and DataLake) are central to bottom-up modeling. These components enable the DT to ingest, process, and learn from real-world data, supporting empirical model refinement and adaptation. From these data, and adopting several techniques for extracting behavioral rules, a more and more accurate behavior model can be built. The **Behavior Engine Module** can thus be continuously updated based on operational data and inferred behavior rules, guaranteeing the DT remains relevant and accurate and that it can derive additional behavior knowledge and representation over time.

The key characteristics of this approach are:

- **Data-centric:** Begins with available data and operational context, emphasizing measurable and observable phenomena [52, 251]. The diversity of data sources often presents integration and harmonization challenges.
- **Incremental Modeling:** Models evolve from individual components, data sources, and observed behaviors, often starting with simple visualization and advancing to complex analytics.
- **Pragmatic Integration:** Emphasizes practical integration with existing systems and workflows, leveraging current data infrastructure.
- **Flexibility:** Enables rapid adaptation to changes in the physical system or data landscape, facilitating quick deployment of initial functionalities.
- **Empirical Validation:** Models are continuously validated and refined using actual data through analytics, machine learning, and statistical methods [185].
- **Incremental Inferring of Behavior:** The combination of historical data and the ability to generate synthetic data representing meaningful scenarios makes it possible to identify and represent behavior rules that the physical system exhibits or that can be implemented in the DT and enforced in the physical system.

The advantages of this approach are several: it enables rapid prototyping and faster usage of the DT functions (e.g., a Passive DT); it is strongly aligned with operational realities and available data (collected by the organization and extensible to grasp additional phenomena), and it supports continuous improvement and adaptation based on observed trends. Its limitations are also relevant. It may lack a holistic view of system goals and requirements without overarching architectural guidance (this can lead to difficulties in understanding what are the most relevant data and features to consider). There is a risk of fragmented or inconsistent models leading to local optima if not governed by higher-level principles [39].

A data-driven approach, as described in Subsections 2.7.3 and 2.7.5, can also exploit the use of general-purpose sensing, where a limited number of sensors captures measurements of the environment. These data can then be transformed, by means of synthetic sensing techniques (i.e., the ability to derive information from general-purpose sensing by means of AI techniques), into relevant information describing the physical system and the correlated objects using it [38, 119, 203, 268]. From this increasingly large dataset, it could be possible to incrementally derive behavior rules for a specific entity [38].

5.1.4.3 Hybrid Approaches

Hybrid approaches that combine the strengths of both paradigms are also possible [251]. The reference architecture is designed to support such an approach: the **MetaModel Module** and **Behavior Engine Module** provide the structured framework and traceability of top-down design, while the **ContextBroker**, **AI/GenAI Module**, **Prognostic Module**, and **Prescriptive Module** enable continuous adaptation and optimization based on actual data. This integration allows for the tuning of formal models using empirical data, and for the extension of DT capabilities from descriptive and predictive to prescriptive and autonomic. Also in this case, behavior templates, used in conjunction with data models that represent the data relevant for the construction of the DT, can provide a top-down behavior definition corroborated by data-driven validation.

The choice between top-down, bottom-up, or hybrid approaches should be guided by project goals, data availability, organizational maturity, and the need for integration versus rapid adaptation. The presented architecture supports the different facets of the *Model First* principle by elevating modeling to a foundational concern, ensuring that the DT can evolve in response to both design intent and operational context. Hybrid approaches are expected to gain wider adoption as organizations seek more comprehensive, adaptive, and intelligent DTs. The realization of improved DT design and implementation capabilities (such as those represented in the DT LifeCycle management module) can largely contribute to the development and deployment of large DTs capable of incrementally encompassing data-driven and model-based approaches. In addition, the ability offered by AI/GenAI to produce useful synthetic data to instruct the DT about how to behave in particular situations can help in gradually empower new capabilities in the DT to respond to a growing set of cases and situations. This means that the DT implementation can start with a baseline behavior corroborated by available data and evolve toward more complex behavior representation supported by new actual, synthetic, and generated data.

5.4.1.4 Interacting DTs

Complex assets or systems are often best represented as compositions or aggregations of sub-DTs, each representing a specific component or aspect. Additionally, DTs may be replicated to provide localized access, bringing the DT closer to customers or distributed operational teams.

Consider the traffic light example: the system controlling a large crossroad could comprise multiple elementary traffic lights (as described previously), each with its own behavior. However, for the crossroad traffic light system to function properly, each individual traffic light must synchronize its behavior with neighboring lights to ensure the crossroad is well regulated, and traffic flows follow a precise policy. This concept can be extended to a network of crossroads' traffic light systems that need to synchronize within a city traffic light system. This higher-level system executes well-defined behaviors at the macro level, while each individual crossroad and each traffic light operate their own localized behaviors, contributing to the overall system coordination.

5.4.1.4.1 Challenges in Interacting and Replicated DTs

The interaction and integration of these complex and potentially replicated DTs present several challenges:

- **Communication Overhead:** Managing communication and data exchange among a large number of interacting DTs can introduce significant overhead and complexity.
- **Coordination and Leadership:** Replication distribution points to the need for coordinating different components to reach their goals. Identifying a coordinator and guaranteeing consensus between different replicas can be challenging in a broadly used DT with several replicated components.
- **Data Consistency:** Maintaining data consistency across replicated DTs is a critical concern, especially when updates are frequent. **Brewer's theorem** (also known as CAP theorem) highlights the trade-offs between consistency, availability, and partition tolerance in distributed systems [269]. When designing interacting and replicated DTs, these trade-offs must be carefully considered to meet application-specific requirements. Ensuring data integrity and consistency is a core aspect of addressing the information problem in distributed DT environments [38].
- **Synchronization Mechanisms:** Robust synchronization is required to ensure that different sub-DTs or replicas collectively provide a consistent and up-to-date representation of the overall physical system.
- **Complexity Management:** The orchestration and monitoring of a large ecosystem of interacting and replicated DTs require sophisticated tools and strategies to manage system complexity and ensure operational reliability.

Addressing these challenges is paramount for realizing the full potential of complex DT deployments. Strategies may include the adoption of well-defined communication protocols, distributed consensus mechanisms (for strict consistency), and/or consistency models (where availability is prioritized). The choice of strategy should be driven by the specific use case and the balance required between consistency, availability, and partition tolerance.

5.5 From Modules to Components and Microservices: A DT Perspective

The architecture should provide guidelines and principles for a full implementation of the DT system. So far, the specification of the architecture has been in terms of functionalities and their context. An initial decomposition into finer-grained components has been pursued. The next step in specification is to arrive at a definition of components in terms of small implementable components and elements.

As previously defined, a **Module** (see Section 5.1.3) is a structural *block* aggregating related functions to implement a coherent set of responsibilities, encapsulating constituent *Parts* for modular design.

Expanding on this, modules are decomposed into **Components**, which are finer-grained functional units encapsulating specific functions or services that collectively realize the module's capabilities. Components provide a more detailed and specialized breakdown of functionality.

Further decomposition leads to **Microservices**, which are highly specialized, loosely coupled, and independently deployable services executing single, narrowly scoped functions [270]. Microservices provide minimal processing capabilities dedicated to specific tasks, promoting scalability, modularity, and independent life-cycle management within the DT ecosystem.

This hierarchical decomposition from modules to components to microservices enables the encapsulation of functionality, clear separation of concerns, and flexible deployment architectures.

This book does not pursue a full architectural decomposition at this level of detail. For the discussion in this and in the following sections, a set of decomposition guidelines and suggestions is provided. This should lead the designers to a next level of specification in terms of more granular components and microservices.

As an example, the internal components of the prognosis module, as depicted in Figure 4.14, can be further decomposed into a set of collaborating, more granular components. This transition from a monolithic module to a microservice-oriented architecture offers several key advantages, aligning with principles of scalability, maintainability, and independent deployment. The rationale behind this finer-grained decomposition stems from the need to address specific concerns and optimize resource utilization for distinct functionalities within the prognosis process.

5.5.1 Rationale for Further Decomposition: DT Specifics

While general microservice principles like separation of concerns and independent scalability are relevant, the decomposition of DT modules requires additional, DT-specific considerations:

- Contextual Data Handling: The prognosis module relies on contextual data provided by the Context Broker. This data has diverse origins (e.g., real-time system state, historical records), formats, and update frequencies. Decomposition must consider how to manage and distribute this data within the prognosis module efficiently. For example, separating services that handle the aggregation of current situation data from the Context Broker from those that integrate historical case data for case-based reasoning.

- Model Granularity and Fidelity: The prognosis module may employ models with varying levels of detail and accuracy. For example, a "Failure Prediction Service" might utilize high-fidelity models with detailed physical parameters to predict specific failure modes. In contrast, a "Scenario Generation Service" could use lower-fidelity, more abstract models to efficiently explore a wide range of potential future trajectories. Decomposition allows each service to employ the most appropriate models, optimizing resource usage and accuracy.
- Synchronization Requirements: Different services within the prognosis module have varying synchronization needs. Services dealing with real-time situation data from the Context Broker require timely updates to maintain accurate analysis (e.g., the situation data aggregation service). Other services, such as those handling historical case data (e.g., the case data service), might tolerate some delay in updates. Decomposition should align with these different needs to ensure both responsiveness and efficiency.
- Digital-physical Advisory Role: While the Prognosis Module does not directly interact with physical systems for control, its microservices are designed to process data originating from these systems (via the ContextBroker) and generate recommendations for actions. Decomposition should consider the nature of this dataflow—real-time streams, historical batches, event-driven updates—and optimize for efficient processing and the generation of timely and relevant advice. For example, a service analyzing real-time sensor data for anomaly detection might be separated from a service generating long-term maintenance recommendations based on historical trends.
- Life-cycle Management: DT components have life-cycles tied to the physical asset. Decomposition should facilitate independent updates and scaling of services without disrupting the overall DT functionality or the physical system's operation. This is particularly important for long-lived assets.

5.5.2 Microservice Design Representation

The process of designing microservices for the prognosis module involves decomposing its core functionalities into independent, deployable units. Figure 5.6 illustrates a potential architecture where these microservices are organized into logical groups based on their domain within the prognosis process, such as "Situation," "Scenario Management," "Case Reasoning Service," and "Rule-based Reasoning."

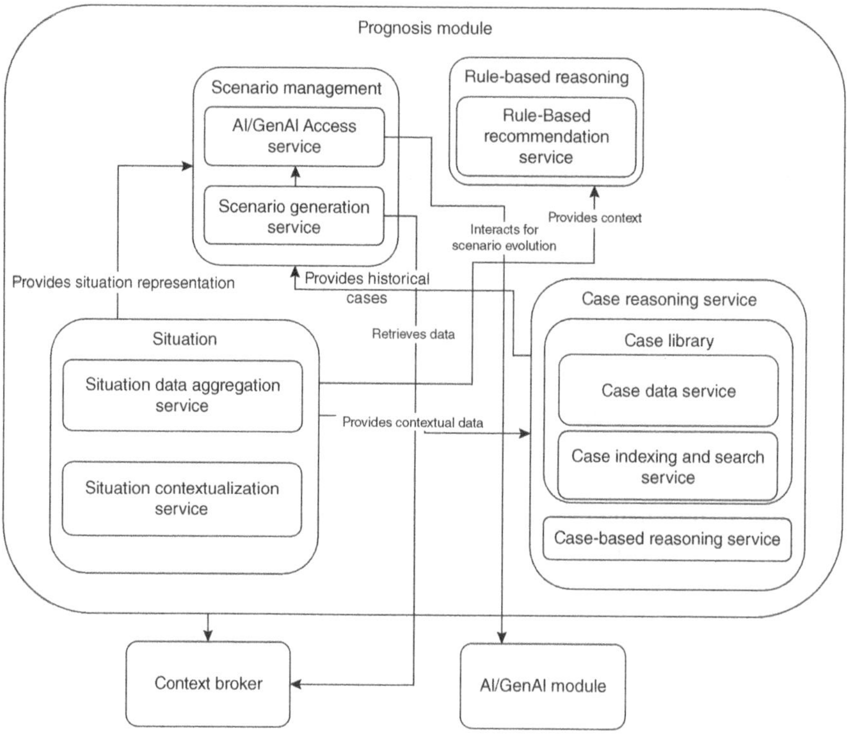

Figure 5.6 Steps toward a microservice decomposition of the prognosis module.

5.5.2.1 Microservice Functions and Characteristics

The decomposed prognosis module comprises the following key microservices. It is designed to leverage a central ContextBroker for real-time data management and delegate AI-related tasks to a dedicated AI/GenAI module:

- Situation
  - Situation Data Aggregation Service: *Function:* Responsible for retrieving specific sets of real-time data, relevant to the current situation, from the ContextBroker. It aggregates and structures this data into a format optimized for the Prognosis Module's internal processing and consumption by other packages. *Characteristics:* High read throughput for querying the ContextBroker, focuses on efficient data aggregation and structuring, provides a tailored view of the situation data, and prioritizes real-time data consistency.
  - Situation Contextualization Service: *Function:* Enriches the aggregated situation data with relevant context by accessing related information available within the ContextBroker. This service transforms the data into

a more meaningful representation of the current situation, preparing it for analysis by other packages. It may also identify and request the collection of additional data points by the Context Broker if needed. *Characteristics:* Data processing intensive, relies on efficient querying of the ContextBroker for related context, potentially involves complex logic to infer deeper meaning from the available context, may trigger requests for new data collection by the ContextBroker, and needs robust data versioning and provenance tracking.

- Case Reasoning Service
  - Case Library
    - Case Data Service: *Function:* Stores and manages historical case records, including past situations (snapshots of relevant data and context IDs from the ContextBroker), observed outcomes, and associated actions or recommendations (potentially generated by the AI/GenAI Module). *Characteristics:* Focuses on data persistence and structured storage, supports data retrieval for case-based reasoning and for training AI models in the AI/GenAI module, and requires efficient versioning and archiving of historical data.
    - Case Indexing & Search Service: *Function:* Indexes the historical cases to enable efficient searching and retrieval of similar past situations based on the current contextualized situation. This service might also facilitate the retrieval of relevant cases for the AI/GenAI Module's analysis. *Characteristics:* Utilizes indexing technologies, optimized for similarity searches based on attributes that may include contextual information, and needs to handle fuzzy matching and similarity metrics relevant to the DT domain.
  - Case-based Reasoning Service: *Function:* Derives mitigation recommendations by identifying and adapting successful strategies from similar past cases. It is based on explicit past experiences rather than trained AI models. Its role is to provide more explicit, human-understandable examples derived from precedent cases compared to AI-driven recommendations. *Characteristics:* Depends on the quality and relevance of the case library, involves similarity assessment of contextualized situations, and requires domain-specific knowledge representation and reasoning capabilities.
- Rule-based Reasoning
  - Rule-based Recommendation Service: *Function:* Generates mitigation recommendations based on predefined rules and the current contextualized situation data. This remains within the core prognosis module, as it is rule-based, not AI-driven. *Characteristics:* Fast execution, relies on a well-defined rule engine operating on contextualized data, must ensure consistency and validity of rules within the DT context.

- Scenario Management
  - AI/GenAI Access Service: *Function:* Provides a standardized interface for the prognosis module to access the various AI-powered functionalities offered by the dedicated AI/GenAI module. This includes requesting predictions (failure, RUL), generating AI-driven recommendations, and generating scenarios using AI models. *Characteristics:* Acts as a client for the AI/GenAI module's APIs, handles data transformation and communication protocols, ensures secure and reliable interaction with the AI/GenAI module, and needs to manage asynchronous communication and handle AI model versioning.
  - Scenario Generation Service: *Function:* Generates potential future scenarios based on current contextualized trends and by orchestrating calls to the AI/GenAI Module for AI-driven scenario projections. The core logic for defining the scope and parameters of scenarios resides here. *Characteristics:* Involves orchestration of data and AI model calls, provides a range of possible outcomes, and requires mechanisms for scenario validation and plausibility checking within the DT domain.

Key Interactions:

- The situation element retrieves real-time data from the ContextBroker (emphasizing real-time dataflow).
- The scenarios management element interacts with the AI/GenAI module for AI functionalities (highlighting AI integration).
- The situation element provides contextual information to the case reasoning service, rule-based reasoning, and scenarios management elements (underscoring the importance of context).
- The case reasoning service provides historical case data to the scenarios management element (illustrating data reuse for scenario generation).

5.5.3 Rationale for Microservice Decomposition: DT Advantages

The core analytical capabilities of the Prognosis Module can now be distributed and accessed through specialized services. These include:

- AI/GenAI Access Service: This service acts as the primary interface to the dedicated AI/GenAI Module, which provides functionalities such as failure prediction, Remaining Useful Life (RUL) prediction, and AI-driven scenario generation. **This decomposition allows for independent scaling and evolution of AI models.**
- Case-based Reasoning Service: This service provides forward-looking insights by leveraging historical case data to identify potential future system states and recommend actions based on past experiences. **This service benefits from**

independent scaling and optimization of the case library and search capabilities.

- Scenario Generation Service: This service generates potential future trajectories, utilizing both current contextual data and potentially AI-driven projections accessed via the AI/GenAI Access Service. **This decomposition enables flexible scenario management and the integration of different prediction models.**

These services leverage the "Situation" data and historical information from the "Case Library" to provide forward-looking insights, predict potential failures, and estimate the RUL of assets. By offering these capabilities, the prognosis module enables proactive decision-making, allowing for timely maintenance interventions, optimized operational strategies, and reduced downtime. The generated scenarios further aid in understanding potential future trajectories and in evaluating the effectiveness of different mitigation actions recommended by the "Rule-based Recommendation Service" and the "Case-based Reasoning Service." In essence, the prognosis module transforms data and historical experiences into actionable intelligence, forming the core value proposition of the prognosis module within the broader DT ecosystem.

In this example, the separation principles for collecting different major functionalities have been applied. AI- and GenAI-related functionalities have been maintained in the dedicated AI/GenAI module, accessed via the AI/GenAI access service within the prognosis module. The proposed architecture, however, is flexible and can support other arrangements. For instance, the prognosis module could, in alternative deployments, comprise instances of machine learning and GenAI functions and related microservices for creating a local implementation capable of encompassing all the needed functionalities. The separation proposed by the architecture is primarily functional, and the system designer retains the flexibility to deploy the DT system in different manners, exploiting the componentization and replication of microservices according to specific needs and resource constraints.

5.5.4 Preparing the Components for Deployment

Each finer-grained microservice can be deployed independently using a variety of strategies. In particular, the system engine components facilitate diverse deployment options, such as containerization with Docker [271] for portability, orchestration via Kubernetes [272] for automated scaling and resilience, cloud-managed services for streamlined operations, and edge deployments to meet low-latency requirements [273]. These strategies ensure the proper allocation and life-cycle management of the prognosis module microservices across the available computational infrastructure.

The optimal deployment strategy depends on factors like the scale of the DT system, performance requirements, infrastructure constraints, and team expertise. Furthermore, system components must be arranged so that execution chains are easily identifiable and coordination among software modules is straightforward and robust. Achieving this organization necessitates selecting an appropriate interaction paradigm (see Section 5.2). Although a client-server approach, often employing REST protocols to integrate and chain microservices, is a popular and streamlined option, this subsection illustrates an alternative approach.

Figure 5.7 depicts an agent–supervisor architecture. In this model, autonomous agents handle local tasks at the edge, while a supervisor coordinates their actions and provides extended functionality. This structure can be especially beneficial when edge processing and local autonomy offer clear advantages over a traditional client-server arrangement.

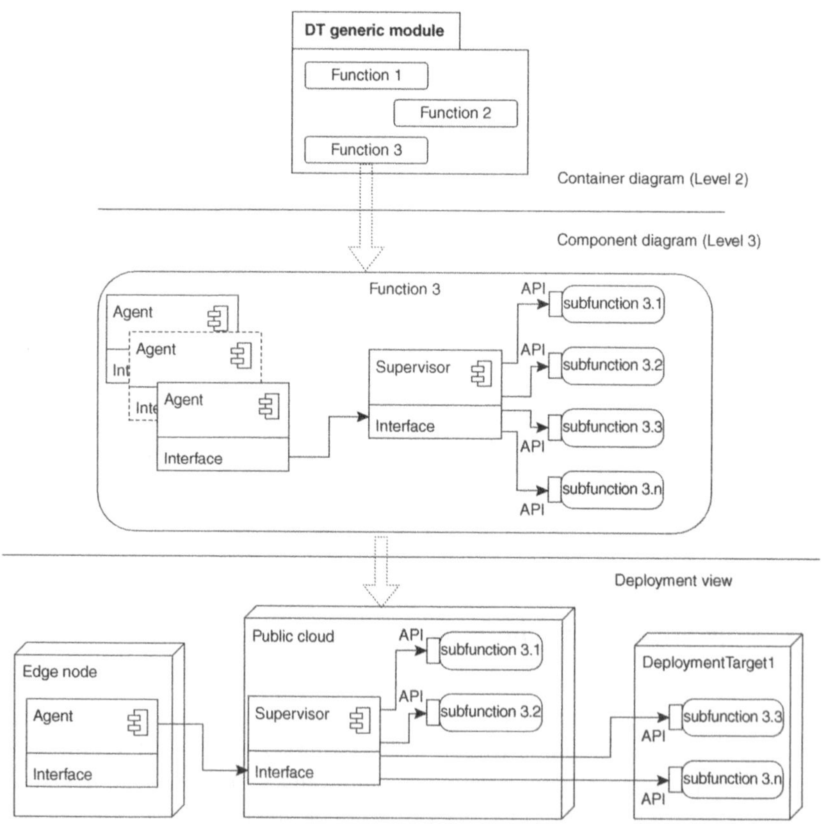

Figure 5.7 A possible control paradigm for the components of the DT architecture.

The traffic light and home automation examples have demonstrated that components often need to autonomously address local events and issues. An agent–supervisor architecture offers a promising approach for implementing such DTs. By decomposing the system into well-defined modules and components, a fine-grained set of functionalities emerges that, when combined, fulfills the overall requirements of the DT engine. These microservices represent the core capabilities of the system and may be directly chained or interwoven to create a powerful yet complex control structure.

While a client-server approach provides a straightforward, streamlined control organization, and can even leverage an API gateway to coordinate complex control chains of microservices, the agent–supervisor model presents an alternative that emphasizes local autonomy and dynamic inter-component interaction. In this configuration, agents act as autonomous components managing local control threads; when necessary, they request coordination and guidance from a supervisor. The supervisor, in turn, orchestrates the agents' activities and accesses additional functions to augment the overall system capability. This structuring is particularly well suited for scenarios where edge processing and local autonomy offer significant advantages.

5.5.5 Comparison of the Architecture with ISO 23247 Standard

The architecture presented in this chapter outlines a detailed, modular, and flexible framework that addresses both foundational and advanced features required for modern DT systems.

5.5.5.1 Common Concepts

This architecture shares several core elements with the ISO 23247 standard for DTs in manufacturing [8]:

- **DT Core Components:** Both include representation of *physical entities*, their *virtual models*, and the *connections* enabling data exchange. The presented architecture structures this via modules such as the *Behavior Module*, *Meta-Model Module*, and *Context Broker* for data contextualization.
- **Data Management:** The use of a *Context Broker* and *DataLake* supports NGSI-LD compliant semantic data management, similar to ISO's emphasis on standardized contextual information models.
- **Behavior Modeling and Simulation:** The architecture places the behavior model as a fundamental architectural element through the behavior Meta-Model and execution engines, consistent with ISO 23247's requirement for explicit behavior synchronization between physical and virtual entities.

- **Life-cycle Management:** Both highlight the importance of managing the DT life cycle, including incremental development, deployment, operation, and evolution facilitated by agents for development and operation.

5.5.5.2 Notable Extensions and Differences

This architecture goes beyond ISO 23247 by incorporating emerging technologies and detailed architectural patterns:

- **AI and Generative AI Integration:** The inclusion of dedicated AI/GenAI modules enables predictive, prescriptive, and autonomic behavior, offering advanced capabilities not explicitly specified by the ISO standard.
- **Microservice and Agent–Supervisor Architectures:** A fine-grained microservice decomposition and agent–supervisor model provide scalability, autonomy, and real-time edge intelligence, extending the standard's general framework toward modern distributed deployments.
- **Advanced Data Architectures:** Use of data lakes and injection chains to curate, validate, and inject data streams, offering an implementation-level richness beyond ISO abstractions.
- **Behavior Templates and Model-driven Development:** Templates and clear model-driven engineering practices support modularity, traceability, and reuse, further structuring the software development process within the DT ecosystem.

5.5.5.3 Summary

The proposed architecture aligns with ISO 23247's core principles, encompassing physical-virtual entity representations, standardized data models, and life cycle considerations. However, it enriches the standard's scope by detailing practical realizations of behavior modeling, AI integration, distributed microservices, and edge computing paradigms. This architecture serves as an implementable evolution beyond the ISO foundation, suitable for contemporary DT deployments.

5.6 Testing and Validation of DTs

The testing and validation of DTs are fundamental activities that ensure these virtual representations reliably reflect the behavior and characteristics of their physical counterparts. This process is crucial because DTs increasingly support critical decision-making in industries ranging from manufacturing to infrastructure and healthcare, where errors or discrepancies can have significant consequences. Validated DTs provide confidence that simulations, predictions, and optimizations derived from the virtual models are accurate and actionable.

5.6.1 Importance of Testing and Validation

Testing and validation activities guarantee that a DT accurately captures the physical system's dynamics and can be trusted to behave consistently over time. Given that DTs are continuously updated with real-time data, validation is not a one-time effort but an ongoing necessity to confirm that the twin remains an accurate reflection of the physical asset or process. Importantly, validated DTs enable cost savings by allowing extensive virtualization of physical system testing. By simulating scenarios virtually—including extreme or rare operating conditions that are difficult or dangerous to reproduce physically—stakeholders can explore system behaviors thoroughly and reduce the risks inherent in physical testing. This virtual experimentation accelerates product development cycles, optimizes operational strategies, and enhances safety protocols.

5.6.2 Continuous Impact Within the Enterprise

It is critical to emphasize that the testing and validation of DTs is a continuous, life-cycle-spanning activity. This continuous nature means that testing has a persistent impact on the people, processes, and resources of the enterprise. Effectively supporting rigorous DT testing requires dedicated teams and sustained investment in personnel and technology infrastructures. The enterprise must embed testing frameworks into operational workflows, quality controls, and governance policies to maintain the DT's accuracy as the physical system evolves. This ongoing commitment necessitates allocation of appropriate budgets and strategic prioritization, underscoring that DT validation is not only a technical challenge but also a comprehensive organizational endeavor [274] with relevant costs associated with it.

5.6.3 Techniques and Approaches for Testing and Validation

As highlighted by Worden et al. [275], the testing and validation of DTs represent a uniquely challenging problem due to their dynamic and evolving nature. Unlike traditional static models, DTs ingest continuous real-time data streams, often blending physics-based and data-driven modeling approaches that introduce layers of complexity and emergent system behaviors. These characteristics require validation frameworks to move beyond classical one-off verification toward ongoing evaluation supported by empirical data and feedback loops.

A key difficulty is the lack of standardized Testing, Evaluation, Verification, and Validation (TEVV) frameworks tailored specifically to DTs [276], leading to variable practices and rigor across industries. Worden and colleagues propose a comprehensive TEVV framework combining formal verification, state-space exploration, assertion-based testing, and continuous empirical validation by domain experts to manage these challenges.

The paper [277] emphasizes virtual testing in manufacturing DTs, where precision in replicating physical processes and detecting rare defects is critical. This work advocates for iterative virtual test cycles integrated within manufacturing workflows and certification standards for DTs. These approaches reduce reliance on costly physical prototyping while increasing model reliability and confidence.

In alignment with these challenges, the International Council on Systems Engineering (INCOSE) emphasizes a model-based test and evaluation approach as part of its systems engineering framework, which is highly relevant to DTs [278]. INCOSE advocates for rigorous Verification, Validation, and Accreditation (VV&A) of digital models, including DTs, using model-driven engineering techniques that assess the twin's fidelity against system requirements continuously. This approach integrates traditional systems engineering life-cycle activities with ongoing empirical validation, formal methods, and simulation-based testing to ensure the DT remains a reliable representation of its physical counterpart throughout its life cycle. INCOSE further stresses that testing DTs must be embedded into enterprise operational practices, incorporating multidisciplinary engineering teams and governance structures to sustain the twin's trustworthiness as the basis for decision-making and operational support.

Testing DTs is resource-intensive and often accounts for a significant share of development costs. While exact percentages vary, industry reports suggest that testing and validation activities may consume a considerable part of the total development budget, reflecting the comprehensive nature of verifying model accuracy, ensuring data integrity, and evaluating behavior under a range of operational conditions [276]. Techniques employed include mathematical and formal verification of models, empirical alignment with real and historical data, expert reviews, and AI-augmented simulation and anomaly detection. AI facilitates synthetic data generation for rare scenarios, accelerates simulations, and automates test generation, reducing some cost and complexity.

5.6.4 Value of a Validated DT

The proposition of validated DTs is valuable. First, validated DTs provide a cost-effective means to virtualize the testing of physical systems, significantly reducing expensive, time-intensive, and potentially hazardous physical trials. This virtualization enables extensive testing, including "what-if" analyses of extreme and rare conditions, which are impractical to reproduce physically. Second, a trusted validated DT empowers stakeholders to utilize predictive maintenance, performance optimization, failure diagnostics, and safety analyses confidently. A validated DT serves as a reliable digital counterpart that drives safer, more efficient, and innovative operation and development throughout the product or system life cycle.

6

Deploying and Operating a Digital Twin

After reading this chapter, you should be able to:

- Explain the complexity of the distribution of DT components.
- Understand the DT life-cycle importance and its relation to implementation and operations.
- Identify the requirements posed by a DT architecture on an edge-cloud infrastructure.
- Evaluate the impact of a DT project on the processes of organizations.

6.1 Distribution of DT Components and Functions

The architectural choices for deploying a Digital Twin (DT) significantly impact its performance, scalability, and resilience. The reference architecture (see Figure 5.1) supports flexible deployment of DT modules across various computational islands (cloud, private infrastructure, edge), driven by factors such as separation of concerns, importance and privacy, and performance requirements. These requisites are managed by the system engine and overseen by agents of the DT life-cycle management. This section discusses centralized and distributed deployment models, along with the implications of interacting and replicating DTs and their components in distributed environments.

6.1.1 Centralized or Distributed DT

The implementation of a DT can range from a fully centralized architecture, where all functional components reside in a cluster of nodes, to more distributed models that leverage different computation islands up to highly distributed edge-cloud computing infrastructures.

Some parts of the DT system exhibit a natural separation of concerns so that the modules and components can be seen as packages that can be deployed in different computational islands. The DT architecture has been conceived in a distributed manner, favoring the loose coupling of functionalities: all the modules and large components can be deployed on different computational islands. And actually, their further decomposition into fine-grained elements, e.g., microservices, is designed to minimize dependencies. This favors the possibility to realize different deployment policies.

At a first level of separation, the identified modules can be deployed separately. For instance, the DT life-cycle management can be decoupled from the DT engine's execution. Ensuring robust communication and high reliability between these parts, especially considering the oversight by the DT operation agent and the management of risky situations by the DT critical events agent, is crucial. This can be achieved by allocating these functions to powerful computational islands with communication redundancy and data/function replication, aiming for high reliability. Similarly, the Data Management system is designed with decoupled functions, where the injection chain can be highly distributed at the edge for efficient data capture and preprocessing before ingestion into the ContextBroker, which itself is a candidate for replication and federation across computational islands. These deployment decisions are made by the development team and translated into constraints and rules for resource allocation by the system engine, enforced by DT Agents during deployment and execution. At a more granular level, the deployment can consider aggregating microservices from different functional modules and packaging them in such a way as to deploy replicas of the DT in different computational islands. Each replica could have access to the needed functionalities in isolation from other replicas. Still, the consistency problem should be coped with synchronization functions supported by redundant communications between the different islands.

6.1.1.1 Centralized Cloud-based DT

Despite its distributed nature, the DT system can be deployed in a centralized manner. In this approach, all aspects of the DT, including data ingestion, processing, model execution, and visualization, are primarily hosted on a cloud infrastructure. This model offers advantages in terms of scalability, access to powerful computing resources, and simplified management. However, it may introduce latency, particularly for applications requiring near real-time interaction with the physical system. Its dependence on network connectivity can also be a limiting factor. Furthermore, organizations might prefer to use their own infrastructure for critical software and data, potentially leading to hybrid public–private cloud solutions where the system engine manages the allocation of sensitive components to private clouds while others reside in public clouds, guided by design-level decisions and deployment policies enforced by DT life-cycle management agents.

6.1.1.2 Distributed Edge-cloud DT

A distributed deployment addresses some of the limitations of a centralized model by allocating selected DT functionalities closer to physical assets, at the network edge. Key aspects of this deployment include:

- **Distributed Data Management:** Elements of the data management segment, such as raw data acquisition and preliminary processing (e.g., using general-purpose and synthetic sensing to enrich environmental data), can be performed at the edge. This reduces the volume of data transmitted to the cloud and enables faster local insights. Efficient data handling at the edge is important for addressing the "information problem" in DTs, particularly in latency- and bandwidth-constrained environments [38].
- **Decoupling of Simulation and Execution Modules:** While cooperating in behavior MetaModel execution, these modules often have different processing and communication needs, making their deployment in separate locations a good practice. Additionally, replicating AI/GenAI modules for specific purposes of execution and simulation/improvement can enhance performance and isolation.
- **Local Model Execution:** Models requiring rapid response or closed-loop control can be deployed at the edge, minimizing communication delays and enhancing system autonomy. This can also be supported by interaction paradigm choices as discussed in Section 5.2.
- **Hybrid System Engine:** The system engine can extend its distributed nature by placing components near the physical asset, thereby improving responsiveness and resilience.
- **Local DT Life-cycle Management:** Executing these functions locally can provide more direct organizational control and potentially enhance resilience in case of network issues, although robust communication with the DT engine remains critical.

The utility of a fully distributed edge-cloud architecture depends on specific application requirements and extends beyond life-cycle management. It can serve as a DT design and development strategy that exploits a broad distribution of components and functionalities at the edge. This approach must be supported during the design and development phases and effectively leveraged during deployment and operational phases. While it can improve latency and resilience, it also introduces complexities in management, security, and data synchronization between edge and cloud components. In addition, for solutions with frequent interactions between elements deployed in different computational islands, the response time due to communication latency can rapidly increase [138, 273].

6.1.2 A Deployment Scenario

The modules, components, and elements can be duplicated and used for creating replicas of the DT or some parts of it. These replicas may have specific goals. They can be considered deployment packages that can collect different functions to serve specific goals in the DT process or life cycle. Figure 6.1 shows three deployment packages: one for development and simulation, one for real-time execution, and one for improvements to the deployment strategies. They replicate some of the modules comprised in the DT architecture. This is done to guarantee isolation and the possibility to keep different activities like development, real-time execution, and improvement of deployment separate. The most critical one is the real-time package. It supports the actual execution of the current version of the DT

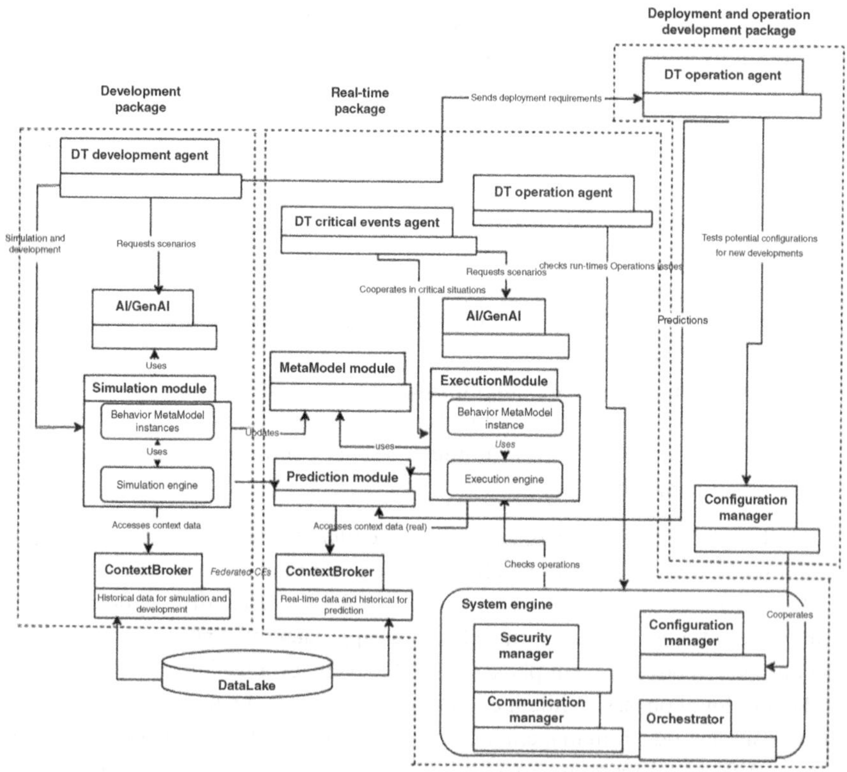

Figure 6.1 Replicating DT functions to support three isolated spaces for development, real-time management, and future deployment policies improvement.

behavior. It can require the allocation of the main version of the system engine, and ContextBroker for example. This package will be deployed on the most performative computational islands to ensure adequate performance. This package supports important functions such as DT critical events and DT operation agents. Due to their relevance, they can be deployed on their own computation cluster; however, the real-time package ensures that they are well- connected and capable of cooperating with modules of the DT engine. The development package replicates some functions in order to create an isolated, but possible distributed functional environment for the development of new functions or improvement of the DT behavior. Also, simulations in particular cases can be supported. For supporting these aims, the simulation module and the AI/GenAI module are replicated. This package may have relaxed requirements on real-time execution, but might require availability of relevant processing capabilities (e.g., Graphics Processing Unit [GPU]) for supporting Artificial Intelligence (AI) processing. The deployment and operation improvement package has the goal of supporting new optimized operation and deployment strategies. For this end, it duplicates a configuration manager for having dedicated capabilities isolated from those used in the real-time Package. The deployment and operational improvement can work on its own goals or can cooperate with the development package to determine the best deployment strategy for newly introduced or modified components.

6.2 Operating the DT

The operational phase of a DT is critical for achieving its intended goals. It involves continuous management and evolution throughout the DT's life cycle. Operating a DT poses significant technical, organizational, and process challenges for those organizations designing, deploying, and managing these solutions. Therefore, key aspects of DT operation and life cycle management require careful consideration to ensure effective and sustainable performance.

6.2.1 Product and DT Life-cycle Management and Phase Transitions

The DT is associated with a product, a physical system, or a process; hence, its life cycle is strongly related to that of the associated object. Figure 6.2 highlights the flow from creation and design; production, i.e., implementation and testing; operations, i.e., usage, adaptation, and extension; up to the disposal phase. During these phases, AI and software development cycles gain increasing importance. The use of AI technologies throughout the different phases of the DT life cycle is introduced in this subsection and further elaborated in Section 6.2.3. A primary guideline driving the DT operation process is that the DT should follow and serve the different phases of its physical system.

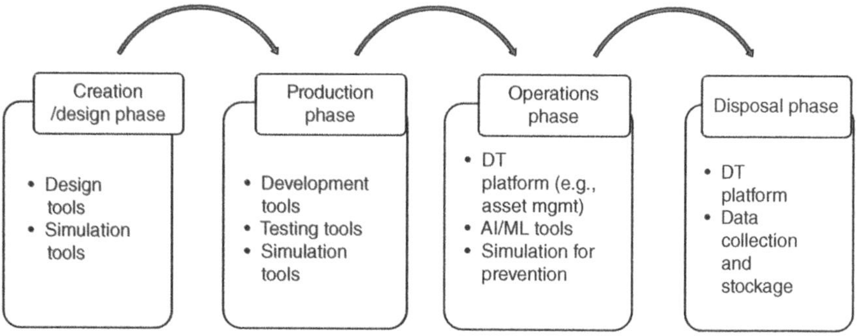

Figure 6.2 Physical object and DT life-cycle phases.

Based on Figure 6.2, a simple description of the different DT phases in its life cycle is provided below.

- **Creation/Design Phase:** This phase supports ideation and involves defining the requirements and objectives for the product and corresponding DT. While the physical system is mainly virtual at the conceptual design phase, the DT can help simulate and prototype relevant aspects of the physical system to enable better design choices. AI can assist by analyzing trends and identifying potential opportunities.
- **Production Phase:** During this phase, the physical system is under development and consolidation. The DT is extensively involved in development choices, testing, and validation. The DT implementation can be actively tested and stressed for various purposes, leveraging implemented processes and models. Simulations and testing of edge situations are prominent. AI tools and techniques are extremely useful in driving these activities toward consolidating a robust physical system and related DT ready for operation.
- **Operations Phase:** This phase is devoted to operating the product or physical system for users and customers. The DT represents the product or physical system "class." It entails gathering consistent information from different instances of the physical object and adapting the DT's behavior to real conditions. Here, the DT represents an "ideal" physical system whose behavior can be modeled accurately. Such a DT can recommend mitigation actions for individual or broader critical situations. Depending on the organization's needs and choices, the DT can evolve from representing a single physical system to a "meta" representation of multiple operating instances, enabling extrapolation of common behaviors or predictions for individual cases.
- **Disposal Phase:** This phase encompasses decommissioning of the physical system while preserving its essential characteristics and critical information within the virtual representation, which remains accessible beyond the

physical asset's end of life. Historical data can help in understanding structural issues and provide explanations of specific behaviors. The DT transitions into a virtual model representing experiences and decisions from the design, production, and operation phases. It can be seen as a SPace-tiME (SPIME) description of the physical system [29].

The physical system (and DT) life cycle is a complex process requiring coordination among specialized teams. Transitions between phases must be carefully managed to ensure a smooth transfer of responsibilities and activation of new phases. Some DT activities span phases—for example, during disposal, certain product instances might still be operational. This complexity is compounded by the fact that at each phase, internal processes related to functional capabilities, data, and AI technology management must be addressed.

6.2.2 Management of DT Functionalities

The DT undergoes a long development process integrated with the product/physical system life cycle. The functionalities of a DT evolve as understanding of the physical system and environment deepens, and new analytical techniques emerge [251, 279]. The DT is a software-intensive artifact requiring various software-related processes throughout its life cycle.

These activities, represented in Figure 6.3, begin during the creation/design phase to provide an initial mock-up that evolves in line with product development.

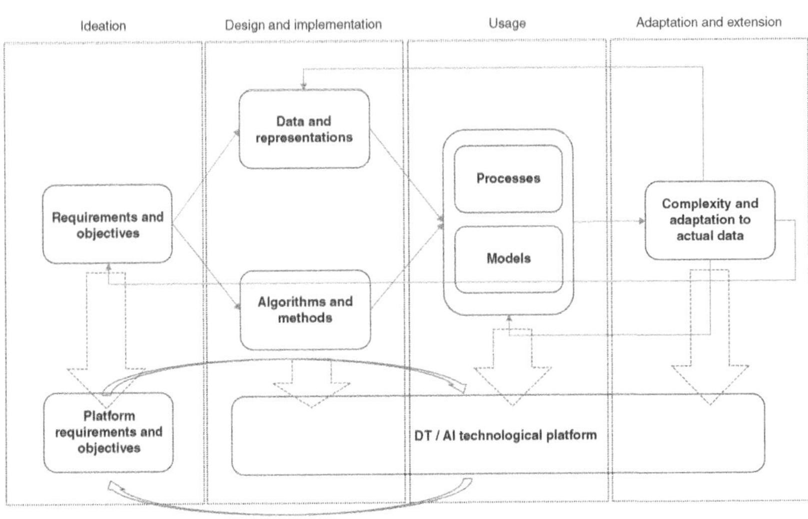

Figure 6.3 DT functional operation and management.

The DT must adapt continuously to new needs and goals of different phases, incorporating new data and processes. Consequently, behavior models adequate for new phases must be introduced or adopted. This process can require substantial rethinking and improvement of the algorithms and methods applied by the DT. A fundamental guideline is that the DT must accommodate and support the evolution and phase transitions of the physical system. The envisaged steps by which the DT follows the progression of the physical system life cycle, supports its various phases, and facilitates smooth transitions between them include:

- **Ideation:** This activity varies throughout the life-cycle phases. It relates to ideation for supporting the DT across its entire life cycle or addresses specific requirements in the current phase. For instance, ideation during creation and design targets designing the DT's function to reflect expected physical system behavior, while in production, it might involve designing "critical situations" and related test suites to stress and assess the physical system's behavior.
- **Design and Implementation:** Solutions conceived during ideation are detailed and implemented according to phase-specific needs, such as behavior mock-ups in the creation and design phase, critical situation evaluations for production and operations, and what-if or reuse scenarios in the disposal phase.
- **Usage:** Here, solutions are used for their intended phase-specific purposes. Data collection, prediction of behavior or failure, and testing suites feature prominently during operation, aiding simulation and evaluation of new or existing products.
- **Adaptation and Extension:** Solutions are adapted and extended to remain effective in current or future phases. Developed solutions may be generalized and made reusable, creating a repository of efficient, preexisting solutions that can improve future physical systems.

These processes mainly involve the DT development management module, especially the DT development agent function, which is a critical focus during DT development and use.

Other aspects complementing functional management of DTs include:

- **Functionality Deployment and Updates:** Managing deployment of new functionalities and updates seamlessly to minimize disruption.
- **Functionality Monitoring and Performance:** Tracking performance and reliability to ensure accurate and timely insights, including Key Performance Indicator (KPI) and Service Level Agreement (SLA) monitoring for user needs.
- **Coordination of Functionality Interdependencies:** Managing interactions among DT functionalities to ensure effective collaboration, e.g., avoiding interference between simulation and execution processes.

- **User Access and Authorization:** Controlling access based on roles and responsibilities, with different permissions for designers, developers, or simulator teams.

The continuous demand for software updates and perspective changes across physical system life-cycle phases requires complex organizational DT-related processes. The operational team must sustain this continuous evolution with relevant technical and domain expertise, mastering diverse technologies and techniques for DT improvement.

Managing DT functionalities is a cyclical process aligned with life-cycle phases, requiring streamlined organizational processes and a unified goal of delivering a consistent solution. Many DT projects face challenges in achieving this, and creating highly general, adaptable solutions is even more difficult than focusing on specific domains. This partly explains why many DT solutions remain specialized.

6.2.3 AI for DT Management and Operation

The DT, like any large software system, undergoes its own life cycle with distinct phases. Integration of AI and Machine Learning (ML) is key to many advanced DTs [18, 27, 280]. AI tools and techniques are pervasive throughout the DT life cycle and should be calibrated to improve processes and solution effectiveness. Figure 6.4 illustrates the growing integration and impact of AI and the varying applicability of AI techniques in supporting DT evolution.

Figures 6.2 and 6.4 provide complementary views on the product/physical system and DT life cycles [3, 13, 17, 281, 282]. Their integration requires correctly phased activities and broad AI support.

A primary consideration when using AI is the different roles it plays: supporting problem domain representation and solution (e.g., managing ambulance passage

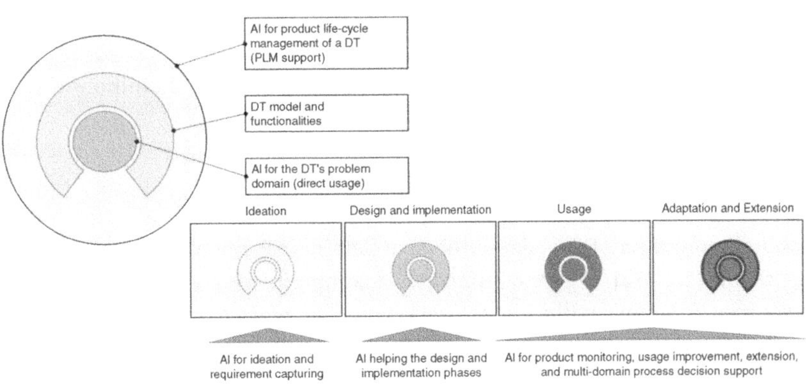

Figure 6.4 DT life cycle with AI integration.

in a traffic system), integrating data and behavior representations with the DT's current state (e.g., transitioning from representing a single physical system to a meta representation), and supporting specific life-cycle phases (e.g., using simulation and generative AI in operation to analyze unexpected discrepancies or molding behavior expectations in creation and production).

Managing phase transitions with deeper AI integration presents operational challenges such as data migration, model updates, platform evolution, and adapting to AI-driven complexity.

Operationally, there are complexities related to AI management and especially in model management:

- **Model Deployment and Versioning:** Managing the deployment of AI models into the DT environment and tracking different versions of models. This could also imply a switch from a model addressing the needs of a phase (e.g., production) to another similar one that copes with the issues of another phase (e.g., operations).
- **Model Monitoring and Performance Evaluation:** This involves continuously monitoring the performance and accuracy of deployed AI models, detecting drift and degradation.
- **Model Retraining and Updates:** Establishing processes for retraining AI models with new data and deploying updated models without disrupting operations. This can have a huge impact on the AI/GenAI module as well as all the others that use these functions.
- **Explainability and Trustworthiness:** Addressing the need for explainable AI (XAI) to ensure the trustworthiness and interpretability of AI-driven insights. Under this perspective, the MetaModel module should be tuned so that it can cooperate in producing explanations aligned with the specific phases of the physical system.
- **Governance and Compliance for AI:** This aspect involves adhering to ethical guidelines and regulatory requirements related to the use of AI.

AI management will acquire an increasing importance in the definition of DTs and their life cycles.

6.2.4 Data Management for the DT

The foundation of any DT is data. Effective data management is paramount for its operation [20, 252]. Figure 6.5 provides a comprehensive view of the various data sources and flows within a DT ecosystem. The main data sources can vary along the life cycle. For instance, the historical data can refer to previous physical systems in the creation and product phases, while there is definitely operational data in the operations phase.

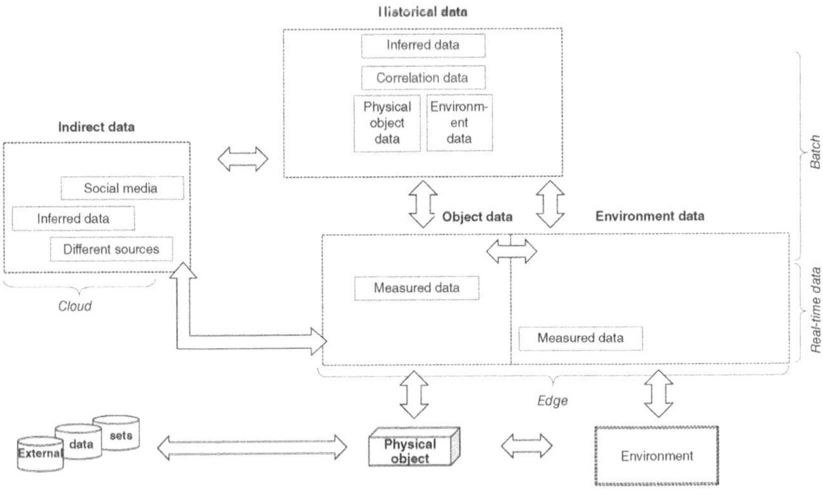

Figure 6.5 The operational data's life cycle for supporting a DT.

The data collected in the different phases create a large data system that can be exploited even when the focus on data has moved from easing and supporting the DT modeling to actual operational value. The data must be stored securely, but depending on different phases, the collection, manipulation, and access to relevant data will have to be prioritized to ease their collection/curation and reduce the DT's reaction time. Certain data sources are then prioritized, and data management components can be moved closer to them to facilitate the transformation into contextualized information. Some behavior components could also be moved to the edge of the infrastructure or closer to physical assets to improve efficiency and response time. Key aspects to consider include:

- **Data Acquisition and Integration:** Continuously acquiring data from physical assets (direct data, both static and dynamic) and their environment(s) (environment data, both static and dynamic), as depicted in Figure 6.5. This also includes integrating indirect data from various sources, potentially residing in the cloud. This external data can change depending on the specific life-cycle phase.
- **Data Storage and Governance:** Implementing robust storage solutions capable of handling the volume and variety of DT data, including historical data (inferred and correlation data) and real-time data streams. Establishing data governance policies ensures quality, security, and compliance across all data types. For instance, moving from a production to an operation phase also means scaling up the number of products that will generate operational

data. The new phase can require a different set of data acquisition policies to keep up with the surge of collected data and their management.

- **Data Processing and Transformation:** Developing and maintaining pipelines for cleaning, transforming, and preparing data for analysis and consumption by various DT functionalities. This involves processing both real-time data at the edge and batch processing historical data in the cloud. The operation phase can require a modification of the configuration of data management components to comply with a considerable increase in data sources. This adjustment could also include the distribution of more functions to the Edge to reduce the concentration of data in a specific cluster and for the early transformation and curation of data.
- **Data Versioning and Lineage:** Tracking data changes and understanding the origin and transformation history of data, from the physical object and the environment, and the identification of phases and periods of analysis, ensures traceability and the reproducibility of insights. This can be seen as a large implementation of SPIME capabilities. Data are collected with references to space (i.e., location), time (with timestamps), and identity (the element that generated the data). The availability of this information can be useful for several tasks of traceability and tracking of specific issues.

6.2.5 Management of the System Infrastructure

A DT relies on a large, distributed IT infrastructure that includes different computational islands, comprising cloud and edge capabilities, interconnected by communication networks [283, 284]. This infrastructure is epitomized in Section 5.3.1 as a system engine whose goals are to provide a working infrastructure as well as the tools and mechanisms to adapt and exploit it to the varying needs of the DT system and its components. Operating this infrastructure at enterprise scale presents several challenges:

- **Isolation and Separation of Critical Functions:** Some functions and data of the DT system are critical and strategic for the organization. There is a need to preserve and protect them from external attempts to access and reuse them. Virtualization may help, but most likely, large organizations will try to host these critical software elements in their own infrastructure (private cloud) and to use public cloud infrastructure for less critical data management and processing. This process may also take different forms in the public cloud where specific SLAs with respect to privacy, isolation, and execution can be negotiated with the cloud provider. In any case, there is a need to guarantee interoperability of different aggregations of components with differentiated levels of privacy and security [285].
- **System Monitoring and Maintenance:** Continuously monitoring the health and performance of the underlying infrastructure and performing

necessary maintenance and upgrades are both essential. This also includes the ability to check the functioning of different computation islands under different administrative domains.

- **Scalability and Elasticity:** Ensuring the infrastructure can scale to handle increasing data volumes and computational demands is a key issue. This poses several challenges: the required processing capabilities may have different characterizations, for instance, at the edge, or be computation-intensive (e.g., GPU for heavy AI tasks), or be categorized as critical and private. A system engine should take care of these needs.
- **Security and Reliability:** Implementing robust security measures to protect sensitive DT data and ensure the high availability and reliability of the system. This aspect should also consider the different phases of the life cycle, while privacy is needed when creating and putting into production a new product, as the operations of a well-known and established product could have very different privacy requirements.
- **Optimization Management:** Optimizing infrastructure costs while meeting performance requirements is always important. The system engine could adopt a Network DT (NDT) approach for representing and governing the infrastructure. This NDT could be supported by a monitoring and optimized template.

6.2.6 Additional Relevant Topics

In addition to the above, the following topics deserve attention with respect to operations and life-cycle management:

- **DT Interoperability:** How different DTs or components of a larger DT ecosystem interact and exchange information.
- **Human-DT Interaction:** Designing effective interfaces and workflows for users to interact with and derive value from the DT.
- **Security of the DT Ecosystem:** Addressing security threats at the data, application, and infrastructure levels.
- **Value Realization and Return Of Investment, Rate on Interest (ROI), Measurement:** Tracking the business value generated by the DT and measuring the return on investment in its operation.

6.3 Example: Traffic Light Service DT

To illustrate deployment and operational principles, consider a DT for a city traffic light system. The context DT architecture (Figure 5.1) enables flexible deployment of modules across cloud and edge environments, supporting both real-time control and long-term optimization.

Within this architecture, modules such as the behavior module can be implemented as a structural cooperation between local agents (deployed at the edge) and centralized components (deployed in the cloud or core). This approach allows the behavior module components to be partitioned and deployed into local and global capabilities: local agents address immediate, site-specific needs, while centralized controllers coordinate system-wide optimization. Similarly, communication and data management are enhanced by deploying edge agents that support local information curation and reliable integration with the central system.

In this scenario, a *Traffic Light Agent* is implemented as part of the behavior module and operates at the edge, close to the physical intersection. It collaborates with the central traffic light behavior module to blend local autonomy with global coordination. The agent is responsible for collecting and aggregating data, executing local control logic, and communicating with both the ContextBroker and higher-level behavior module components.

6.3.1 Deployment Mapping

The deployment can have this configuration:

- **At the Edge (near the physical traffic light):**
  - *Traffic Light Agent*: A lightweight software component responsible for:
    - Collecting sensor data (e.g., vehicle detectors, pedestrian buttons).
    - Performing basic data filtering and validation.
    - Handling local actuation (e.g., fallback signal plans if disconnected).
    - Communicating with the central DT system.
    - Implementing basic logic and behavior either autonomously or under orchestration from the central behavior module.
- **In the Cloud/Central DT System:**
  - *Communication Manager* (System Engine): Manages secure, reliable communication with all edge agents.
  - *ContextBroker* (Data Management): Aggregates real-time context from all intersections and provides it to other DT modules.
  - *Traffic Light Behavior Module* (DT Engine): Implements city-wide traffic control logic, leveraging global states and models. It interacts with multiple agents in the field to coordinate higher-level synchronization and policy enforcement. The module may include several agent-based components at runtime.
  - *AI/GenAI Module* (DT Engine): Provides components for historical data analysis and traffic pattern prediction, working in conjunction with the behavior module and others.
  - *Prescriptive Module* (DT Engine): Optimizes signal timing strategies based on analytics and predictions, in cooperation with the behavior module.

- *Visualization Module* (DT Engine): Offers dashboards and real-time monitoring for city traffic operators.
- *DataLake* (Data Management): Stores historical and real-time traffic data, in collaboration with the ContextBroker.
- *Orchestrator, Security Manager, Configuration Manager* (System Engine): Manages the deployment, security, and configuration of distributed DT components, including resource allocation to support seamless integration between edge agents and cloud modules.

6.3.2 Operational Workflow

The expected flow and coordination of the operation, baseline, is the following:

1. **Data Collection:** Traffic light agents gather data from their respective intersections, including sensor readings and inferred metrics such as intersection occupancy, and transmit it to the *ContextBroker* via the *Communication Manager*.
2. **Context Aggregation:** The *ContextBroker* integrates data from all intersections, maintaining an up-to-date, system-wide state.
3. **Behavior and Control:** The *Behavior Module* analyzes the aggregated context to determine optimal traffic light actions city-wide and issues policy directives to local agents.
4. **Command Dispatch:** The *Communication Manager* transmits control commands or policies from the central system to the appropriate edge agents, which then actuate the local traffic lights policies.
5. **Data Archiving and Analytics:** The *DataLake* archives all relevant data, which the *AI/GenAI Module,* through the contextualization of the ContextBroker analyzes for long-term pattern detection and prediction.
6. **Optimization and Prescription:** The *Prescriptive Module* leverages analytic results to refine and optimize traffic policies and command plans, working in concert with the behavior module for implementation.
7. **Operator Interaction:** Traffic operators access real-time and historical data, as well as control dashboards, via the *Visualization Module.*
8. **Continuous Feedback:** The system continuously adapts to changing traffic conditions, updating both local and global strategies.

Figure 6.6 represents a deployment architecture scenario for the discussed example, considering the real-time needs (e.g., real-time package of Figure 6.1). Three different computational islands are assumed: an edge closer to the traffic light system, a public cloud for deployment of a large part of the DT system's components, and a private infrastructure that hosts DT life-cycle management functionalities readily usable by the organization operating the traffic light DT.

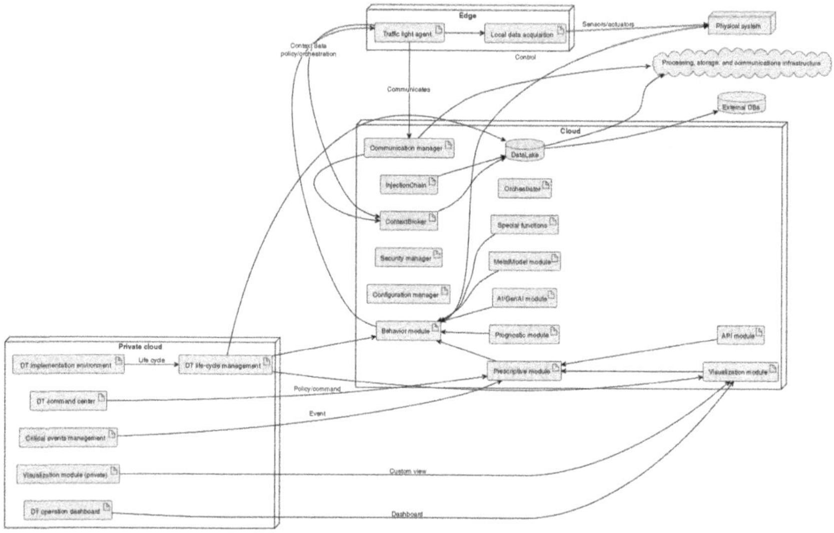

Figure 6.6 Deployment of DT components on a large heterogeneous computing infrastructure.

The increasing complexity of managing DT implementations that span over different computing infrastructures is obvious. However, these options will be increasingly adopted if common functionalities (not strategically competitive) can be allocated to powerful and secure public cloud solutions. The definition of complex deployment plans is left to the designers of the DT system.

6.3.3 Benefits

This DT deployment has several advantages; in fact, it:

- Minimizes latency for real-time control by using traffic light agents for local sensing and actuation.
- Enables advanced analytics and optimization in the cloud, leveraging the full context DT architecture.
- Provides a unified operational dashboard for city operators.
- Ensures resilience and scalability by separating lightweight edge functions from system-wide intelligence and management.
- Supports flexible integration and coordination between local autonomy and global optimization.

6.4 DT Impact on Organization Processes

The adoption and effective management of a DT within an organization have profound implications for organizational processes, culture, and structure. As illustrated in the context DT architecture (Figure 5.1), a DT is not merely a technological solution but a cross-functional system that requires organizational transformation and strong commitment at multiple levels.

6.4.1 Breaking Down Information Silos

Implementing a DT necessitates dismantling traditional organizational information silos. Data and knowledge must flow freely across departments such as R&D, business units, operations, IT, and maintenance. The DT's value depends on integrating heterogeneous data sources and processes, which often requires organizations to rethink established boundaries and fosters a culture of transparency and collaboration.

6.4.2 Cross-departmental Cooperation and Commitment

A successful DT initiative requires a cooperative attitude and willingness to share expertise and resources among diverse organizational units. This cooperation must be supported by clear management commitment and leadership, as the DT's life-cycle spans multiple phases, from design and implementation to operation and evolution involving different departments. For example, during transitions between life-cycle phases (such as from product design to operation), different processes may run in parallel, requiring close coordination and joint efforts between departments to ensure operational continuity and knowledge transfer.

6.4.3 Integration of Diverse Technologies

One of the most significant challenges is the integration of a wide range of technologies. DTs require not only domain-specific solutions (e.g., traffic control algorithms for a traffic light service) but also robust software engineering, data management, and AI/analytics capabilities. Additionally, technologies supporting the DT's own development (e.g., simulation environments, testing frameworks) and those required for life-cycle management (e.g., versioning, deployment orchestration, critical event monitoring) must be harmonized. Achieving seamless interoperability between these segments of functionalities is complex and often demands new skills, tools, and governance models.

6.4.4 Organizational Change and Digital Maturity

The journey toward a DT-enabled organization is as much about organizational change as it is about technology. It requires:

- **Willingness to Change:** Staff and management must be open to new ways of working, including increased reliance on data-driven decision-making and automation.
- **Digital Skills Development:** Upskilling and reskilling are necessary to enable teams to work with advanced data management, AI, and integration platforms. Particularly important are AI and software development proficiency.
- **Governance and Security:** New governance structures may be needed to ensure data quality, privacy, and security across the DT ecosystem.
- **Continuous Improvement:** DTs enable continuous monitoring and feedback, which should be leveraged to drive ongoing process improvement.

6.4.5 Additional Organizational Challenges

Other issues that organizations involved in DT transformation may encounter include:

- **Change Management:** Resistance to change can slow DT adoption. Clear communication and involvement of stakeholders are critical.
- **Data Ownership and Stewardship:** Defining who owns and manages data within the DT is essential for accountability and compliance.
- **Legacy Systems Integration:** Many organizations must integrate DTs with existing legacy systems, which can be technically and organizationally challenging.
- **Alignment with Business Goals:** Ensuring that the DT initiative remains aligned with broader business objectives and delivers measurable value.

In summary, the implementation of a DT is a catalyst for organizational transformation. It requires not only technical innovation but also a cultural and structural shift toward greater collaboration, transparency, and agility. Organizations that adopt these changes are better positioned to realize the full potential of DT technologies. The DT's ability to support digital transformation must be viewed from a long-term perspective, as its development often involves extended cycles before delivering comprehensive capabilities and benefits. Continuous support for the development, deployment, and refinement of the DT solution within the enterprise is essential for sustained success.

6.5 Life-cycle Insights from Industrial Experiences

The implementation and operation of DTs in industrial contexts follow a structured life cycle: **design**, **development**, **deployment**, and **operation**. While the concept is widely promoted, real-world applications reveal a complex interplay of technological, organizational, and strategic factors. This section synthesizes lessons learned from documented industrial use cases and academic literature to outline high-level processes and barriers to exploitation [13]. It is important to state that this analysis is not exhaustive. It presents a set of illustrative and well-known industrial DT projects such as BMW's *iFactory* [286], NASA Langley's facility-scale twin, and others that provide meaningful insights relevant to the themes of design, implementation, deployment, and operation. Many other significant use cases exist, such as emerging healthcare or logistics twins, that warrant future detailed treatment. For example, recent studies (like [287]) describe innovative healthcare twins, which were not included here due to scope and focus. Similarly, the ISO 23247 standard [8] on manufacturing DTs provides emerging guidelines essential to enablers and barriers and should be considered foundational in industrial settings. Before delving into examples, a critical observation arises from recent literature [288, 289]: the industry lacks a fully standardized and reusable DT platform. Enterprises mostly construct DT systems combining best-of-breed technological components and strategic know-how. These proprietary platforms implement valuable intellectual property, limiting transparency and knowledge sharing across competitors. Current major commercial DT platforms (e.g., Microsoft Azure DTs, Amazon Web Services IoT TwinMaker [290, 291]) tend to offer robust data management and asset modeling but are lightweight regarding embedded behavioral and simulation models [289]. This gap motivates many companies to develop proprietary, domain-tuned DT capabilities and platforms. These factors create difficulties in obtaining comprehensive insights about DT development and operational projects, since strategic details are often confidential. This environment underscores the complexity and the competitive sensitivity surrounding DT technology [289].

6.5.1 Life-cycle Phases

Design begins with identifying the physical asset or system to be mirrored and defining its functional boundaries. For example, NASA Langley Research Center developed a facility-scale DT integrating Geographic Information System (GIS) and Building Information Modeling (BIM) to support spatial planning, hazard mitigation, and energy efficiency [292]. Similarly, BMW's *iFactory* initiative used high-resolution 3D scans to create virtual replicas of production sites, enabling layout optimization and early-stage planning [293]. In shipbuilding, DT design integrates Computer-aided Design (CAD) models with hydrodynamic simulations to capture complex physical behaviors [294]. **Development** involves creating simulation models, integrating diverse data sources, and configuring digital infrastructure. Tata Steel's HIsarna project developed a DT to simulate novel steel-making processes using real-time sensor data and thermal models [293]. Kaeser compressors implemented DTs allowing predictive maintenance and dynamic service contracts via cloud and Internet of Things (IoT) technologies [295]. Shipbuilding development benefits from modular and scalable architectures managing complex CAD data and multiphysics environmental interactions [294]. Manufacturing processes increasingly rely on DT technologies to enhance efficiency, quality management, and supply chain resilience. The paper [296] emphasizes challenges in mapping entire plants and reconfigurable production lines, calling for advanced integration techniques and reactive control. Dassault Systèmes advances the field via its *Virtual Twin Experiences* powered by the 3DEXPERIENCE platform, which integrates advanced simulation, AI, and collaboration tools, connecting product design with real-world behavior to accelerate innovation across aerospace, automotive, construction, and healthcare sectors [103]. The paper [297] proposes a systemic architectural framework emphasizing modular components, standard interfaces, and federated models that enable DT scalability and adaptability. It highlights the criticality of robust governance, security measures, and compliance mechanisms embedded early in the design and development processes.

Operations, Maintenance, Repair, and Overhaul (MRO) are pivotal stages where DTs enable continuous product life-cycle data integration to optimize systems and predict failures. The paper [298] highlights how virtual twins facilitate digitizing manual MRO workflows, leveraging AI to assist mechanics in aviation, thus enabling flexible, modular, and transferable shop floor processes. This approach exemplifies elevating traditional MRO with DTs' systemic connectivity.

For complex projects, the contribution [299] discusses DT frameworks that tackle multi-stakeholder collaboration and project complexity through modular, federated twin ecosystems, stressing the importance of scalable architectural components that support project life-cycle management. This work provides an essential viewpoint for digital twins not only as products but as integrated entities across project stages.

In the oil and gas sector, DTs accelerate project delivery and operational excellence by integrating asset life-cycle data with real-time operational monitoring. This process, analyzed by the paper [300] involves dynamic DTs that enhance risk assessment, optimize maintenance schedules, and improve safety protocols specifically tailored to the energy industry's needs.

Deployment entails embedding DTs into operational workflows, validating models against empirical data. Thames Water's leak detection twin integrates acoustic sensors combined with GIS and Supervisory Control and Data Acquisition (SCADA) systems to optimize maintenance [293]. NASA Langley's DT supports over 300 applications, including space allocation, routing, and emergency response [292]. Deployment is an iterative process involving Enterprise Resource Planning (ERP) and Product Life-cycle Management (PLM) integration, organizational training, and continuous refinement [13, 17, 301, 302]. Paper [289] details deployment strategies emphasizing human-in-the-loop designs and continuous validation routines that cultivate user trust and system robustness. It discusses transitioning DTs from static digital replicas to dynamic, behavior-driven systems that leverage continuous data and AI to inform predictive and prescriptive analytics. **Operation** focuses on continuous monitoring, predictive analytics, and decision-support mechanisms. BMW's virtual factories facilitate real-time collaboration across 31 industrial sites, decreasing planning cycles by 30% [293]. Kaeser's DTs maintain near-perfect uptime and underpin dynamic pricing schemes [295]. In shipbuilding, DTs optimize life-cycle maintenance through sensor-driven feedback and simulation [294]. These operational twins enable adaptive control and proactive anomaly detection [292]. The paper [289] further explores how the operation phase is evolving toward autonomous DTs that self-adapt and learn, incorporating federated ML and edge computing paradigms to sustain scalability and privacy.

6.5.2 Exemplary Industrial DT Projects

This subsection groups industry-specific DT implementations collected from several sources ([6, 289, 293, 296, 297, 303], and [295], and others).

6.5.2.1 Automotive

BMW's *iFactory* initiative exemplifies advanced DT deployment, integrating CAD, IoT sensors, and logistics to reduce planning time by 30% and enable adaptive manufacturing across 31 plants [293]. Ford utilizes DTs to simulate supply chain disruptions influencing vehicle production [295]. The paper [303] describes how DTs provide the automotive industry with transformational advantages through detailed virtual replication of manufacturing and operational systems, enabling agile product development and sustainable innovation.

6.5.2.2 Aerospace

Rolls-Royce's *IntelligentEngine* program combines telemetry and physics-based simulations to optimize engine maintenance, safety, and fuel efficiency, operating within rigid certification frameworks [6, 94, 301, 302]. SpaceX uses DTs for detailed rocket flight and reentry simulations [295]. The paper [297] adds that aerospace DTs increasingly integrate federated learning models to protect sensitive data across collaborators.

6.5.2.3 Shipbuilding

Shipbuilding utilizes DTs for simulating hull dynamics, fuel consumption, and maintenance, interfacing complex CAD and hydrodynamic models with sensor data [294]. While the paper [289] emphasizes the challenge of integrating heterogeneous data sources while achieving coherent behavior simulation.

6.5.2.4 Energy and Utilities

Thames Water's DT incorporates acoustic sensing with GIS and SCADA technologies to detect leaks and optimize repair schedules [293]. Energy sector DTs focus on grid reliability and asset management through real-time data and analytics [295].

6.5.2.5 Retail and Smart Cities

Lowe's Innovation Labs utilize DTs for augmented reality-assisted shelf management [293]. Smart city projects like Virtual Singapore model infrastructure and environmental dynamics for urban planning and disaster response [295].

6.5.2.6 Manufacturing

Tata Steel's HIsarna DT merges sensor data and thermal modeling for process optimization [293]. GE integrates DT-equipped turbines for predictive maintenance and operational efficiency [295].

6.5.2.7 Healthcare

Siemens Healthineers pioneered personalized medical DTs for patient-specific decision-making, combining imaging, and real-time biological data [295].

6.5.3 Enablers and Barriers to Industrial Exploitation

The ISO 23247 standard [8] emerges as a pivotal enabler toward standardization and interoperability of DTs in manufacturing, addressing gaps in architecture definitions and life-cycle processes. This international initiative complements the technological enablers like IoT, cloud/edge computing, and AI outlined previously [301, 302]. A recent paper [288] investigates DT applications in complex engineering systems, highlighting deployment challenges such as integration complexities, multi-stakeholder collaboration, and the criticality of high-fidelity systemic modeling. Their findings reinforce many of the barriers and enablers presented in this chapter, advocating for structured governance models and iterative validation to realize operational resilience.

6.5.3.1 Barriers and Enablers to DT Development and Adoption

Despite the growing interest and benefits of DTs, their development and widespread adoption face significant challenges, particularly in complex industrial domains such as process industries. DT projects span several years across all life-cycle phases, contrasting with shorter software development cycles [13, 301]. Their operation often transforms corporate asset management practices and strategic decision-making over the long term [292, 293]. The long duration and the constant refinement of models and data are essential features to consider when starting a new DT project.

Based on systematic literature reviews and empirical studies [288, 301], the following key barriers and enablers have been identified:

Barriers:

- *High Initial Investment Costs:* Deploying DT technology requires substantial capital for IoT sensors, data infrastructure, simulation software, and skilled personnel, often limiting adoption among small and medium enterprises [301]. Modeling, constant refinement, and improvements to extend the reach of a DT representation can last for several years. Furthermore, the DT must keep pace with the intended evolution of the physical system. These features require sustained dedication and organizational support over a considerable span of time. Additionally, the initial development and usage phases of the DT may deliver fewer advantages than expected due to the complexity of the objectives. It is important to support these early phases through strong management backing and continuous support.
- *Data Integration and Interoperability Issues:* Heterogeneity of data formats, legacy systems, and lack of standardized interfaces hinder smooth integration of various data sources into cohesive DTs [288].
- *Workforce Skill Gaps:* Adequate expertise in data science, simulation modeling, and system integration is essential, yet often scarce, posing a significant obstacle to effective DT development [301].
- *Cybersecurity and Data Privacy Concerns:* The interconnected nature of DTs increases vulnerability to cyberattacks and raises concerns regarding the handling of sensitive operational and personal data [301].
- *Organizational Resistance and Change Management:* Resistance to adopting new technologies, inadequate change management strategies, and unclear value propositions can impede DT projects [288].
- *Complexity of Modeling and Validation:* Capturing accurate behavioral and operational models for complex physical systems entails high complexity and iterative validation efforts [288].

Enablers:

- *Robust Data Architecture and Standards:* Establishing interoperable data models, adopting standards like ISO 23247, and leveraging cloud-edge computing architectures facilitate seamless data flow and integration [301].

- *Incremental and Modular Implementation:* Phased deployment strategies that build DTs incrementally and modularly may reduce complexity and investment risk [301].
- *Cross-Disciplinary Collaboration:* Integration of domain experts, IT and OT professionals, and business stakeholders enhances knowledge sharing and accelerates effective adoption [288].
- *Advanced Analytical and AI Capabilities:* ML and AI-driven analytics enhance prediction accuracy, anomaly detection, and decision-support functions within DTs [301].
- *Management Support and Clear Value Proposition:* Strong executive sponsorship, explicit objectives aligned with business goals, and demonstration of ROI build organizational commitment [288].
- *Cybersecurity and Privacy By Design:* Embedding security and privacy measures from the outset reduces risks and builds trust among users and partners [301].

Addressing these barriers with the enablers outlined provides a pathway toward more mature and widespread deployment of DT solutions [13, 17], ultimately realizing their transformative potential in industrial operations.

6.5.4 Advantages and Enterprise Effort

DTs foster enhanced asset efficiency, cost reduction through predictive and prescriptive analytics, accelerated innovation, and improved risk management [13, 293, 295]. Realizing these gains demands significant organizational commitment, including governance structures, continuous training, and cultural adaptation [17, 289, 297].

7

Some Examples of Applicability of the Digital Twin Architecture

After reading this chapter, you should be able to:

- Capture the differences and the applicability of top-down or bottom-up strategies for Digital Twin development within specific problem domains.
- Grasp the complexity of problem domains and their representation by means of a Digital Twin.
- Explain the relationship between Metaverse and Digital Twin concepts.

7.1 Introduction

This chapter illustrates some of the possibilities offered by the proposed Digital Twin (DT) architecture to develop, operate, and exploit the DT capabilities. It tries to provide views and hints about how to use the solutions described in Sections 7.2, 7.3, and particularly 7.4 and 7.5 to support the DT developments in different contexts. Actually, the most investigated scenarios, as manufacturing, are disregarded, because there is a lot of literature available about these well-known subjects (e.g., [6, 20, 304, 305]. This chapter tries to provide a view about different ways for building DT. For instance, the bottom-up and Top-down approaches, as discussed in Sections 2.7.5 and 5.4, are demonstrated, as well as hybrid combinations of them. The focus on new fields of application poses new challenges to the DT definition and its implementation. These new application scenarios can contribute to enlarging the investigations about the evolution of DT. Models and modeling approaches, functional decomposition, and module/component definition and implementation discussed in previous chapters are utilized to illustrate possible DT applications.

This chapter will discuss the following DT services:

- DTs for smart cities.
- Network Digital Twin (NDT) for edge-cloud continuum.
- DTs for cultural heritage.
- DT as an integral part of the Metaverse.

7.2 Developing DTs for Smart Cities: A Bottom-up Approach

This section describes a bottom-up methodology for developing DTs for smart cities, beginning with a focused, small-scale DT and gradually expanding it to model more complex urban systems.

The development of DTs for smart cities is a complex, iterative process that benefits from a bottom-up methodology. These complex systems have not been formally designed as a physical entity. Rather than attempting to model the entire city from the outset, it is often more effective to start with a focused, small-scale DT targeting a specific urban problem or asset. For instance, the example described in Section 2.7.3 provides an insight about how to proceed from small to larger models [132]. Over time, this DT can be extended and specialized by leveraging general-purpose sensing, synthetic sensing, and advanced data analytics. These capabilities are all supported by the flexible, modular architecture introduced in Section 5.1.3.

7.2.1 From Simple DTs to Specialized Behavior

Initially, a DT may be deployed to monitor and manage a single asset or process, such as a traffic intersection, waste bin, or environmental pollution. The core requirements at this stage are:

- **General-purpose Sensing:** Deploying basic sensors to collect fundamental data (e.g., temperature, traffic flow, bin fill level) without the need for a highly specialized and not reusable sensor infrastructure.
- **Data Management:** Using the *InjectionChain* and *ContextBroker* components (see Figure 5.1) to ingest, curate, and store contextualized data and keep the raw ones in the *DataLake* for further analysis.
- **Simple Behavior Model:** Designing and implementing a basic *Behavior Module* to respond to sensed events (e.g., trigger alerts, change traffic signals).

As data accumulates and operational experience grows, the DT can be enhanced:

- **Synthetic Sensing:** Deriving new insights by combining multiple data sources, using analytics or AI/GenAI modules to infer states not directly measured (e.g., estimating congestion from multiple sensors).

- **Specialized Behavior:** Evolving the *Behavior Module* into a more sophisticated set of microservices, integrating domain knowledge and predictive capabilities (e.g., adaptive traffic control, predictive maintenance).
- **Microservice Orchestration:** Leveraging the *Orchestrator* and *Configuration Manager* to deploy, scale, and update DT modules independently as the system evolves.

7.2.1.1 Behavior Modeling for a Smart Roundabout

The behavior modeling of a roundabout is a prime example of how DT architecture enables advanced, data-driven management of urban mobility. Leveraging general-purpose sensors and synthetic sensing, the DT can capture and analyze the flow of vehicles through entry and exit points, derive normal operational patterns, and detect anomalies in real time.

Figure 7.1 represents the case in which a general-purpose sensor capability is used to monitor a roundabout. A behavior agent (as described in Section 5.2 and represented in Figure 5.7) is deployed at a node nearby the roundabout to capture data related to the scene, determine vehicles, their trajectories, and possible local anomalies. The data collected by the general-purpose sensing is transformed into synthetic, well-formed data by the agent and injected into the ContextBroker. The ContextBroker notifies the behavior module that new information is available. This module requests the services of the prescriptive module (Section 4.6.2) to analyze the situation and the AI/GenAI Module to check if new rules can be extracted from the data. The returned information is used to determine if the behavior of behavior module and its components (e.g., the local agent) should be changed. In this case, the agent is notified and can instruct actuators (if present) to instantiate new policies.

7.2.1.1.1 Data Collection and Local Processing

At the edge, an agent capable of dealing with general-purpose sensing and other functions is deployed at the roundabout node. This agent is responsible for:

- **Scene Capture:** Collecting data that can provide information related to the status of the roundabout.
- **Scene Analysis:** Analyzing the measurements to determine vehicle type, trajectory, and detect anomalies (synthetic sensing).
- **Local Data Management:** Curating and formatting derived information, then injecting it into the ContextBroker.
- **Actuator (Optional):** Used by the agent to implement policies determined by the global behavior module in cooperation with other functions.

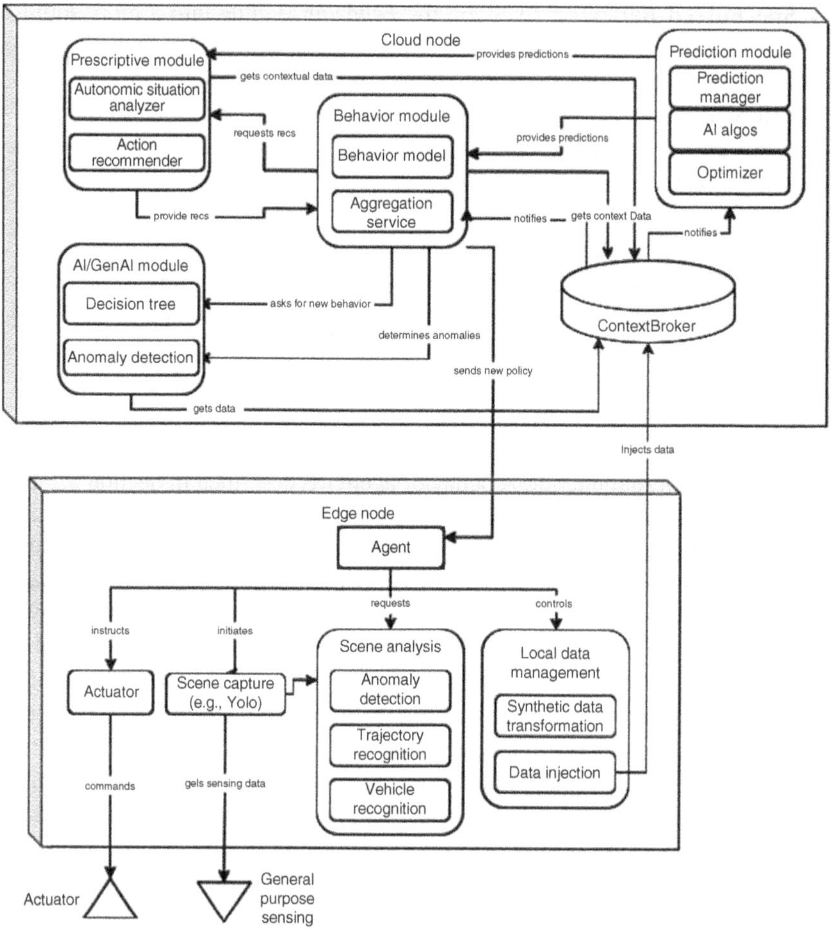

Figure 7.1 DT behavior modeling for a smart roundabout.

7.2.1.1.2 Centralized Behavior Modeling and Anomaly Detection

Once data is ingested by the *ContextBroker*, the following steps occur:

- **ContextBroker:** Notifies subscribed modules when new data is available.
- **Behavior Module:** Checks the received data and decides whether to update the behavior model and extract new insights (e.g., anomaly detection). It may invoke the prescriptive and AI/GenAI modules. Based on their feedback, it can request the agent to update its models or actuate mitigation policies. Otherwise, it continues functioning as expected.
- **Prescriptive Module:** Analyzes the situation and, if needed, recommends new policies and actions to the behavior module.

- **AI/GenAI Module:** Extracts new rules from the available data (e.g., via decision trees), detects additional anomalies, and updates both the ContextBroker and the behavior module.

This process enables the DT to:

- Learn normal roundabout operation and peak usage patterns.
- Detect and classify anomalies in real time.
- Continuously improve local agent intelligence by deploying updated rules and models.
- Provide actionable insights for traffic management and safety interventions.

7.2.2 Microservices and Component Flexibility

The context DT architecture (Figure 5.1) is designed for flexibility and scalability through its modular approach. Its high-level components have been further decomposed to achieve more granular control, as represented in Section 5.3, and further refined with specific identification of microservices in Section 5.5.2. This process of decomposition of functions should arrive at the point of identifying the small services that can be used in a coordinated manner to provide the Smart City expected functions. At this general representation, some needed components can be identified and are candidates for further decomposition. In general:

- The DT engine for providing the needed bottom-up DT functionalities. Each DT engine component (e.g., behavior, AI/GenAI, or others such as visualization) can be further refined and implemented as independent microservices, allowing for incremental development and deployment.
- The *ContextBroker* enables seamless data sharing and integration between modules, supporting both simple and advanced DT scenarios.
- The architecture supports the addition of new modules or the replacement of existing ones with minimal disruption, thanks to standardized APIs and clear separation of concerns. For instance, the special function can extend the capabilities offered by the DT.

7.2.3 Integrating Heterogeneous Data Streams for Holistic Urban Insights

A key advantage of the modular DT architecture is its ability to integrate multiple, heterogeneous streams of data, such as traffic, pollution, and weather measurements, to provide a comprehensive understanding of city dynamics. By fusing these data sources, the DT can uncover correlations (e.g., between traffic congestion and air quality), anticipate future scenarios, and support the design of effective urban policies.

For example, by combining real-time traffic data with pollution sensor readings and weather forecasts [203, 306, 307], the DT can:

- Identify areas where traffic congestion leads to spikes in pollution, especially under certain weather conditions.
- Recommend dynamic traffic management policies (such as rerouting, congestion pricing, or adaptive signal timing) to reduce emissions in critical zones.
- Support city operators in evaluating the effectiveness of interventions and adjusting strategies in real time.

This holistic approach is enabled by the architecture's data management and AI/-GenAI module, which can ingest, analyze, and correlate diverse datasets to generate actionable insights for sustainable urban management.

This bottom-up approach to DT development enables cities to start small, demonstrate value quickly, and evolve their DT systems as needs and opportunities grow. The modular, microservice-oriented architecture supports incremental deployment, integration of new data sources, and continuous improvement of behavior models, making it suited for the dynamic environment of smart cities.

7.3 NDT: The Edge-cloud Continuum Representation

This section details a top-down approach for designing a NDT, which begins by defining the overall infrastructure and then breaking it down to accommodate the needs of various stakeholders.

The concept of NDT applies the DT paradigm to the domain of networked infrastructures, enabling advanced monitoring, optimization, and management of complex, distributed digital ecosystems. In line with recent research results [137, 138] NDTs are essential for providing both providers and customers with actionable, real-time insights into the performance and health of an edge-cloud continuum infrastructure.

7.3.1 A Top-down Approach for NDT Design

In this example, the NDT is designed using a top-down methodology. While in practice network deployments often grow bottom-up, here the definition of an edge-cloud infrastructure from scratch is assumed, and it is associated with a corresponding NDT. The starting point is the overall processing, storage, and communication infrastructure, typically composed of resources and services from multiple stakeholders (e.g., telecom operators, cloud providers, edge infrastructure owners). There is also a strong need to support customers in understanding how their applications are distributed within the infrastructure and which resources are allocated.

The NDT must therefore support a holistic, unified view for both providers and customers, enabling all stakeholders to access both global and segment-specific (edge, public cloud, private cloud) perspectives on their allocated resources. All stakeholders should be able to establish optimization strategies according to their own interests. This creates a complex situation in which contrasting requirements of different stakeholders must be mediated. The NDT should identify these requirements and constraints and determine allocation and optimization policies that accommodate disparate needs. Under this perspective, this DT somehow stresses optimization management and functions within the DT behavior model. It is particularly focused on the monitoring and optimization needs to accommodate the needs of the stakeholders.

7.3.2 NDT Template: Monitoring and Optimization

A typical NDT implementation follows a monitor-optimize template (see Section 5.3.4), with two main functional pillars:

- **Monitoring:** Continuous collection and aggregation of network telemetry, resource usage, and service KPIs from all segments (edge, cloud, private cloud) and all stakeholders. This is achieved through distributed monitoring agents and robust data management pipelines.
- **Optimization:** Data-driven analysis and decision-making, using advanced analytics, AI/GenAI modules, and prescriptive logic to recommend or enact changes that improve network performance, reliability, and efficiency for customers, segments, or the global infrastructure.

7.3.3 Stakeholder Views and Insights

The NDT architecture supports multiple, customizable views:

- **Provider (Holistic) View:** Aggregates data from all stakeholder infrastructures, enabling end-to-end monitoring, anomaly detection, and optimization across the entire continuum.
- **Customer (Global) View:** Presents a unified actionable representation (view or dashboard) of all resources and services allocated to the customer, regardless of their physical or administrative location.
- **Customer (Segment) View:** Offers detailed insights and visualizations for specific segments (e.g., edge, public cloud, private cloud), supporting fine-grained management and troubleshooting. This segmented view can be offered to both providers and customers for monitoring and policy assignment according to stakeholder goals.

7.3.4 NDT Architecture Overview

The NDT architecture (shown in Figure 7.2), adapted to the edge-cloud continuum scenario, features a modular structure that leverages the context DT architecture (Figure 5.1) and its componentization as presented in Section 5.5.2, with specialized components for network monitoring, optimization, and stakeholder interaction. Also, in this case, local agents need to be deployed in the computing infrastructures or have access to the relevant data. These local agents can be considered as the front-end of the infrastructural islands that compose the monitored NDT infrastructure and gather data about their behavior, format them according to the NDT NGSI-LD-based data model, and send them to the ContextBroker. The behavior module considers the current execution and progress of the entire infrastructure by accessing contextualized data of the ContextBroker, and determines which stakeholder views and requirements can be satisfied. The behavior module interacts with the prognostic module to anticipate issues or problems in all the infrastructural islands and on different composed infrastructures or customer environments, and with the prescriptive module to determine action plans that support the requirements of all platform stakeholders.

7.3.5 Optimization and Prognosis: Example Workflows

The modular NDT architecture enables advanced workflows for network optimization and prognosis. The NDT can deploy agents in the various computing, storage, and communication infrastructures to collect relevant information about resource allocation and consumption. If this is not possible, the DT should be able to access or receive relevant information to reconstruct an accurate

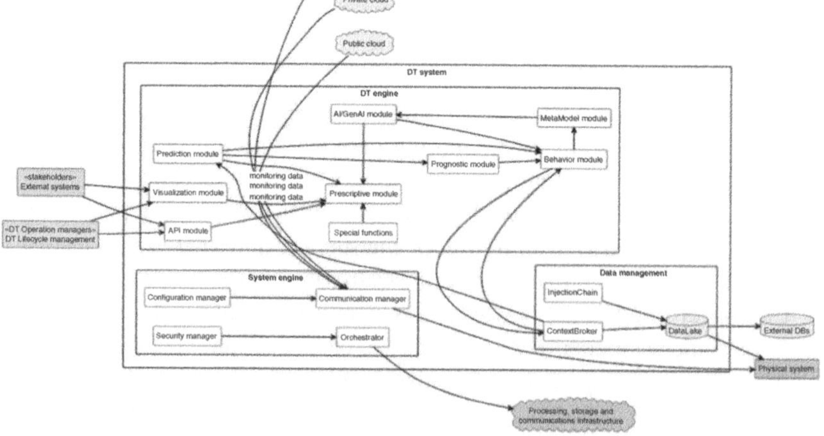

Figure 7.2 Network DT basic architecture.

representation of the monitored infrastructure's status. Conversely, agents deployed locally should be able to interact with local orchestrators or policy managers to instruct them on actions to take. If this is not feasible for security reasons, the agent should run in the DT system but must be able to send policy and actuation requests to external systems through secure and trusted APIs.

7.3.5.1 Optimization Example

Figure 7.3 depicts major interactions between modules that support the NDT implementation. When the behavior module detects suboptimal resource allocation or performance degradation (e.g., network congestion across edge and cloud segments), it interacts with the prescriptive module to analyze the situation. The prescriptive module, leveraging real-time and historical data, recommends reconfiguration actions (e.g., traffic rerouting, resource scaling). The behavior module identifies the agents to be involved in this change of policy and sends them the

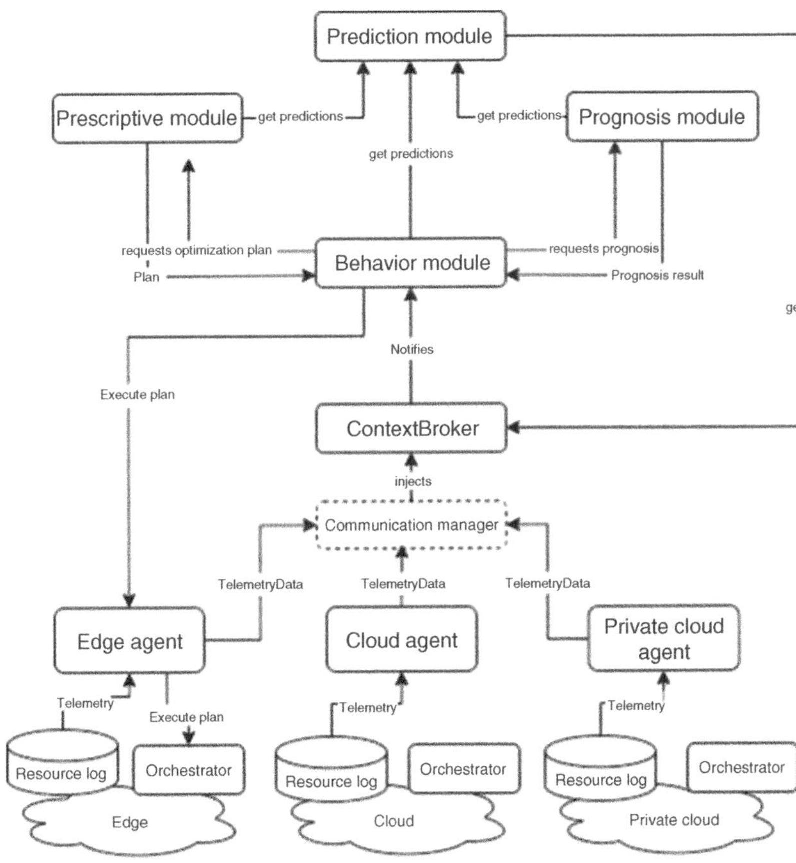

Figure 7.3 NDT basic interactions between modules.

command to implement the plan. Each agent is responsible for interacting with the local orchestrator and making sure that the local policies are changed according to the behavior module decision.

It is important not to confuse the fact that the DT itself may run on a similar infrastructure. Here the NDT is running on its own infrastructure that is different from the edge/cloud/private cloud infrastructure. If the infrastructure is directly controlled by the system engine orchestrator, commands and policies can be directed to these components; otherwise, instructions should be sent outside of the DT system toward appropriate elements (via secure and private APIs), most likely to other orchestrators or external actuators. In the first case, the designer needs to put particular attention in separating the infrastructure supporting the DT (that could be seen as a stakeholder) and the global infrastructure supporting all the stakeholders.

7.3.5.2 Prognosis Example

In this example, the prognostic module continuously analyzes trends in network telemetry and health indicators collected and organized in the DT ContextBroker. If it predicts a possible malfunction (e.g., impending hardware failure or capacity exhaustion), it notifies the behavior module, which can proactively trigger mitigation strategies or alert operators.

The NDT enables a holistic, actionable representation of the edge-cloud continuum, supporting both providers and customers with tailored insights and optimization capabilities. Its modular, top-down architecture ensures scalability, interoperability, and advanced automation, paving the way for resilient, efficient, and intelligent networked infrastructures.

7.4 The Challenge of DTs for Cultural Heritage

This section explains why a hybrid bottom-up and top-down approach is essential for cultural heritage DTs, as it allows for the integration of physical, data-driven precision with broader historical and contextual information.

DTs are increasingly recognized as transformative tools for the preservation, study, and valorization of cultural heritage. While initial applications often focus on visual representation (e.g., 3D models), the true potential of DTs lies in their ability to capture and integrate the multifaceted nature of cultural artifacts. Applying DTs to cultural heritage presents unique challenges and opportunities compared to industrial or infrastructure domains. The complexity and richness of cultural heritage objects necessitate a hybrid approach, combining bottom-up (object-centric, data-driven) and top-down (contextual, interpretative) perspectives [7, 250].

7.4.1 A Hybrid Approach: Bottom-up and Top-down

Cultural heritage artifacts possess inherent complexity, embodying physical, functional, historical, and artistic dimensions. Describing these artifacts from a single perspective is often insufficient. A comprehensive understanding requires a multi-faceted approach, capturing relevant features from various viewpoints. This presents a dual challenge:

1. Identifying the essential perspectives needed to fully represent the artifact's significance and value.
2. Representing the key features relevant to each perspective in a meaningful and accurate way.

For instance, a statue can be analyzed from a physical perspective (material composition, current environmental conditions), a functional perspective (its role in architectural or social space), a historical perspective (its evolution in meaning and interpretation over time), and an ownership perspective (its provenance and associated cultural significance). These perspectives are often intertwined and influence each other. A purely bottom-up approach, focusing solely on the physical object's attributes, may neglect the crucial contextual information that gives the artifact its cultural value. Conversely, a purely top-down approach may lack the precision and objectivity offered by detailed physical measurements.

In the cultural heritage context, a bottom-up approach starts with the detailed digital representation of individual artifacts, capturing their physical properties (shape, dimensions, material) and environmental conditions (temperature, humidity, light exposure) through IoT-enabled sensing. Functional aspects can also be described in a bottom-up manner, by identifying the components and their interactions.

A top-down approach complements this by embedding the artifact within its broader historical, artistic, social, and geographical contexts. This involves incorporating historical narratives, artistic interpretations, social significance, and location-based information.

A hybrid methodology, integrating bottom-up precision with top-down contextualization, enables the DT to serve as a dynamic, multi-perspective knowledge system, offering a richer and more complete understanding of cultural heritage.

7.4.2 Multi-view D for Artifacts

Drawing from the initial works on DT for cultural heritage [7, 250], several key, interrelated views for the DT of a cultural artifact can be considered:

- **Physical View:** Represents the tangible properties of the object (dimensions, material, color, texture), and integrates real-time environmental data from

IoT sensors (temperature, humidity, light). This view supports conservation, preventive maintenance, and material analysis.

- **Functional View:** Describes the intended function or use of the artifact (e.g., tapestry, clock, painting, tool), enabling classification, comparative analysis, and understanding its role within a cultural context.
- **Content View:** Captures the semantic or iconographic content expressed by the object, such as the depiction of a landscape, a person, a symbolic motif, or a narrative scene. This view is essential for art historical analysis and interpretation.
- **Historical View:** Provides a temporal perspective, documenting how interpretations, significance, function, and uses of the artifact have evolved across different historical periods. This view supports studies of cultural change and reception.
- **Ownership View:** Traces the provenance and ownership history of the artifact, offering insights into its journey, authenticity, cultural value, and potential legal or ethical issues.
- **User Perspective:** Adapts the DT's representation and narrative to the specific user's profile, knowledge level, and interests. For instance, providing technical details for conservators, historical narratives for historians, or contextual information for tourists.
- **Social View:** Analyzes public sentiment, social engagement, and cultural impact of the artifact, potentially using sentiment analysis of social media data or visitor feedback.
- **Contextual View:** Situates the artifact within its geographical, cultural, and institutional context. For example, linking an artifact to its original location, associated buildings, or related cultural practices. This view is particularly relevant for tourism and education.

7.4.3 Web of Related DTs

The DT approach enables the interconnection of multiple artifact twins, forming a "web" of related DTs. By identifying shared attributes (material, style, provenance), thematic links (iconography, historical period), or contextual relationships (artifacts from the same site or collection), the system can reveal complex patterns, influences, and connections across collections, periods, and geographies.

AI and advanced analytics modules within the DT architecture can support the discovery of communalities and intersection points, fostering new research and curatorial insights. For example, clustering artifacts based on stylistic similarities or identifying temporal correlations in their ownership histories.

7.4.4 Personalized and Adaptive Experiences

The context DT architecture (see Figure 5.1) and its componentization in Section 5.3 facilitate the creation of DT representation that can offer personalized and adaptive user experiences. The behavior module can tailor the information and interaction modalities based on the user's profile, preferences, and context. AI/GenAI module can generate personalized narratives, recommend related artifacts, or provide customized explanations. The visualization module can offer different dashboards, interactive maps, or immersive experiences for diverse audiences.

7.4.5 Case Study: Egyptian Scarabs and the Power of DTs

Consider the case of Egyptian scarabs, small, carved artifacts with specific colors linked to manufacturing techniques that evolved over time [308]. Traditional documentation, even with high-resolution photographs, may be insufficient for experts to accurately determine the subtle color variations and attribute the artifact to a particular era or workshop. Figure 7.4 depicts a possible interaction between components, modules, and stakeholders for supporting the Egyptian scarab application. A DT for scarab can encode detailed colorimetric data (beyond RGB values, perhaps spectral data), material analysis (e.g., composition of the glaze), and provenance information. Leveraging the data management and AI/GenAI modules, the system can:

- Compare the color attributes of a given scarab to a database of other scarabs, identifying clusters with similar hues and manufacturing signatures. The AI/GenAI module can employ clustering algorithms to group scarabs based on color similarity.
- Discover connections to other objects, potentially from different countries or epochs, that share similar color characteristics. For instance, finding similar glaze colors in Roman glass or Chinese ceramics suggests potential trade

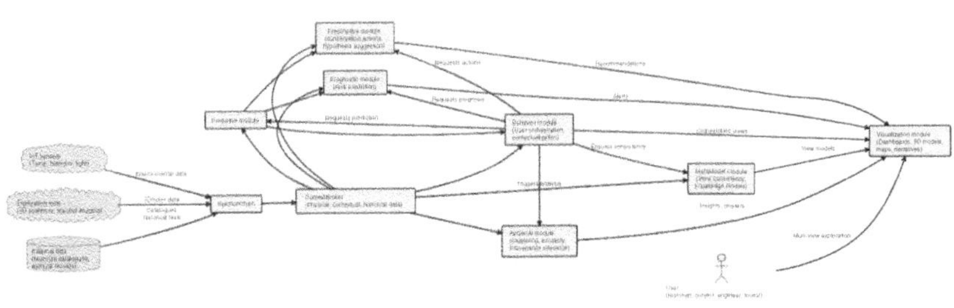

Figure 7.4 DT architecture supporting Egyptian scarab application.

routes or technological exchange. The AI/GenAI module can perform similarity searches and pattern recognition across different artifact types.

- Support experts in attributing artifacts more accurately, providing curators and the public with interactive visualizations of these relationships. The visualization module can offer comparative color palettes and three-dimensional (3D) models with color-coded regions.
- Enable the behavior module to trigger new analyses or recommendations when new data is ingested (e.g., a newly digitized scarab). For example, if a new scarab is added, the system can automatically re-cluster the data and update the visualizations.

7.4.6 Context DT Architecture Support for Cultural Heritage

The proposed DT architecture provides a robust framework for implementing these multi-view DTs and supporting the described functionalities:

- **Data Acquisition:** IoT sensors and digitization tools (3D scanners, spectral imaging devices) feed physical and environmental data through the InjectionChain into the ContextBroker. This includes data for the physical view and potentially contextual data. It also stores contextualized data from various sources, supporting complex queries and analytics. This allows the management of diverse data types associated with different artifact views (e.g., images, sensor readings, historical texts) and integration with external databases and systems (e.g., museum catalogs, archival records).
- **Behavior Module:** Orchestrates user interactions, situation-aware recommendations, and triggers advanced analyses. It can tailor the presentation of the DT based on the user perspective and manage the flow of information between different modules.
- **AI/GenAI Module:** Performs clustering, similarity analysis, pattern recognition, and generates new insights (e.g., color matching, provenance inference). This module is essential for supporting the comparative analysis across different artifact views and for discovering hidden connections.
- **Visualization Module:** Presents multi-view dashboards, interactive maps, 3D models, and supports personalized narratives. It allows users to explore the artifact from different perspectives and facilitates a deeper understanding of its context and significance.
- **Prescriptive and Prognostic Modules:** Suggest conservation actions (based on environmental data from the physical view) or predict potential risks to the artifact's preservation. These modules can also assist historians in evaluating hypotheses by suggesting further lines of inquiry or data to examine.

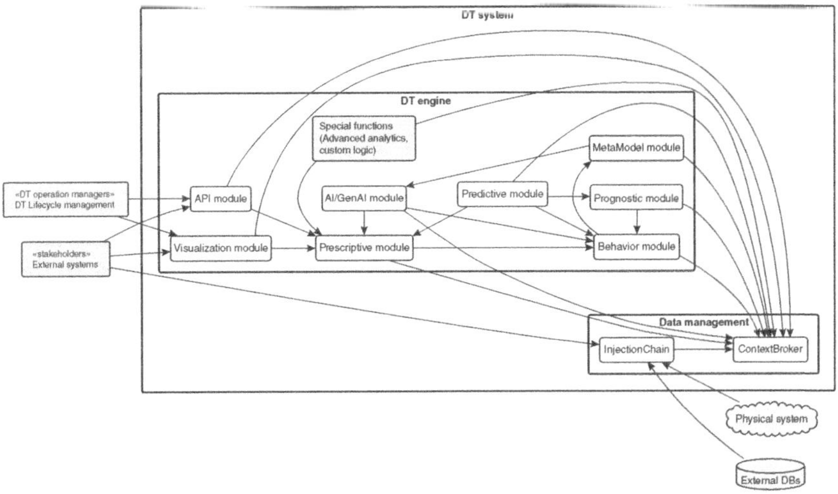

Figure 7.5 DT architecture supporting cultural heritage applications.

- **MetaModel Module:** Manages the evolving data and knowledge models that underpin the multiple artifact views. This module ensures consistency and interoperability between different representations of the same artifact.

Figure 7.5 represents a simplified instance of components and modules supporting cultural heritage applications.

DTs for cultural heritage demand a hybrid, multi-view approach to capture the richness and complexity of artifacts and their contexts. The modular DT architecture provides a robust foundation for integrating diverse data sources, supporting personalized experiences, and uncovering new connections, ultimately enhancing both scholarship and public engagement with cultural heritage. The use of AI enables the discovery of hidden patterns and relationships across different artifact views.

7.5 DT as an Integral Part of the Metaverse

This section discusses how DTs can be integrated into the metaverse, providing real-world data fidelity and predictive capabilities that enhance the realism and utility of virtual environments.

The metaverse is rapidly evolving into a persistent, shared, immersive, and often 3D virtual environment where users can interact with each other and with digital representations of objects, spaces, and processes. Conceptually, the metaverse can be viewed as a behavior model of hypothetical and, potentially, real worlds, a dynamic space where both imagined and real phenomena are simulated, visualized, and experienced. It is characterized by features such as presence (the feeling of being there), interoperability (the ability to move seamlessly between experiences), standardization (ensuring compatibility), and persistence (the continuity of experiences).

In this context, DTs are a bridge between physical systems (PSs) and the metaverse. While DTs focus on creating accurate, data-driven, and often real-time models of existing entities, systems, and processes, the metaverse offers visualization, interaction, and engagement capabilities that make these models accessible, understandable, and actionable for users. DTs ground the metaverse in reality, providing data fidelity and behavioral accuracy, while the metaverse amplifies the value of DTs by enabling immersive exploration, manipulation, and collaborative use.

The integration of DT and metaverse technologies is a natural and mutually reinforcing convergence [309–313]. DTs contribute fidelity, real-time data synchronization, and predictive capabilities, enhancing the realism and utility of the metaverse. Conversely, the metaverse amplifies the value of DTs through immersive visualization, enhanced user engagement, and collaborative interaction, transforming data-driven models into dynamic, interactive experiences. This synergy enables not only the monitoring and analysis of existing systems but also their exploration, manipulation, and collaborative use in rich virtual settings, opening up new possibilities across various domains. For instance, the metaverse could be a way to represent different views of the same cultural heritage artifact.

7.5.1 State of the Art of Metaverse Platforms and Mapping to the Context Digital Architecture

The landscape of metaverse platforms is diversified, with each platform offering unique capabilities for visualization, interaction, and integration with actual data. Understanding how these platforms align with the DT architecture can facilitate the development of robust and scalable metaverse applications leveraging DTs functions, realizing an even closer integration between these technologies. This can bring mutual benefits: the DT can gain better and compelling visualization and user engagement capabilities; the metaverse can benefit from an alignment with and exploitation of data and behavior models. Some prominent metaverse platforms are:

- **Unity and Unreal Engine**: These are leading real-time 3D creation tools used to develop immersive, interactive environments [314]. They map primarily to the *Visualization Module* of the DT architecture, providing the graphical rendering, user interface, and interactive elements of the metaverse experience. They can also leverage the *API Module* to access data from other parts of the architecture.

- **Roblox, Decentraland, and Spatial**: These platforms emphasize user-generated content, social interaction, and persistent virtual worlds [315]. They rely heavily on APIs and data integration features, corresponding to the *API Module* and *ContextBroker* in the context digital architecture, to connect users, assets, and data within their virtual spaces. The *Behavior Module* needs to extend its capabilities to better manage complex user interactions and social dynamics as supported by these platforms.
- **Microsoft Mesh and NVIDIA Omniverse**: These platforms are geared towards enterprise and industrial applications [316], supporting real-time collaboration, simulation, and integration with IoT and DTs. They leverage advanced AI and simulation engines, aligning with the *AI/GenAI Module*, *Behavior Module*, and *MetaModel Module* of the context digital architecture, to visualize complex systems and predict their behavior. The *ContextBroker* facilitates the integration of real-time data from PSs.
- **Sensor and IoT Integration**: Many metaverse platforms now support real-time data feeds from PSs through APIs and data streaming protocols [317]. This capability aligns directly with the *InjectionChain* and *ContextBroker* components of the DT architecture, enabling the metaverse to reflect the current state of actual systems.

This mapping demonstrates the modularity and adaptability of the DT architecture, making it well-suited to serve as a robust backbone for metaverse applications. By providing a structured framework for data management, analytics, and integration, the architecture supports the development of scalable, interoperable, and data-driven metaverse experiences.

7.5.2 Integration Points and Mutual Enhancement

DT architectures and metaverse platforms share several key integration points and can mutually enhance each other, creating a synergy that extends the capabilities of both technologies:

- **Visualization and User Engagement**: The metaverse excels at delivering immersive, interactive, and engaging experiences, which can be significantly enhanced by the real-time, multi-view data and accurate behavior models provided by DTs. DTs bring fidelity and accuracy to the metaverse, while the metaverse makes DT data more accessible and understandable.
- **Data Synchronization**: The *ContextBroker* ensures that changes in the PS, captured by DTs, are accurately and promptly reflected in the metaverse, and potentially vice versa. This bidirectional synchronization supports

real-time monitoring, control, and interaction between the physical and virtual realms.

- **Simulation and Prediction**: The *AI/GenAI Module*, *Prescriptive Module*, *Prognostic Module*, and *Simulation Engine* of the DT architecture can significantly enrich metaverse environments by providing predictive analytics, scenario simulation, and automated recommendations. This enables users to explore "what-if" scenarios, optimize processes, and make informed decisions within the metaverse.
- **Contextualization and Personalization**: The *Behavior Module* and *Meta-Model Module* allow the metaverse to adapt content and interaction modalities to the user's context, preferences, and role. This enables personalized and situation-aware experiences, enhancing user satisfaction and engagement.
- **Collaborative Spaces**: The metaverse provides shared virtual spaces where multiple users can interact with the same DTs, enabling collaborative analysis, design, decision-making, and training. This fosters teamwork, knowledge sharing, and distributed expertise.
- **Interoperability and Standards**: Future integration will benefit from standardization efforts to ensure interoperability between different metaverse platforms and DT systems. This will allow seamless data exchange and the creation of more open and interconnected virtual worlds.

Conversely, the metaverse can enhance the DT architecture by providing advanced visualization capabilities, richer user interfaces, new modalities for user engagement and collaboration, and the ability to create shared virtual spaces for interacting with DT data. Under this perspective, the DT architecture needs to improve its capability to manage and support highly interactive processes with users. This can be achieved by means of *Special Functions* or, even better, through a new dedicated *Interaction Manager* function that can be introduced in the DT architecture. It is a bridge between the visualization and behavior modules, enabling a smoother integration between the user's needs to "manipulate" and change the physical representation and the behavior representation of the PS supported by the behavior module.

Figure 7.6 encompasses this important change in the DT engine part.

7.5.3 Use Cases: Education, Tourism, and Factory Management

The convergence of DTs and metaverse offers the possibility to explore and exploit existing and new scenarios.

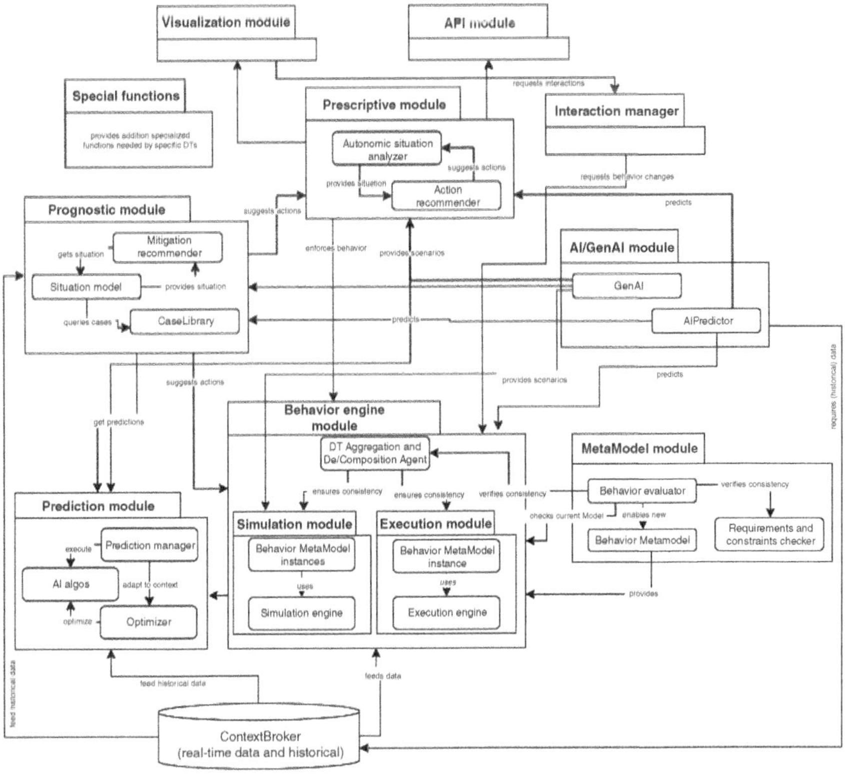

Figure 7.6 Extended DT engine part for accommodating metaverse applications.

7.5.3.1 Education

The integration of DTs and the metaverse enables immersive, interactive, and engaging learning experiences that transcend the limitations of traditional classrooms [318]. For example:

- Students can explore detailed DTs of complex scientific equipment (e.g., a particle accelerator, a human heart) in a virtual laboratory, conducting experiments and manipulating parameters in a safe and controlled environment.
- Historical artifacts and sites can be brought to life in the metaverse, allowing students to virtually visit ancient Rome, examine Egyptian mummies, or witness historical events as they unfolded.
- Collaborative learning environments in the metaverse enable students from different locations to work together on projects, share insights, and learn from each other in real-time.

- The metaverse's visualization and engagement capabilities make abstract concepts tangible and memorable, while the DT ensures fidelity to real-world behavior and data.

7.5.3.2 Tourism and Cultural Heritage

The combination of DTs and the metaverse can impact the tourism and cultural heritage sectors [319], offering new ways to experience, preserve, and promote different cultural experiences:

- DTs of heritage sites and artifacts can be embedded in persistent virtual worlds, allowing users to virtually visit and explore cultural assets from anywhere in the world, at any time.
- Interactive narratives and contextual information, driven by AI and linked to the DT, can provide rich and engaging experiences for virtual visitors.
- For example, a DT of an Egyptian scarab can be examined in detail, with AI-driven narratives and contextual information about its history, symbolism, and manufacturing techniques provided through the metaverse interface.
- Virtual tours can be personalized based on user preferences and interests, offering tailored experiences for different audiences.
- The metaverse can also be used to raise awareness and generate funding for the preservation of endangered cultural heritage sites.

7.5.3.3 Factory and Industrial Management

In manufacturing and industrial settings, the metaverse and DTs are enabling real-time monitoring, simulation, optimization, and training [320]:

- Managers and engineers can enter a virtual representation of the factory floor, interact with DTs of equipment and processes, and monitor key performance indicators in real-time.
- Predictive simulations can be run in the metaverse to optimize production schedules, identify potential bottlenecks, and plan maintenance activities.
- Training scenarios can be conducted in the metaverse, allowing workers to practice complex or dangerous procedures in a safe and virtual environment, leveraging the behavioral fidelity of DTs to ensure realistic training.
- Remote collaboration is facilitated, enabling experts from different locations to work together on troubleshooting problems or designing new production lines.
- The GenAI module ability to create synthetic scenarios can be used to educate people to cope with critical situations but also to get input from experienced persons about how the situation should be tackled in the best way.

DTs and the metaverse are converging to create powerful, data-driven, immersive, and interactive environments that enhance user engagement, enable collaborative exploration, and bridge the gap between real and virtual worlds. The modular DT architecture provides a robust foundation for this integration, supporting a wide range of applications across diverse sectors, including education, cultural heritage, industry, and beyond. This convergence promises to further enrich the capabilities of platforms for improving their capabilities to support compelling applications.

7.6 Implementing Services with the Envisaged Architecture

This section provides a few remarks about how the envisaged architecture can be used for implementing the services discussed in this chapter.

The modular, microservice-oriented context DT architecture provides a robust and flexible framework for implementing the diverse services discussed in this chapter. Its core strength lies in the clear separation of concerns, where each component is responsible for a specific function, allowing for tailored and scalable solutions.

The central role of the **ContextBroker** is key to enabling these services. It acts as a shared data bus, ensuring seamless data sharing and integration between all modules, from simple data streams to complex, contextualized information. This capability is fundamental to services that rely on heterogeneous data fusion, such as those for smart cities, which combine traffic, pollution, and weather data to provide holistic insights.

The DT services are realized through the intelligent orchestration of specialized modules:

- The **Behavior Module** is essential for all services, as it orchestrates interactions and manages the overall system logic. In smart cities, it responds to sensed events; in cultural heritage, it adapts the user experience based on profile; and in the metaverse, it manages complex user interactions and social dynamics.
- The **AI/GenAI Module** is leveraged across services for advanced analytics and new insight generation. It is used to extract new rules in smart city traffic management, perform similarity searches for cultural heritage artifacts, and enrich metaverse environments with predictive analytics and scenario simulations.
- The **Prognostic** and **Prescriptive Modules** enable proactive problem-solving. They are used to anticipate network issues in the NDT example, and to suggest conservation actions for cultural heritage artifacts, demonstrating their crucial role in risk mitigation and forward-looking analysis.

This architectural approach ensures that each service can be built by combining and leveraging the appropriate modules for its specific needs, without requiring a complete redesign of the underlying system. The modularity also supports the replication property, allowing for dedicated instances of the DT to be created for specific analyses, such as "what-if" scenarios for the NDT, without affecting the primary operational DT.

Overall, the architecture's flexibility, as demonstrated in the chapter, allows it to support bottom-up, top-down, and hybrid modeling approaches. This adaptability confirms that the principles and components used in the architecture can effectively satisfy a wide range of requirements and modeling needs across different domains, from smart cities to cultural heritage and the metaverse.

8

The Digital Twin of the Future

After reading this chapter, you should be able to:

- Evaluate the applicability of a DT to a specific problem domain.
- Foresee the possible evolution of DT techniques and tools.
- Explain the need for an improved operation process for DTs.
- Evaluate the DT concept impacts on society and its relationships with privacy, ethics and human experience.

8.1 The Evolution of DT

Digital Twin (DT) technology has gradually expanded beyond its origins in manufacturing and industrial automation, becoming an increasingly adopted approach for modeling, monitoring, and optimizing complex systems across diverse domains. This evolution is characterized by several major axes discussed in this section.

Higher Integration of Data-driven and Behavior Models: Two main approaches have developed in parallel: Model-based Systems Engineering (MBSE), which emphasizes structural and behavioral modeling, and IoT-driven DTs, which focus on collecting and visualizing data from physical systems. The next evolutionary step is a greater unification of these approaches, enabling DTs to not only represent what is happening, but also why and how it happens. This integration supports simulation, prediction, and prescriptive analytics, making DTs active participants in system management rather than passive mirrors.

Agile Construction and Incremental Evolution: There is a growing need to simplify the DT construction process to rapidly realize its benefits. Agile and data-driven methodologies enable quick implementation of a basic DT, which can be incrementally enriched with new behaviors, data models, and functions. This is facilitated by further componentization of DT architectures, the use of well-formed behavior templates, and the availability of rich libraries of modular functional components (e.g., microservices) deployable on distributed infrastructures. Another aspect is the benefit of a parallel definition and construction of the physical system and its DT.

Explicit Representation of the Environment: As DTs are deployed in increasingly complex and dynamic scenarios, explicitly representing the environment in which a physical system operates becomes critical. The environment can significantly impact the system behavior and performance. Developers should represent the environment when external factors (such as temperature, humidity, user presence, or regulatory constraints) affect the system's states. Best practices include modular environmental models and situation-aware data integration, enabling the DT to adapt its behavior as environmental conditions change. A practical guideline is to model the environment whenever its variability can influence key performance indicators or operational safety.

Organizational Commitment and Methodologies: Successful DT development and deployment require the involvement and commitment of the entire organization, including technical teams, domain experts, operators, and decision-makers. Methodologies such as agile development, DevOps for DTs, and cross-disciplinary project management are emerging as best practices. Early and continuous stakeholder engagement, iterative prototyping, and clear role definitions are essential to manage the inherent complexity of DT projects.

Expansion of Application Domains: While DTs are well established in "native" domains such as manufacturing and Industry 4.0, their adoption is rising in fields like healthcare, smart cities, transportation, and energy. This expansion brings new challenges, including the need to balance top-down (knowledge-driven, model-based) and bottom-up (data-driven) approaches. The ability to incrementally build and evolve a DT, starting with a minimal viable model and growing as requirements and understanding mature, is increasingly recognized as a major requirement for future DT solutions.

Operations and Life-cycle Management: The operation and life-cycle management of DTs, from creation and deployment to maintenance, evolution, and decommissioning, are critical challenges. Seamless transitions between life-cycle phases, robust versioning, and support for continuous integration and delivery are necessary to ensure that DTs remain accurate and effective as the physical systems they represent evolve.

Development Methodologies and Environments: There is a growing need for dedicated development methodologies and environments tailored to the unique requirements of DTs. These should support the entire life cycle of both the

DT and the physical system, enabling rapid prototyping, modular design, extensibility, and integration with existing enterprise systems.

The following sections will explore whether DTs can be considered a general solution for all problems, identify the most promising application domains, and discuss the expected evolution of DT technologies, including platforms, modular architectures, AI integration, interoperability, and future methodologies for development, operation, and assessment.

8.2 Evaluating DTs as a General Solution

Despite the interest around DT technologies, it is important to recognize that DTs are not a universal solution for every problem. The construction and operation of a DT is a resource-intensive process, requiring significant investment in time, expertise, integration, and technology. In many cases, traditional solutions, such as conventional monitoring systems, dashboards, or targeted simulations, may be more cost-effective and sufficient to meet the needs of a given application.

A cost-benefit analysis should precede any decision to pursue a DT solution. The literature highlights the importance of structured evaluation frameworks and decision-support methodologies to figure out the value of DT adoption [20, 39]. These frameworks typically consider factors such as system complexity, required fidelity, life-cycle duration, integration requirements, and the potential for value creation through simulation, prediction, and optimization.

Certain domains, such as manufacturing, aerospace, and energy, are naturally suited to DT adoption due to their inherent complexity, scale, and demand for real-time monitoring and predictive analytics. In contrast, other domains may find simpler and more traditional solutions preferable, at least in the short term.

The contextual codevelopment of the physical system and its DT can sometimes lead to quicker and more cost-effective implementations, especially when requirements are well understood, and the system can be incrementally modeled and built. Designing a physical system together with its DT can increase the cost marginally and could open to the benefits of having a powerful tool for controlling the functioning of the PS.

A key consideration in DT construction is the potential for reusability and extensibility. Building a monolithic DT for a single application can result in high costs, rigidity, and maintenance challenges. Instead, an open and modular architecture enables the development of multiple applications on top of the same DT platform, supporting long-term evolution and adaptability.

The decision to implement a DT should be guided by a clear understanding of the problem domain, a careful analysis of costs and benefits, and a commitment to open, modular, and evolvable architectures.

8.3 Promising Application Domains

DT technology has found its most mature and impactful applications in domains such as manufacturing, energy, and aerospace [321]. These sectors share characteristics that make them especially suitable for DT adoption: high-value assets, complex processes, long life cycle, and the need for real-time monitoring, predictive maintenance, and optimization. In aerospace, for example, DTs are improving efficiency and safety by enabling enhanced production planning, predictive maintenance, and collaborative design [321]. In manufacturing and energy, DTs support life-cycle management, process optimization, and risk reduction. As discussed in Ref [6], there is a growing adoption of DTs in smart cities, healthcare, transportation, and cultural heritage. The suitability of DTs depends on factors such as measurability, process complexity, and the potential for incremental modeling. Some of the most cited and promising domains for DT applications include:

- Manufacturing and Industry 4.0
- Aerospace and Aviation
- Energy and Utilities
- Transportation and Mobility
- Smart Cities and Infrastructure
- Healthcare and Life Sciences
- Asset and Life-cycle Management
- Construction and Built Environment
- Telecommunications and Networks

The potential of DTs extends beyond the "native" domains. Literature and recent frameworks [322] suggest that the suitability of DTs in new domains depends on several factors and that a one-size-fits-all approach is rarely optimal. Instead, the choice of DT methodology, top-down, bottom-up, or hybrid, should be informed by the nature of the domain and the measurability of its environment.

Having criteria for deciding if a DT solution is viable could help decision makers. Some possible points to consider are:

- **Measurability and Data Availability:** Domains such as transportation, smart cities, and asset management offer rich opportunities for DTs because they are increasingly instrumented with sensors and IoT devices. These environments lend themselves to bottom-up modeling, where incremental, data-driven DTs can be built and refined as more measurements become available [322]. The initial focus may be on creating passive DTs that represent the current state, with behavioral intelligence and advanced analytics added over time.
- **Process Orientation and Complexity:** Domains involving well-defined, complex processes, such as construction, pharmaceutical manufacturing, or

even the medical device industry and biomedical engineering, are also candidates for DTs. Here, the process-oriented nature allows for top-down modeling, leveraging existing knowledge and standards to build DTs that mirror the life cycle of products or assets. The discriminant in these cases is the complexity of the process: highly complex, high-value processes benefit most from DT adoption [323], but are more difficult to implement and manage.

- **Incremental and Hybrid Approaches:** In domains where both measurable data and process knowledge are available, a hybrid approach can be adopted. For example, in healthcare, the complexity of biological systems is high, but the potential benefits of DTs, from personalized medicine to hospital management, are substantial. Here, the key is to evaluate the expected benefits against the complexity and cost of DT implementation, often starting with a limited-scope DT and expanding as value is demonstrated [323].
- **"Chaotic" or Less-structured Domains:** Domains such as cities or large-scale infrastructure, which have evolved organically and lack centralized control, present unique challenges. For these, the discriminant is the availability of reliable measurements. If sufficient sensor data can be collected to create a valid initial representation, a passive DT can be established and then incrementally enriched with behavior and predictive capabilities.

8.3.1 Initial Criteria for DT Suitability

The following initial criteria can help the evaluation of DT adoption in new domains:

1. **Is the environment measurable and instrumented?**
2. **Is the process or system complex, high-value, or safety-critical?**
3. **Can the DT be built incrementally (bottom-up), or does it require a top-down, process-driven approach?**
4. **Is there potential for multiple applications and long-term value creation?**

These criteria, combined with rigorous cost-benefit analysis and stakeholder engagement, help ensure that DT investments are targeted where they deliver value.

8.4 Anticipated Evolution of DT Technologies

DT technologies are rapidly evolving, driven by advances in distributed computing, artificial intelligence (AI), IoT, and cloud-edge architectures. The modular DT system architecture illustrated in Figure 5.1 and the detailed DT engine representation of Figure 7.6 reflect the trend toward highly composable, scalable, and interoperable solutions. In this section, some key technological components and directions shaping the future of DTs are briefly discussed.

8.4.1 DT Platforms

Modern DT platforms provide the infrastructure for building, deploying, and operating DTs at scale. As illustrated in Figures 5.1 and 7.6, these platforms typically integrate data ingestion pipelines, real-time analytics, simulation engines, and user interface modules. Leading industry solutions are evolving toward supporting plug-and-play modules, microservices, and standardized APIs, which enable rapid integration with physical systems, external databases, and business processes.

Despite these advances, several challenges and opportunities for future evolution remain:

- **Flexible and On-demand AI Integration:** While AI is increasingly embedded in DT platforms, current solutions often require custom integration of specific algorithms for each application. Future platforms should provide a flexible AI layer, allowing users to select, configure, and run multiple AI techniques in parallel or on demand. This would enable continuous experimentation and exploitation of new AI advancements as they become available.
- **Support for AI Training and Validation During Operation:** Effective AI integration requires the ability to train and validate models concurrently with the normal operation of the DT. DT platforms must provide mechanisms for strict isolation and segregation of training and validation processes, ensuring that these activities do not disrupt real-time execution or compromise system stability (e.g., the Development Package represented in Section 6.1.2). At the same time, operational data should be accessible for use in training and validation, enabling models to learn from the most current and relevant system states (the possibility of federating different ContextBrokers). The availability of well-formed, reusable AI modules and pipelines, together with robust data management strategies, will significantly reduce development time, improve reliability, and support continuous improvement of AI-driven functionalities.
- **Streamlined Data Management and Injection Chains:** Data management, particularly the configuration of injection chains and data models, remains a significant bottleneck. The process of selecting, transforming, and injecting new data into the ContextBroker is time-consuming and error-prone. Future platforms should offer more automated and adaptive data ingestion pipelines, with tools for rapid data model definition, mapping, and validation.
- **Resilient and Distributed Context Management:** The ContextBroker is a critical component but also a potential deadlock. Evolving toward a more distributed and federated context management approach would enhance

resilience, scalability, and performance. Such an approach would also facilitate the simultaneous use of data for training, simulation, and operational decision-making (see Section 6.1.2).

- **Enhanced User Interaction and Visualization Integration:** As DTs become more complex and widely used, seamless integration with advanced visualization and user interaction modules is essential (see Figure 7.6). Platforms should support immersive, real-time dashboards, collaborative interfaces, and adaptive user experiences to maximize the value of DT insights for diverse stakeholders.

The next generation of DT platforms must go beyond baseline functionalities, embracing modularity, flexibility, and intelligence. They should enable on-demand integration of AI, automate and distribute data management, and provide rich, user-centric visualization capabilities. These evolutions will be key to supporting the growing scale, complexity, and diversity of DT applications.

8.4.2 DT Creation and Development

The development of a DT typically combines both top-down (model-driven) and bottom-up (data-driven) approaches. MBSE methodologies, such as SYSML, provide structural and behavior models that guide the initial design, while IoT-driven development leverages sensor data for real-time state estimation and monitoring. Agile and incremental development practices are increasingly adopted, enabling teams to start with a minimal viable DT and iteratively enrich its capabilities as requirements evolve.

Despite these advances, there is a clear need for improved development environments and methodologies tailored specifically to DTs. Even with the introduction of SYSML v. 2.0, the ecosystem lacks a consistent and mature set of tools that fully support the end-to-end DT development life cycle. Current environments often fall short in providing seamless integration between models, simulation, data management, and deployment.

Future DT development environments should address several key requirements:

- **End-to-end Methodological Support:** Methodologies should guide developers from ideation through deployment, supporting the entire life cycle of the DT. This includes requirements capture, model definition, simulation, integration, testing, and operational deployment.
- **Behavior Templates and Rich Data Models:** Access to a library of well-formed behavior templates, to be tailored to specific problem domains, would greatly accelerate development. These templates should be easily customizable and tightly integrated with a rich set of reusable data models, enabling rapid adaptation to new use cases. This will be complemented

by a rich set of well-designed but customizable microservices and different control paradigms (see Section 5.2) for facilitating the implementation of solutions.

- **Integrated Simulation and Scenario Analysis:** Creation and development environments should provide built-in simulation capabilities, allowing teams to explore different scenarios, validate design choices, and identify potential issues early in the life cycle. This simulation capability should also extend to runtime, supporting continuous validation and the ability to suggest improvements as new requirements or operational data emerge.
- **Extensible and Evolvable Behavior Models:** The environment should enable developers to operate on a single, coherent behavior model that can be incrementally extended and refined. This ensures that modifications to the model because of results of simulations or changes due to the introduction of new requirements are immediately available to the execution and simulation engines. In this way, the DT remains aligned with the evolving physical system and stakeholder needs.

The architecture of modern DT systems should integrate such advanced development environments (as discussed and shown in previous chapters and represented in Figure 8.1). By providing comprehensive methodological support, reusable templates, and robust simulation tools, future DT creation and development platforms will significantly reduce time-to-value and improve the quality and adaptability of DTs.

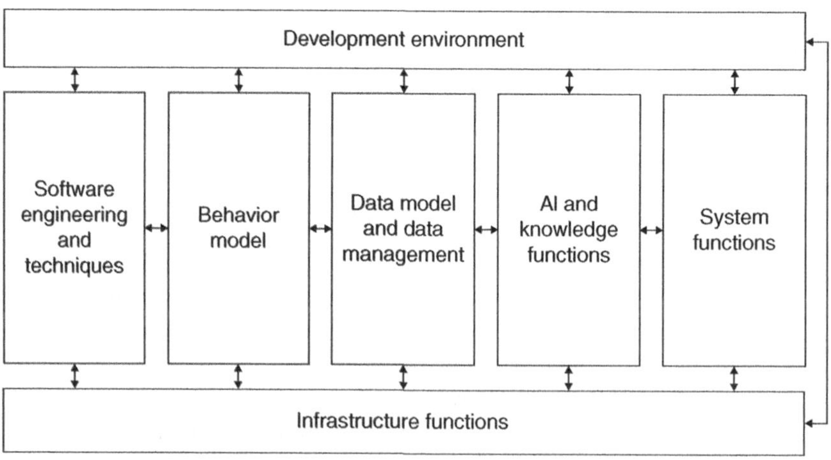

Figure 8.1 A possible high-level infrastructure for a DT development environment.

8.4.3 Decomposition of Modules

A key evolution in DT technology is the move away from monolithic systems toward architectures composed of fine-grained, reusable components. The presented DT modules, such as Visualization, API, Behavior, AI/GenAI, MetaModel, and Prescriptive/Prognostic components, are an initial step toward the identification and organization of component-based DT architecture and an integrated development environment. There is still a major need to further decompose them into smaller, independent, reusable services.

This fine-grained decomposition is essential for several reasons:

- **Reusability:** Smaller, well-defined components can be reused across different DT implementations, reducing development time and effort.
- **Parallel Development and Independent Scaling:** Teams can develop, test, and deploy components in parallel, and scale only those parts of the system that require additional resources.
- **Flexible Coordination Models:** Decomposition enables support for a variety of coordination models, including client-server, event-driven, and intelligent agent-based architectures. This flexibility allows DTs to adapt to different operational requirements and integration scenarios.
- **Integration with Development Environments:** The availability of fine-grained, ready-to-use functional components within DT development environments accelerates the creation and evolution of DTs. Developers can assemble new DT solutions by composing existing components, ensuring consistency and reducing errors.
- **Open and Evolvable Architectures:** Avoiding monolithic designs in favor of open, modular architectures ensures that DT systems remain adaptable to new requirements, technologies, and domains.

The ongoing decomposition of DT modules is therefore not just a technical trend, but a foundational requirement for building scalable, maintainable, and future-proof DT systems.

8.4.3.1 Coordination of Functionalities

Coordination of DT functions can be achieved using different interaction patterns besides simple chaining and client-server:

- **Agent–Supervisor Approach:** Hierarchical structures where high-level supervisors coordinate the actions of specialized agents (e.g., Figure 5.7).
- **Actor Model:** Fully decentralized, peer-to-peer architectures where equal actors communicate asynchronously, supporting scalability and resilience.

These paradigms can be chosen dynamically depending on the applications' needs and the envisaged deployment configuration of the solution.

8.4.4 Extensible Architecture

DT systems must be designed for extensibility, allowing new modules, data sources, and analytics to be integrated over time. Open architectures, standardized interfaces, and support for third-party extensions are essential for long-term sustainability and adaptability. The example of Interaction Manager discussed in Section 7.5.2 is indicative of the need to have an open and extensible platform able to accommodate new functionalities and components. The Special Function Module in the proposed architecture can be considered as a sort of placeholder for additional functions already integrated in the architectural framework.

8.4.5 Integrated Methodologies

Successful DT development demands integrated methodologies that bring together systems engineering, software development, and deep domain expertise. The complexity and modularity of modern DT architectures require a holistic approach that bridges the gap between conceptual modeling, data-driven design, and operational deployment.

While current methodologies such as MBSE provide strong support for structural and behavioral modeling, they could improve in several key areas when applied to DTs:

- **End-to-end Coverage:** MBSE and similar approaches often stop at the model level and do not extend seamlessly to code generation, deployment, or integration with real-time data streams. There is a pressing need for methodologies that support the full DT life cycle, from ideation and codesign (simultaneously developing the physical system and its DT) through to implementation and operation.
- **Codesign with Physical Systems:** Effective DT development should enable the concurrent design of the physical system and its digital representation. Current methodologies rarely support this level of integration, leading to misalignment and increased rework as systems evolve.
- **Data-driven Development Gaps:** The data-driven approach, while powerful, is even less mature in terms of methodological support. Much of the burden is left to individual designers and developers, with little guidance on best practices for data model selection, data pipeline construction, or integration with behavior models.
- **Life-cycle Integration:** There is a critical need for methodologies that integrate all phases of the DT life cycle, from requirements capture and design, through simulation and validation, to deployment, monitoring, and

evolution. This integration ensures traceability, consistency, and the ability to adapt as requirements and operational contexts change.

To address these gaps, modern DT environments need to offer better development environments with comprehensive toolchains that support modeling, simulation, code generation, deployment, and monitoring, enabling a smoother transition from design to operation. Well-formed templates, such as libraries of reusable blueprints for common DT patterns, which accelerate development, promote best practices, and ensure consistency across projects.

Looking forward, the integration of methodologies with advanced simulation, codesign capabilities, and life-cycle management tools will be instrumental in reducing development time, improving quality, and ensuring that DTs remain aligned with both the physical system and stakeholder needs throughout their life cycle.

8.4.6 AI Integration

AI is becoming a cornerstone of modern DT systems, enabling advanced analytics, pattern recognition, predictive maintenance, and autonomous decision-making. As depicted in Figure 7.6, the AI/GenAI module interacts with behavior, prescriptive, and visualization components to provide actionable insights and drive continuous system improvement. This module has to be designed to encompass and exploit a library of existing AI tools and algorithms. These may evolve and increase over time. Figure 8.2 depicts a generic set of AI functionalities needed to support a DT architecture.

In addition, more that one algorithm can be executed in parallel to provide the best results if combined. Behind this module, there needs to be a supporting continuous training and validation functionality that automatically updates and validates the used solution in such a way as to provide the system with always updated and well-trained algorithms.

Despite its growing importance, several challenges and opportunities characterize the current and future evolution of AI integration in DT platforms:

- **Lack of On-demand and Preintegrated AI Solutions:** Presently, the integration of AI into DTs is highly manual; designers must select, implement, and integrate algorithms themselves. There is a clear need for platforms to offer on-demand, preintegrated AI modules that can be easily configured and deployed as needed, reducing development time and lowering barriers to adoption.
- **Continuous Training and Validation on Operational Data:** Most current DT platforms do not support continuous training and validation of AI models using up-to-date operational data. To maintain accuracy and relevance, AI solutions should be capable of ongoing learning and adaptation, leveraging

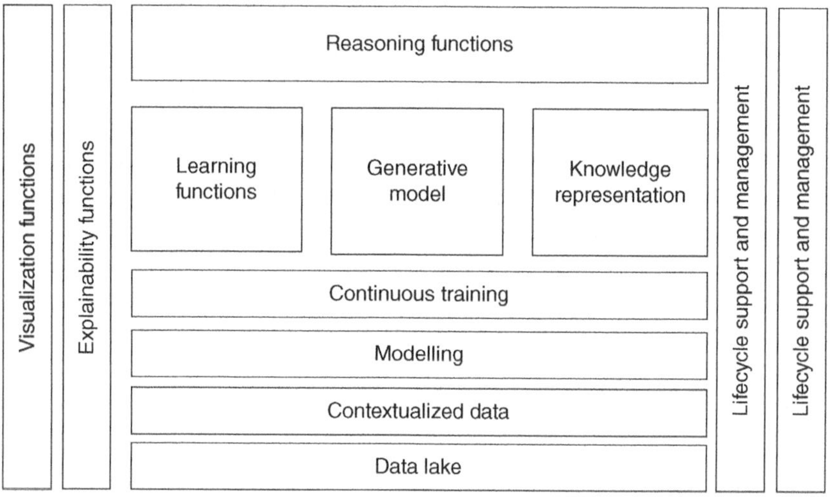

Figure 8.2 An AI infrastructure for the DT.

the latest data streams from the physical system. This requires robust data-sharing mechanisms and automated pipelines for retraining and validating models without disrupting normal DT operation.

- **Automated Operations and Life-cycle Management:** The process of updating, validating, and deploying AI algorithms should be fully automated and integrated into the DT operational life cycle. This includes automatic replacement of outdated models with newly validated ones, minimizing manual intervention and ensuring that the DT consistently delivers optimal performance.
- **Segregated Execution with Shared Data Access:** Training and validation processes must be isolated from real-time operations to avoid performance degradation or system instability. However, these processes should have access to the same operational data, enabling efficient learning while maintaining system integrity.
- **Parallel Execution and Ensemble Decision-making:** Advanced DT platforms should enable the parallel execution of multiple AI algorithms, allowing for ensemble approaches where results are merged to enhance decision accuracy and robustness. This capability supports experimentation and the adoption of best-performing models in real time.

Addressing these challenges will require the next generation of DT platforms to provide seamless, automated, and flexible AI integration, transforming AI from an add-on feature into a core, continuously evolving component of the DT ecosystem.

8.4.7 Testing and Assessment

Robust testing and assessment frameworks are critical for ensuring the reliability, safety, and performance of DT systems. The modular and distributed nature of modern DT architectures demands comprehensive strategies that go beyond traditional verification and validation.

Looking to the future, several key advancements are needed to address the increasing complexity and collaborative nature of DT development:

- **Multi-view and Multi-role Testing Support:** DT testing and validation must accommodate the needs of diverse teams, engineers, domain experts, operators, and business stakeholders, each with different perspectives and goals. Future frameworks should provide customizable testing environments that allow each role to define, execute, and assess test scenarios relevant to their objectives.
- **AI-driven and GenAI Testing Suites:** The development and integration of generative AI (GenAI) testing suites can significantly accelerate the creation of test cases, automate scenario generation, and enhance coverage. AI can assist in identifying edge cases, predicting failure modes, and continuously updating test suites based on operational feedback.
- **Automated Structural Analysis and Deployment Optimization:** Advanced testing and validation tools should be capable of generating detailed graphs that represent the structure and interdependencies of DT components. These graphs can be analyzed using AI-driven clustering algorithms to identify optimal deployment configurations, such as grouping highly interactive components within the same computational island to minimize latency and maximize performance [273].
- **Continuous Monitoring and Feedback Loops:** Testing and assessment should not be limited to predeployment phases. Continuous monitoring, real-time validation, and automated feedback loops are essential for detecting anomalies, validating updates, and ensuring ongoing alignment between the DT and its physical counterpart.

By embracing these advancements, future DT testing and assessment frameworks will enable faster, more reliable development cycles, support collaborative and role-specific validation, and optimize deployment strategies through intelligent analysis of system structure and behavior.

8.5 Improved Operations

As DT systems become more sophisticated and integral to the management of complex physical assets, the operational phase emerges as a critical component of their success. The proposed architecture, Figure 5.1, illustrates the interplay between DT modules, data management, and system engines, all of which must be supported by robust, future-oriented operational practices. Improved operations require a holistic approach that covers the entire DT life cycle, supports multi-skilled teams, and enables continuous development and adaptation.

8.5.1 Life-cycle Management

Modern DT operations must be guided by comprehensive life-cycle management frameworks that extend from initial deployment to dismissal. This includes:

- **Operational Guidelines for the Full Life Cycle:** The development of clear operational guidelines is essential to ensure consistency and quality throughout the DT life cycle. These guidelines should be open and accessible to multi-skilled teams, fostering collaboration among developers, domain experts, operators, and management.
- **Continuous Development and Update:** DT systems must support ongoing updates and enhancements, reflecting changes in the physical system, new requirements, and advances in technology. Continuous integration and delivery pipelines, as depicted in the system engine of the architecture diagrams, are vital for enabling rapid, low-risk evolution of DT functionalities.
- **Servitization Support:** DTs enable the servitization of physical systems, transforming products into ongoing services. This requires operational processes that support not only just the monitoring and optimization of assets, but also the delivery of value-added services throughout the asset's life cycle.
- **Mapping DT Development Processes to the Life Cycle:** It is crucial to map DT development and operational processes to the various phases of the physical system life-cycle, ensuring alignment and traceability from design to operation and beyond.
- **Long-term Commitment and Capability Assessment:** Organizations must commit to the long-term success of DT projects, ensuring that both internal and external capabilities are available to support ongoing development and operation. Regular assessments of skills, resources, and partnerships are necessary to sustain DT initiatives.

8.5.2 Managing the Switch of States

One of the challenging aspects of DT operations is managing transitions between different life-cycle phases or operational states. This includes:

- **Identification of Critical Transition Points:** Critical points often occur at phase transitions, such as moving from development to production or from production to operation. These transitions can introduce risks and require careful planning and mitigation strategies.

- **Strategies for Mitigating Transition Issues:** Operational guidelines should include strategies for mitigating issues at phase switches, such as robust versioning, rollback mechanisms, and staged deployments.
- **Coordination of Complex DTs in Multiple Phases:** In many cases, different parts of a complex DT may be in different life-cycle phases simultaneously (e.g., one module in operation while another is still in production or development). Effective coordination and synchronization mechanisms are needed to ensure consistency and reliability across the DT ecosystem.

8.5.3 Operations Tools

The complexity and criticality of DT operations demand advanced tools and methodologies:

- **Comprehensive Operations Tooling:** Tools are needed for monitoring, diagnostics, configuration management, security, and orchestration, as depicted in the system engine of the proposed architecture. These tools must support both routine operations and exceptional events, providing visibility and control over the entire DT system.
- **Support for Multi-skilled Teams:** Operations tools should be designed for use by multidisciplinary teams, providing role-based interfaces and customizable dashboards that cater to the needs of different stakeholders.
- **Methodological Integration:** The integration of operational tools with development environments and life-cycle management frameworks is essential for enabling seamless transitions between development, testing, deployment, and operation.
- **Capability and Resource Management:** Tools should also support the assessment and management of organizational capabilities and resources, helping to ensure that all necessary skills and assets are in place for successful DT operation.

In summary, improved operations for DT systems require a comprehensive, life-cycle-oriented approach that supports continuous development, robust state management, and the effective use of advanced tools and methodologies. These capabilities are essential for realizing the full potential of DTs in enabling adaptive, service-oriented, and resilient management of complex physical systems.

8.6 Interoperability and Standards

Interoperability and adherence to standards are relevant for the sustainable evolution of DT systems. As DT ecosystems grow in complexity, integrating diverse modules, external systems, and stakeholders, the ability to seamlessly exchange data, models, and operational commands becomes a critical enabler for scalability, flexibility, and long-term value creation. The proposed architecture highlights modularity and openness, but, obviously, several opportunities remain for further strengthening interoperability and standardization.

8.6.1 Standardization Efforts

Ongoing standardization initiatives, such as those led by ISO (e.g., ISO 23247 for manufacturing DTs), IEC, and industry consortia like the DT Consortium, are helping to define common frameworks, reference architectures, and vocabularies for DT systems. These efforts are essential for:

- Ensuring compatibility across platforms, vendors, and domains.
- Facilitating integration with legacy systems and future technologies.
- Enabling the exchange of models, data, and control flows between DTs and external systems.

A forward-looking improvement for the proposed architecture is the explicit alignment of each module, especially those in the DT Engine and Data Management layers, with emerging standards. This would support plug-and-play extensibility and foster a rich ecosystem of reusable DT components.

8.6.2 Open APIs and Data Models

Open APIs are the backbone of interoperability in DT systems. While the current architecture provides APIs for integration with external systems, a next-generation approach should extend API coverage to include comprehensive operational functions, such as life-cycle management, monitoring, and orchestration, enabling external tools and stakeholders to interact with the DT not only just for data access but also for operational control.

Similarly, data models should not only represent the real-time state and structure of the physical system, but also encapsulate life-cycle information, versioning, and operational metadata. Standardized, open data models would facilitate:

- Seamless migration and synchronization of DTs across platforms and environments.
- Efficient mapping of DT processes to different life-cycle phases, supporting continuous evolution and traceability.
- Enhanced support for servitization and multi-stakeholder collaboration.

Future improvements to the architecture could include:

- Embedding standardized API endpoints for both operational and life-cycle management functions in the API module.

- Adopting or contributing to open data model standards that capture not only system state but also life cycle and operational context.
- Ensuring that the ContextBroker and Data Management segments are designed for easy adaptation to evolving standards and interoperability requirements.

To fully realize the promise of interoperable DT systems, future architectures should:

- Embrace dynamic discovery and negotiation of capabilities between DT modules and external systems.
- Support automated compliance checking with relevant standards.
- Foster an open ecosystem where third-party modules and services can be seamlessly integrated, upgraded, or replaced.

By prioritizing interoperability and standards, DT architectures will be better positioned to support complex, distributed, and collaborative applications-ensuring adaptability, resilience, and long-term sustainability in rapidly evolving digital ecosystems.

8.7 Ethical, Privacy, and Trust Considerations in DT Systems

DT systems are becoming increasingly sophisticated and pervasive, demanding careful attention to ethical concerns, data privacy, and trust—especially when these systems interact with or represent human users. The modular architecture inherent in DTs creates several points at which sensitive data may be accessed, processed, or shared. This complexity underscores the necessity for robust and comprehensive frameworks that secure both the technical infrastructure and its human implications.

DTs often rely on the collection and processing of personal data, such as behavior patterns, preferences, and even health information—a dependency clearly observed in sectors like e-health, smart tourism, and personalized services. In such areas, the DT may require extensive access to personal information, thereby elevating the risks of unauthorized access, misuse, or unintended disclosure. One promising strategy to mitigate these risks is to empower users by allowing them to decide which data to disclose and under what conditions, as discussed in [324]. Adhering to strict principles of data minimization and purpose limitation, where only the data necessary for DT operation is collected, is essential. Complementing these policies with strong technical safeguards, including encryption, access control, and anonymization, is equally important, particularly in critical components like the data management and system engine modules. Ensuring compliance with data protection regulations, such as the GDPR, further reinforces these security measures across different jurisdictions.

Ethical challenges arise prominently when DTs serve in roles that involve human representation or decision-making. Consider, for instance, cultural heritage applications where the digital portrayal of artifacts, sites, or historical narratives may be influenced by national, cultural, or gender perspectives, thereby risking bias and misrepresentation. To address these issues, AI modules within DTs must be engineered to promote fairness and avoid discrimination; doing so ensures that representations and recommendations are both equitable and respectful of diverse viewpoints. Equally important is fostering transparency and explainability so that users and stakeholders can understand the rationale behind AI-driven decisions, a substantial factor when such decisions materially affect individuals or communities. Ultimately, responsible AI deployment should incorporate oversight mechanisms to prevent unintended outcomes, particularly in sensitive contexts.

As DT systems evolve toward greater autonomy, capable of making independent decisions and taking actions without constant human oversight, establishing trust grows ever more important. Stakeholders must be confident that these automated systems are reliable, secure, and aligned with shared human values. Trust can be nurtured by implementing robust validation processes that delineate when human intervention is required, especially in novel or critical scenarios, and then gradually reducing oversight as confidence in automated decisions solidifies. Moreover, maintaining comprehensive logs of decisions and actions enhances auditability and accountability, which facilitates thorough post-analysis if issues arise. Trust, inherently dynamic, is sustained through continuous monitoring, validation, and transparent communication with all stakeholders.

In summary, addressing the ethical, privacy, and trust dimensions is essential to the responsible design and operation of DT systems. By embedding privacy-by-design principles, ethical AI standards, and consistent trust-building mechanisms into the DT architecture, these systems can deliver significant benefits while safeguarding the rights and values of all stakeholders.

8.8 Human-in-the-loop and User Experience

DT systems are not only technical constructs but also socio-technical systems where human users play a pivotal role. The future evolution of DTs will increasingly emphasize human-in-the-loop paradigms, user-centric design, and advanced visualization to ensure usability, trust, and acceptance.

8.8.1 User-centric Design

A user-centric approach is essential for DT adoption and effectiveness. Future DT architectures should embed explainability features, enabling users to understand, interrogate, and trust the system's recommendations and decisions. This is particularly important when DTs incorporate AI/GenAI and prescriptive modules, which must provide transparent reasoning for their outputs and recommendations. In addition, behavior modeling within DTs should consider human habits, cognitive limitations, and regulatory requirements (e.g., limiting screen time or adapting to accessibility needs), ensuring that the system remains aligned with user well-being and legal frameworks.

8.8.2 Visualization and Immersive Interfaces

Advanced visualization and immersive interfaces translate complex system states and predictions into actionable insights for diverse stakeholders. Future DT platforms will integrate real-time dashboards, 3D/AR/VR environments, and collaborative tools, allowing users to interact intuitively with both the physical and digital worlds. Such interfaces not only enhance situational awareness but also support effective decision-making and foster greater engagement across multidisciplinary teams. The visualization and interaction managers as well as the behavior module will have an impact on the human acceptance and usage of the DT solutions. At the same time, the user reactions will be used to mold and smooth the way the DT will interact with humans.

8.9 Sustainability and Societal Impact

The deployment of DTs brings both opportunities and responsibilities in terms of sustainability and societal impact. As resource-intensive projects, DTs must be evaluated for their net contribution to sustainable development and social good.

8.9.1 DTs for Sustainable Development

While DT development can be costly, their potential to drive sustainability is significant, especially in domains such as smart cities, energy management, and network optimization. For example, Network DTs can help reduce the carbon footprint of data centers by enabling more efficient resource allocation and predictive maintenance. In urban contexts, DTs can support the optimization of transportation, energy use, and infrastructure planning, directly contributing to environmental and economic sustainability.

8.9.2 Societal Impact and Digital Inclusion

The societal impact of DTs extends beyond technical efficiency. The acceptability of DTs, especially those that represent or interact with humans, such as Human DTs, can encounter resistance due to concerns about privacy, autonomy, and representation. Ensuring digital inclusion requires that DT systems are accessible, transparent, and respectful of diverse user needs and societal values. Proactive engagement with stakeholders, clear communication of benefits and risks, and the incorporation of ethical guidelines are essential for fostering trust and maximizing positive societal outcomes.

8.10 Future Steps

This work has explored the evolution, challenges, and opportunities in DT technologies, with particular attention to architecture, development methodologies, operations, interoperability, ethics, and societal impact. The architecture presented in Figure 5.1 exemplifies the inherent complexity of DT system development and integration.

While the proposed architecture is primarily intended as an explicative and demonstrative model, it offers guidelines for addressing the technical and organizational demands of next-generation DTs. In particular, it highlights the importance of fostering openness and collaboration, as the design encourages broad participation from both users and developers by supporting modularity, extensibility, and seamless integration with external systems and stakeholders. Equally significant is the explicit integration of AI and behavioral modeling. By coupling AI/GenAI modules directly with adaptable behavior models, the architecture enables advanced analytics, improved explainability, and adaptive decision-making within the DT engine.

The model also accommodates both top-down and bottom-up approaches, allowing for model-driven as well as data-driven development. This flexibility facilitates incremental and agile DT creation that can adapt to changing requirements. In addition, the inclusion of dedicated modules for configuration, security, and orchestration ensures comprehensive life cycle and operations management, which is vital for continuous development, deployment, and adaptation throughout the DT life-cycle. Attention to a user-centric design which integrates human-in-the-loop paradigms, explainability, and ethical considerations, will further position the architecture for responsible and inclusive deployment in diverse domains.

Compared to several existing DT frameworks and platforms, this architecture distinguishes itself by aiming at a modular decomposition into fine-grained identification of reusable components, and providing templates and libraries of well-formed components designed to democratize DT solution development. It explicitly has the goal to integrate operational and life-cycle management as first-class concerns and places a strong emphasis on interoperability through the use of open APIs and extensible data models that include life-cycle and operational metadata. Moreover, the architecture is prepared for AI-driven automation, continuous validation, and the design of explainable user interfaces.

Future consolidation of such architectures will require ongoing research and collaboration across disciplines, the development of comprehensive DT development environments, and the adoption of open standards and best practices. By addressing these challenges, the DT community can accelerate the creation of sustainable, trustworthy, and impactful DT systems for the future.

A

Listings and Details

This chapter is intended for readers interested in technical details. It complements other chapters by providing listings and a more detailed description of specific implementation-related aspects. However, it does not aim to present a complete software design for a DT.

A.1 Descriptive Modeling

This section comprises listings and details from Section 3.

A.1.1 Data Model and Application Programming Interfaces

APIs can be differentiated in terms of goals, intent, and accessibility to better meet stakeholders' needs. Different types are listed in the following:

1. **Infrastructure API:**
   Purpose: Managing the life cycles of DT or their components, allowing the creation, deletion, and configuration of instances of DT elements (controllers, sensors, and actuators) and their relationships.

   Endpoints:
   - `POST /twins/{twinType}`: Creates a new twin instance (e.g., `POST /twins/controller`).
   - `GET /twins/{twinId}/{metadata}`: Retrieves metadata about a specific twin, including its type, properties, and relationships.
   - `DELETE /twins/{twinId}`: Deletes a twin instance.

- `PUT /twins/{twinId}/relationships/{relationshipName}`: Creates or updates a relationship between twins.
- `DELETE /twins/{twinId}/relationships/{relationshipName}`: Deletes a relationship.

Security Considerations: Role-based access control (RBAC) could be established to clearly identify who can create, delete, or modify twins and relationships. This means implementing a system where users are assigned roles that grant specific permissions to interact with the infrastructure API. The API checks and enforces these permissions to ensure only authorized users can perform specific actions on DTs and their relationships.

2. **Data Ingestion API:**
Purpose: Used for initialization of components and elements and for correction of a DT's state when needed or under the supervision of system managers.

Endpoints:
- `PUT /twins/{twinId}/{properties}`: Sets multiple property values on a twin (e.g., name, location).
- `PUT /twins/{twinId}/properties/{propertyName}`: Sets a single property value on a twin.

Example Request (PUT /twins/controller/properties):

```
{
 "name": "Living Room Controller",
 "location": "Living Room"
}
```

Security Considerations: This operation needs security checks to avoid possible malfunctions or malicious intentions. Examples of checks: Input validation to prevent injection attacks; rate limiting to prevent abuse; auditing of all data ingestion operations.

3. **Streaming API:**
Purpose: Managing continuous or high-frequency data streams feeding into the twin. It includes data formatting and validation, ensuring data is usable by components. It then feeds the data into Context Broker, either formatting the message to match Context Broker requirements, or receiving the streams as one of its subscribers.

Endpoints: (Typically uses protocols like MQTT, WebSockets, or gRPC)
- `/streams/{streamId}`: An endpoint to which sensors or other data sources push data. Clients subscribe to specific data streams to receive updates.

Example (MQTT):

- Topic: `home/controller/temperature`
- Payload: `23.5`

Security Considerations: To make this arrangement effective, some checks are to be performed: authentication and authorization for data streams; encryption of data in transit; DoS protection.

Implementation Note: There are two primary approaches for implementing the streaming API's interaction with the Context Broker:

(a) **Streaming API Pushes to Context Broker:** The `/streams/{streamId}` endpoint receives raw data, performs formatting and validation, and then pushes the data to the Context Broker using its API (e.g., NGSI).

(b) **Context Broker Subscribes Directly:** The Context Broker subscribes directly to the data streams (e.g., via MQTT or WebSockets). The Context Broker handles data formatting and storage.

4. **Event API:**

Purpose: Handling discrete, significant events that occur within the system or are users generated.

Endpoints:

- `POST /events/{eventType}`: Publishes a new event.
- `GET /events?from={timestamp}&to={timestamp}`: retrieves events from a specified timestamp
- `GET /events/{eventID}`: Get specified event (Typically uses Webhooks or Server-Sent events for subscriptions)

Example Request (POST /events/doorOpen):

```
{
 "controllerId": "controller001",
 "timestamp": "2025-04-27T14:00:00Z"
}
```

Security Considerations: Event generation should be authorized for avoiding security issues, for instance, authentication and authorization for event publishing. This feature can be managed using tokens. Clients must present a valid access token with the appropriate scopes to publish events. The event API validates the token to ensure that the client has the necessary permissions.

5. **Mediation API:**
   Purpose: Collecting, transforming, enriching, and validating data before they are used to update the twin's state.

   Endpoints: (This API is typically internal to the DT platform, e.g., between endpoints and the ContextBroker)
   - Functions or services that collect and transform data from raw sensor readings to structured data model elements.
   - Validation rules to ensure data quality and consistency.
   - Enrichment services that add metadata (e.g., location, unit of measurement) to the data.

   Security Considerations: Some security checks could comprise: checks of sensor's identity; code reviews to ensure the transformations are secure and do not introduce vulnerabilities; regular updates to data validation rules.
6. **Security API:**
   Purpose: Managing authentication, authorization, and access control for the entire DT system.

   Endpoints:
   - `POST /auth/token`: Obtains an access token (e.g., using OAuth 2.0).
   - `POST /auth/refresh`: Refreshes an access token.
   - `GET /users/{userId}/permissions`: Retrieves the permissions for a specific user.
   - `PUT /roles/{roleId}/permissions`: Updates the permissions for a specific role.

   Example Request (POST /auth/token):

   ```
   grant_type=password&username=john.doe&password=secret
   ```

   Response (JSON):

   ```
   {
    "access_token": "...",
    "token_type": "Bearer",
    "expires_in": 3600
   }
   ```

   Security Considerations: Strong authentication mechanisms (e.g., multi-factor authentication); least privilege principle; regular security audits; encryption of sensitive data (e.g., passwords).

A.1.1.1 Example of the Relationship Between Data Model and API

The DT embodies a smart home controller orchestrating various sensors and actuators. To simplify the examples, a reduced data model containing only the attributes relevant to the example scenarios is depicted:

Listing A.1: JSON Data Model

```
{
        "controllerId": "controller001",
        "temperature": {
                "value": 23.5,
                "unit": "Celsius",
                "timestamp": "2025-04-27T13:00:00Z"
        },
        "heatingThreshold": 20.0,
        "actuators": [
        {
                "actuatorId": "thermostat001",
                "actuatorType": "thermostat",
                "targetTemperature": 22.0
        }
        ],
        "sensors": [
        {
                "sensorId": "tempSensor001",
                "sensorType": "temperature",
                "status": "active"
        }
        ]
}
```

Scenario 1: Temperature Threshold Exceeded

1. **Event Generation (Sensor):** The `tempSensor001` detects that the `temperature.value` has exceeded a predefined threshold (e.g., 28 °C).
2. **Event API (Publish):** The sensor publishes a `temperatureExceeded` event via the Event API:

```
POST /events/temperatureExceeded
     {
     "controllerId": "controller001",
     "sensorId": "tempSensor001",
     "temperature": 28.5,
     "timestamp": "2025-04-27T15:00:00Z"
     }
```

3. **Controller Reaction (Event Handler):** The `controller001` receives the `temperatureExceeded` event.
4. **Action (Controller):** The controller uses the `actuators` information (specifically, the `thermostat001`) from its data model to take action. It calls the streaming API to lower the `targetTemperature` of the thermostat:

```
PUT /twins/thermostat001/properties/targetTemperature
     {
     "targetTemperature": 22.0
     }
```

   The Context Broker is updated with the new value for `targetTemperature`.

Scenario 2: User Sets Temperature Threshold

1. **User Action:** A user wants to set the temperature threshold for heating to 18 °C.
2. **API Call (Data Ingestion API):** The user interface makes a call to the data ingestion API to update the `heatingThreshold` property on the `controller001`:

```
PUT /twins/controller001/properties/heatingThreshold
     {
     "heatingThreshold": 18.0
     }
```

3. **Context Broker Update:** The Context Broker is updated with the new `heatingThreshold` value for `controller001`.
4. **Controller Logic:** The controller uses the `heatingThreshold` property from its data model to determine when to activate the heating system.

These examples illustrate how the attributes defined in the data model (e.g., `temperature`, `targetTemperature`, `heatingThreshold`) are used to facilitate interaction between sensors, controllers, users, and the Context Broker through the defined APIs.

A.1.1.2 Role of the ContextBroker

The ContextBroker plays a central role in this home automation DT:

- **Data Storage:** It stores the current state of all entities (controllers, sensors, and actuators).
- **Data Abstraction:** Provides a uniform API to access and update entity data, regardless of the underlying data sources.

- **Real-time Updates:** Publishes updates (context changes) to subscribed components, enabling real-time reactivity.
- **Complex Queries:** Supports complex queries across multiple entities.
- **Relationship with APIs:**
  - *Streaming API:* Feeds continuous sensor data to the ContextBroker.
  - *Event API:* Alerts the ContextBroker about important occurrences.
  - *Data Ingestion API:* Initializes or corrects the state of the twin within the ContextBroker.
  - *Mediation API:* Ensures data is properly formatted before being sent to the ContextBroker.

A.1.2 Extending the Data Model to Fit Stakeholder Needs

This example refers to Section 3.6. It is extending the mapping of requirements to stakeholders.

A.1.2.1 Stakeholder 2: Tenant/User (Focus: Comfort and Control)

Stakeholder Need (Requirement): The tenant needs to understand the current environmental conditions and, where permitted, adjust the target temperature for their comfort. They might also provide feedback on their perceived comfort level.

Extension to the Requirements Set Considering Users' Views:

- `REQ-USER-001 (Environmental Monitoring): The system shall provide the current temperature within the controlled environment.`
- `REQ-USER-002 (Adjustable Setpoint): The system shall allow the user to adjust the targetTemperature of the Thermostat within defined constraints.`
- `REQ-USER-003 (Comfort Feedback): The system may allow the user to provide feedback on their perceived comfortLevel.`

User Constraints:

- `CON-TEMP-001 (Temperature Limits): The targetTemperature set by the user shall be within the range of 18°C to 22°C.`

Also in this case, a few extensions to the data model are needed. **NGSI-LD Extensions (aligning with Requirements and Constraints):**

- Metadata on `targetTemperature` (Property within `actuators` Relationship): Provides additional information (**Metadata**) related to the `targetTemperature` property, addressing `REQ-USER-002` and potentially `CON-TEMP-001`. `description`: "Desired temperature set by the system or user.", `editableByUser: true`, `constraint` (Potential Metadata): `minTemperature`: 18.0, `maxTemperature`: 22.0.
- `comfortLevel` (Property): Represents a subjective **Property** providing user feedback, addressing `REQ-USER-003`. Value: Textual (e.g., "comfortable", "too warm", "too cold"), `observedAt`: Timestamp, Metadata (Context): `userFeedback`: "Acceptable".
- `userSetPoint` (Property): Represents a **Property** reflecting the user's desired setting, related to `REQ-USER-002`. Value: Numeric (e.g., 21.0), Unit: `unitCode`: "CEL", `observedAt`: Timestamp, Metadata (Context): `source`: "userInterface".

A.2 Behavior Modeling

This section comprises listings and details from Section 4.

A.2.1 NGSI-LD Data Model for Traffic Light Behavior

To represent the behavior of the traffic light system described by the state machine of Figure 4.2 and the activity diagram of Figure 4.6, the following NGSI-LD data model can be considered. This model includes entities for the controller and traffic light actuator, capturing their states and properties relevant to the system's operation. The traffic light controller is represented in Listing A.2, and the Traffic Light in Listing A.3.

Listing A.2: NGSI-LD Entity: TrafficLightController

```
{
        "id": "urn:ngsi-ld:TrafficLightController:
            controller001",
        "type": "Controller",
        "currentTime": {
                "type": "Property",
                "value": "<current ISO 8601 timestamp>"
        },
        "dayOfWeek": {
                "type": "Property",
                "value": "<current day of the week>"
        },
```

```
        "timeContext": {
                "type": "Property",
                "value": "Day",
                "metadata": {
                        "description": "Indicates the
                            current time context (Day,
                            Night, Sunday)."
                }
        },
        "cycleTimer": {
                "type": "Property",
                "value": "<remaining time in seconds>",
                "metadata": {
                        "unitCode": "s"
                }
        },
        "controls": {
                "type": "Relationship",
                "object": "urn:ngsi-ld:TrafficLight:
                    trafficlight001"
        }
}
```

The `TrafficLightController` entity manages the overall logic of the traffic light. It tracks the `currentTime` and `dayOfWeek` to determine the `timeContext`, which influences the traffic light's state transitions. The `cycleTimer` property indicates the remaining time in the current light state. The `control` relationship links the controller to the specific `TrafficLight` actuator it manages.

Listing A.3: NGSI-LD Entity: TrafficLight

```
{
        "id": "urn:ngsi-ld:TrafficLight:trafficlight001",
        "type": "Actuator",
        "currentState": {
                "type": "Property",
                "value": "Green",
                "metadata": {
                        "description": "The current color
                            being displayed (Green, Yellow,
                             Red, BlinkingYellow)."
                }
        },
        "nextState": {
                "type": "Property",
                "value": "Yellow",
                "metadata": {
                        "description": "The next state the
                            traffic light will transition
                            to."
                }
```

```
        },
        "transitionTimerDuration": {
            "type": "Property",
            "value": "<duration in seconds>",
            "metadata": {
                "unitCode": "s"
            }
        }
    }
```

The `TrafficLight` entity represents the physical traffic light. Its `currentState` indicates the currently active color. The `nextState` property can be used for predictive purposes. The `transitionTimerDuration` property stores the duration for the current state, corresponding to the timing values (Tg, Ty, Tr) in the state machine.

This NGSI-LD data model provides a structured way to represent the state and behavior of the traffic light system, enabling situation-aware management and potential integration with other smart city applications.

References

1 INCOSE. *INCOSE Systems Engineering Handbook*. John Wiley & Sons, 2023.
2 Jerome Hugues, Anton Hristosov, John J Hudak, and Joe Yankel. TwinOps-DevOps meets model-based engineering and digital twins for the engineering of CPS. In *Proceedings of the 23rd ACM/IEEE International Conference on Model Driven Engineering Languages and Systems: Companion Proceedings*, pages 1–5, 2020.
3 Michael Grieves and John Vickers. Digital twin: mitigating unpredictable, undesirable emergent behavior in complex systems. In Franz-Josef Kahlen, Shannon Flumerfelt, and Anabela Alves, editors, *Transdisciplinary Perspectives on Complex Systems: New Findings and Approaches*, pages 85–113. Springer Cham, 2017.
4 Michael W Grieves. *Digital Twins: Past, Present, and Future*, pages 97–121. Springer International Publishing, 2023. ISBN 978-3-031-21343-4. https://doi.org/10.1007/978-3-031-21343-4_4.
5 Barbara Rita Barricelli, Elena Casiraghi, and Daniela Fogli. A survey on digital twin: definitions, characteristics, applications, and design implications. *IEEE Access*, 7:167653–167671, 2019.
6 Noel Crespi, Adam Drobot, and Roberto Minerva, editors. *The Digital Twin*. Springer, 2023.
7 Roberto Minerva, Gyu Myoung Lee, and Noel Crespi. Digital twin in the IoT context: a survey on technical features, scenarios, and architectural models. *Proceedings of the IEEE*, 108(10):1785–1824, 2020.

8 International Organization for Standardization (ISO). ISO 23247: digital twin framework for manufacturing. Technical report, International Organization for Standardization (ISO), 2021. Defines digital twin model types, fidelity, and data synchronization. https://www.iso.org/standard/79660.html

9 W3C Digital Twin Community Group. Digital twin conceptual and data standards. https://www.w3.org/community/agentprotocol/, 2023. Developing open standards for digital twin interoperability.

10 Tianle Zhang, Xiangtao Liu, Zongwei Luo, Fuqiang Dong, and Yu Jiang. Time series behavior modeling with digital twin for internet of vehicles. *EURASIP Journal on Wireless Communications and Networking*, 2019:1–11, 2019.

11 Peter Augustine. Chapter four - The industry use cases for the digital twin idea. In Pethuru Raj and Preetha Evangeline, editors, *The Digital Twin Paradigm for Smarter Systems and Environments: The Industry Use Cases*, volume 117 of *Advances in Computers*, pages 79–105. Elsevier, 2020. https://doi.org/10.1016/bs.adcom.2019.10.008.

12 Larry Schmitt and David Copps. The business of digital twins. In *The Digital Twin*, pages 21–63. Springer, 2023.

13 Noel Crespi, Adam T Drobot, and Roberto Minerva. *The Digital Twin in Action and Directions for the Future*, pages 1201–1217. Springer International Publishing, Cham, 2023. ISBN 978-3-031-21343-4. https://doi.org/10.1007/978-3-031-21343-4_38.

14 Marc Andreessen. Why software is eating the world. *The Wall Street Journal*, 8:20, 2011.

15 Lev Manovich. *Software Takes Command*. Bloomsbury Academic, 2013.

16 Siemens AG. Digital Twin — Siemens Software. https://www.sw.siemens.com/en-US/technology/digital-twin/, 2025. [Online; accessed September 23, 2025].

17 Noel Crespi, Adam T Drobot, and Roberto Minerva. The digital twin: What and why? In *The Digital Twin*, pages 3–20. Springer, 2023.

18 Adil Rasheed, Omer San, and Trond Kvamsdal. Digital twin: values, challenges and enablers from a modeling perspective. *IEEE Access*, 8:21980–22012, 2020.

19 Concetta Semeraro, Mario Lezoche, Hervé Panetto, and Michele Dassisti. Digital twin paradigm: a systematic literature review. *Computers in Industry*, 130:103469, 2021.

20 Werner Kritzinger, Matthias Karner, Georg Traar, Jan Henjes, and Wilfried Sihn. Digital twin in manufacturing: a categorical literature review and classification. *IFAC-PapersOnLine*, 51(11):1016–1022, 2018.

21 Capstera. Digital twin definition. https://www.capstera.com/glossary/digital-twin/, 2023.

22 Paolo Bellavista, Nicola Bicocchi, Mattia Fogli, Carlo Giannelli, Marco Mamei, and Marco Picone. Measuring digital twin entanglement in industrial Internet of Things. In *ICC 2023-IEEE International Conference on Communications*, pages 5897–5903. IEEE, 2023.

23 Paolo Bellavista, Nicola Bicocchi, Mattia Fogli, Carlo Giannelli, Marco Mamei, and Marco Picone. ODTE: a metric for digital twin entanglement. *IEEE Open Journal of the Communications Society*, 5:2377–2390, 2024.

24 Marco Picone, Stefano Mariani, Roberto Cavicchioli, Paolo Burgio, and Arslane Hamza Cherif. The degree of entanglement: cyber-physical awareness in digital twin applications. In *2024 IEEE 21st Consumer Communications & Networking Conference (CCNC)*, pages 736–744. IEEE, 2024.

25 Thomas Bergs, Sascha Gierlings, Thomas Auerbach, Andreas Klink, Daniel Schraknepper, and Thorsten Augspurger. The concept of digital twin and digital shadow in manufacturing. *Procedia CIRP*, 101:81–84, 2021.

26 Samad ME Sepasgozar. Differentiating digital twin from digital shadow: elucidating a paradigm shift to expedite a smart, sustainable built environment. *Buildings*, 11(4):151, 2021.

27 Roberto Minerva, Noel Crespi, Reza Farahbakhsh, and Faraz M Awan. Artificial intelligence and the digital twin: An essential combination. In *The Digital Twin*, pages 299–336. Springer, 2023.

28 Ralph Barthel, Kerstin Leder Mackley, Andrew Hudson-Smith, Angelina Karpovich, Martin De Jode, and Chris Speed. An internet of old things as an augmented memory system. *Personal and Ubiquitous Computing*, 17:321–333, 2013.

29 Corina Maiwald. With spime to circular service design: introducing service design to an IoT platform provider's delivery process. 2018. https://files01.core.ac.uk/download/pdf/161431389.pdf

30 B Sterling. The internet of things: what is a spime and why is it useful. *Google Tech Talk*, 2007.

31 Bruce Sterling. *Shaping Things*. The MIT Press, Cambridge, 2005.

32 Abdullah Aziz, Shailesh Singh Chouhan, Olov Schelén, and Ulf Bodin. Distributed digital twins as proxies-unlocking composability and flexibility for purpose-oriented digital twins. *IEEE Access*, 11:137577–137593, 2023.

33 Prasad Talasila, Cláudio Gomes, Lars B Vosteen, Hannes Iven, Martin Leucker, Santiago Gil, Peter H Mikkelsen, Eduard Kamburjan, and Peter G Larsen. Composable digital twins on digital twin as a service platform. *Simulation*, 101(3):287–311, 2025.

34 Ljiljana Stojanovic, Thomas Usländer, Friedrich Volz, Christian Weißenbacher, Jens Müller, Michael Jacoby, and Tino Bischoff. Methodology and tools for digital twin management—the FA^{3}ST approach. *IoT*, 2(4):717–740, 2021.

35 Jim Scheibmeir and Yashwant Malaiya. An API development model for digital twins. In *2019 IEEE 19th International Conference on Software Quality, Reliability and Security Companion (QRS-C)*, pages 518–519. IEEE, 2019.

36 Boschert Stefan and Rosen Roland. Digital twin—the simulation aspect. In Hehenberger Peter and Bradley David, editors, *Mechatronic Futures: Challenges and Solutions for Mechatronic Systems and Their Designers*, pages 59–74. Springer, Cham, 2016. https://doi.org/10.1007/978-3-319-32156-1_5.

37 Kazuma Kobayashi and Syed Bahauddin Alam. Explainable, interpretable, and trustworthy AI for an intelligent digital twin: a case study on remaining useful life. *Engineering Applications of Artificial Intelligence*, 129:107620, 2024.

38 Roberto Minerva. *Digital Twin and the Information Problem*. PhD thesis, Sorbonne University, 2024.

39 David Jones, Chris Snider, Aydin Nassehi, Jason Yon, and Ben Hicks. Characterising the digital twin: a systematic literature review. *CIRP Journal of Manufacturing Science and Technology*, 29:36–52, 2020.

40 Christian Kowalkowski, Heiko Gebauer, Bart Kamp, and Glenn Parry. Servitization and deservitization: overview, concepts, and definitions. *Industrial Marketing Management*, 60:4–10, 2017.

41 Wolfgang Ulaga and Christian Kowalkowski. Servitization: a state-of-the-art overview and future directions. In Edvardsson Bo and Tronvoll Bård. *The Palgrave Handbook of Service Management*, pages 169–200, 2022.

42 Junaid Ahmed. Digital twin, servitization, circular economy, and lean manufacturing: a step toward sustainability. In *Human Factors in Engineering*, pages 135–154. CRC Press, 2023.

43 Jürg Meierhofer, Shaun West, Mario Rapaccini, and Cosimo Barbieri. The digital twin as a service enabler: from the service ecosystem to the simulation model. In *Exploring Service Science: 10th International Conference, IESS 2020,* Porto, Portugal, February 5–7, 2020, *Proceedings 10*, pages 347–359. Springer, 2020.

44 Shaun West, Jürg Meierhofer, Oliver Stoll, and Lukas Schweiger. Value propositions enabled by digital twins in the context of servitization. In *Advanced Services for Sustainability and Growth*, page 152, 2020.

45 Ibrahim A Halloun. *Modeling Theory in Science Education*, volume 24. Springer Science & Business Media, 2007.

46 Barbara E Hof. The cybernetic "general model theory": unifying science or epistemic change? *Perspectives on Science*, 26(1):76–96, 2018.

47 Herbert Stachowiak. *General Model Theory*. Springer, 1973.

48 Katerina Lepenioti, Alexandros Bousdekis, Dimitris Apostolou, and Gregoris Mentzas. Prescriptive analytics: a survey of approaches and methods. In *Business Information Systems Workshops: BIS 2018 International Workshops,* Berlin, Germany, July 18–20, 2018, Revised Papers 21, pages 449–460. Springer, 2019.

49 Debashish Roy, Rajeev Srivastava, Mansi Jat, and Mustafa Said Karaca. A complete overview of analytics techniques: Descriptive, predictive, and prescriptive. In *Decision Intelligence Analytics and the Implementation of Strategic Business Management*, pages 15–30, 2022.

50 Ashish K Sharma, Durgesh M Sharma, Neha Purohit, Saroja Kumar Rout, and Sangita A Sharma. Analytics techniques: Descriptive analytics, predictive analytics, and prescriptive analytics. In *Decision Intelligence Analytics and the Implementation of Strategic Business Management*, pages 1–14. Springer 2022.

51 Rogardt Heldal, Patrizio Pelliccione, Ulf Eliasson, Jonn Lantz, Jesper Derehag, and Jon Whittle. Descriptive vs prescriptive models in industry. In *Proceedings of the ACM/IEEE 19th International Conference on Model Driven Engineering Languages and Systems*, pages 216–226, 2016.

52 Fei Tao, Bin Xiao, Qinglin Qi, Jiangfeng Cheng, and Ping Ji. Digital twin modeling. *Journal of Manufacturing Systems*, 64: 372–389, 2022. ISSN 0278-6125. https://doi.org/10.1016/j.jmsy.2022.06.015.

53 Ivan Markovsky and Florian Dörfler. Behavioral systems theory in data-driven analysis, signal processing, and control. *Annual Reviews in Control*, 52:42–64, 2021. ISSN 1367-5788. https://doi.org/10.1016/j.arcontrol.2021.09.005. URL https://www.sciencedirect.com/science/article/pii/S1367578821000754.

54 Valentin Stegmaier, Walter Schaaf, Nasser Jazdi, and Michael Weyrich. Efficient creation of behavior models with variable modeling depths used in digital twins. *arXiv preprint arXiv:2411.07883*, 2024.

55 ETSI. Context information management (CIM); feasibility of NGSI-LD for digital twins. 2022. Group Report GR CIM 017 v1.1.1, ETSI, https://www.etsi.org/deliver/etsi_gr/CIM/001_099/017/01.01.01_60/gr_CIM017v010101p.pdf

56 Daniel González-Sánchez, Luis Bellido, Ignacio D Martinez-Casanueva, David Martínez-García, David Fernández, and Diego R Lopez. Towards building a digital twin for network operation and management. *IEEE Open Journal of the Communications Society*, 2025.

57 JaeSeung Song and Franck Le Gall. Digital twin standards, open source, and best practices. In *The Digital Twin*, pages 497–530. Springer, 2023.

58 Florian Stadtmann, Henrik Andreas Gusdal Wassertheurer, and Adil Rasheed. Demonstration of a standalone, descriptive, and predictive digital twin of a floating offshore wind turbine. In *International Conference on Offshore Mechanics and Arctic Engineering*, volume 86908, page V008T09A039. American Society of Mechanical Engineers, 2023.

59 Sumit Singh, Essam Shehab, Nigel Higgins, Kevin Fowler, Dylan Reynolds, John A Erkoyuncu, and Peter Gadd. Data management for developing digital twin ontology model. *Proceedings of the Institution of Mechanical Engineers, Part B: Journal of Engineering Manufacture*, 235(14):2323–2337, 2021.

60 Weiwei Qian, Yu Guo, Kai Cui, Pengxing Wu, Weiguang Fang, and Daoyuan Liu. Multidimensional data modeling and model validation for digital twin workshop. *Journal of Computing and Information Science in Engineering*, 21(3):031005, 2021.

61 Francesco Flammini. Digital twins as run-time predictive models for the resilience of cyber-physical systems: a conceptual framework. *Philosophical Transactions of the Royal Society A*, 379(2207):20200369, 2021.

62 Matthias Kunze and Mathias Weske. *Behavioural Models*. Springer, 2017.

63 Jinsong Bao, Dongsheng Guo, Jie Li, and Jie Zhang. The modelling and operations for the digital twin in the context of manufacturing. *Enterprise Information Systems*, 13(4):534–556, 2019.

64 Ícaro Aragão Fonseca and Henrique Murilo Gaspar. Challenges when creating a cohesive digital twin ship: a data modelling perspective. *Ship Technology Research*, 68(2):70–83, 2021.

65 Azad M Madni, Carla C Madni, and Scott D Lucero. Leveraging digital twin technology in model-based systems engineering. *Systems*, 7(1):7, 2019.

66 Jens Happe, Heiko Koziolek, Umesh Bellur, Holger Giese, Wilhelm Hasselbring, Robert Laddaga, Tiziana Margaria, Josu Martinez, Christian Müller-Schloer, and Roland Reichle. The role of models in self-adaptive and self-healing systems. In *Self-Adaptive and Self-Healing Systems*. Schloss Dagstuhl–Leibniz-Zentrum für Informatik, 2009. https://drops.dagstuhl.de/storage/16dagstuhl-seminar-proceedings/dsp-vol09201/DagSemProc.09201.4/DagSemProc.09201.4.pdf

67 Daniel Lehner, Santiago Gil, Peter H Mikkelsen, Peter G Larsen, and Manuel Wimmer. An architectural extension for digital twin platforms to leverage behavioral models behaviors. In *2023 IEEE 19th International Conference on Automation Science and Engineering (CASE)*, pages 1–8. IEEE, 2023.

68 Johan Cederbladh, Antonio Cicchetti, and Jagadish Suryadevara. Early validation and verification of system behaviour in model-based systems engineering: a systematic literature review. *ACM Transactions on Software Engineering and Methodology*, 33(3):1–67, 2024.

69 Christine Hofmeister, Robert L Nord, and Dilip Soni. Describing software architecture with UML. In *Software Architecture: TC2 First Working IFIP Conference on Software Architecture* (WICSA1) 22–24 February 1999, *San Antonio, Texas, USA*, pages 145–159. Springer, 1999.

70 Flavio Oquendo. Formally describing the software architecture of systems-of-systems with SosADL. In *2016 11th System of Systems Engineering Conference (SoSE)*, pages 1–6. IEEE, 2016.

71 Ahmed Al-alshuhai and François Siewe. An extension of UML activity diagram to model the behaviour of context-aware systems. In *2015 IEEE International Conference on Computer and Information Technology; Ubiquitous Computing and Communications; Dependable, Autonomic and Secure Computing; Pervasive Intelligence and Computing*, pages 431–437. IEEE, 2015.

72 Sameera Abar, Georgios K Theodoropoulos, Pierre Lemarinier, and Gregory MP O'Hare. Agent based modelling and simulation tools: a review of the state-of-art software. *Computer Science Review*, 24:13–33, 2017.

73 Lina Naciri, Maryam Gallab, Aziz Soulhi, Safae Merzouk, and Mario Di Nardo. Modeling and simulation: a comparative and systematic statistical review. *Procedia Computer Science*, 232:242–253, 2024.

74 Christian Nigischer, Sébastien Bougain, Rainer Riegler, Heinz Peter Stanek, and Manfred Grafinger. Multi-domain simulation utilizing SysML: state of the art and future perspectives. *Procedia CIRP*, 100:319–324, 2021.

75 Melanie Schranz, Alessandra Bagnato, Etienne Brosse, and Wilfried Elmenreich. Modelling a CPS swarm system: a simple case study. In *MODELSWARD*, pages 615–624, 2018.

76 Haifan Jiang, Shengfeng Qin, Jianlin Fu, Jian Zhang, and Guofu Ding. How to model and implement connections between physical and virtual models for digital twin application. *Journal of Manufacturing Systems*, 58:36–51, 2021. Digital Twin towards Smart Manufacturing and Industry 4.0. ISSN 0278-6125. https://doi.org/10.1016/j.jmsy.2020.05.012.

77 Daniel Lehner, Sabine Sint, Martin Eisenberg, and Manuel Wimmer. A pattern catalog for augmenting digital twin models with behavior. *at-Automatisierungstechnik*, 71(6):423–443, 2023.

78 Qinglin Qi, Fei Tao, Tianliang Hu, Nabil Anwer, Ang Liu, Yongli Wei, Lihui Wang, and Andrew YC Nee. Enabling technologies and tools for digital twin. *Journal of Manufacturing Systems*, 58:3–21, 2021.

79 Joze M Rozanec, Jinzhi Lu, Aljaz Kosmerlj, Klemen Kenda, Kiritsis Dimitris, Viktor Jovanoski, Jan Rupnik, Mario Karlovcec, and Blaz Fortuna. Towards actionable cognitive digital twins for manufacturing. *SeDiT@ ESWC*, 2615:1–12, 2020.

80 David J Wagg, Christopher Burr, Jason Shepherd, Zack Xuereb Conti, Mark Enzer, and Steven Niederer. The philosophical foundations of digital twinning. *Data-Centric Engineering*, 6:e12, 2025.

81 Louise Wright and Stuart Davidson. How to tell the difference between a model and a digital twin. *Advanced Modeling and Simulation in Engineering Sciences*, 7:1–13, 2020.

82 TAO Fei, SUN Xuemin, Jiangfeng Cheng, ZHU Yonghuai, LIU Weiran, WANG Yong, XU Hui, HU Tianliang, LIU Xiaojun, LIU Tingyu, et al. makeTwin: A reference architecture for digital twin software platform. *Chinese Journal of Aeronautics*, 37(1):1–18, 2024.

83 Enxhi Ferko, Alessio Bucaioni, and Moris Behnam. Architecting digital twins. *IEEE Access*, 10:50335–50350, 2022.

84 Bedir Tekinerdogan and Cor Verdouw. Systems architecture design pattern catalog for developing digital twins. *Sensors*, 20(18):5103, 2020.

85 Chetna Gupta and Varun Gupta. C4 skills in the engineering graduate: a study to align software engineering education with market-driven software industry needs. *IEEE Transactions on Education*, 67(1):31–43, 2024. https://doi.org/10.1109/TE.2023.3301625.

86 Azad M Madni and Michael Sievers. Model-based systems engineering: motivation, current status, and research opportunities. *Systems Engineering*, 21(3):172–190, 2018.

87 Yübo Wang, Tanja Steinbach, Jonathan Klein, and Reiner Anderl. Integration of model based system engineering into the digital twin concept. *Procedia CIRP*, 100:19–24, 2021.

88 Manas Bajaj, Sanford Friedenthal, and Ed Seidewitz. Systems modeling language (SysML v2) support for digital engineering. *Insight*, 25(1):19–24, 2022.

89 Wolfram Zischka and Daniel Finnegan. System integration for modular open system approach compliant integrated avionics architectures. In *2023 IEEE/AIAA 42nd Digital Avionics Systems Conference (DASC)*, pages 1–7. IEEE, 2023.

90 Jerker Delsing, Géza Kulcsár and Øystein Haugen. SysML modeling of service-oriented system-of-systems. *Innovations in Systems and Software Engineering*, 20(3):269–285, 2024.

91 Alexander Korn, Samuel Gorsch, and Andreas Vogelsang. LLMREI: automating requirements elicitation interviews with LLMs. In *Proceedings of the ACM/IEEE 46th International Conference on Software Engineering: Software Engineering in Practice (ICSE-SEIP)*, pages 123–132, 2024. https://arxiv.org/pdf/2507.02564.pdf

92 Schultz Carl Peter Leslie, Jahangir Muhammad Farhan, and Kamari Aliakbar. A review of drivers and barriers of digital twin adoption. *Journal of Information Technology in Construction*, 2024. https://www.itcon.org/papers/2024_08-ITcon-Jahangir.pdf

93 Jerome Hughes, Anton Hristozov, John Hudak, and Joseph Yankel. TwinOps combines digital twins and DevOps for better cyber-physical systems. *Annual Reviews.* Software Engineering Institute, Carnegie Mellon University, 2020.

94 Rolls-Royce PLC. Digital twin case study: predictive maintenance and operational efficiency. https://ismguide.com/ism-digital-twin-case-studies/, 2024. [Online; accessed September 2025].

95 Pieter van Schalkwyk. Digital twins: a framework that unlocks business value and enables digital transformation at scale. Technical report, Digital Twin Consortium, 2024.

96 International Organization for Standardization. ISO/IEC 3017 3: 2023 - digital twin terminology and concepts. Technical report, International Organization for Standardization, 2023. https://www.iso.org/standard/81442.html

97 Digital Twin Consortium. Digital twin consortium: driving innovation and standardization. https://www.digitaltwinconsortium.org/, 2023.

98 Industrial Digital Twin Association (IDTA). Industrial digital twin association: standardizing digital twins for Industry 4.0. https://industrialdigitaltwin.org/, 2024.

99 Guodong Shao. Manufacturing digital twin standards. Technical report, National Institute of Standards and Technology (NIST), 2024. https://www.nist.gov/publications/manufacturing-digital-twin-standards

100 Industrial IoT Consortium (IIC). IIC journal of innovation: digital twin edition. https://www.iiconsortium.org/news/journal-of-innovation-2019-nov/, 2019.

101 Jeffrey Voas, Peter Mell, Phillip Laplante, and Vartan Piroumian. Security and trust considerations for digital twin technology. Technical Report NIST IR 8356, National Institute of Standards and Technology (NIST), 2025. https://tsapps.nist.gov/publication/get_pdf.cfm?pub_id=957183. Comprehensive report on definitions, standards, and cybersecurity for Digital Twins.

102 General Electric Company. Ge digital twin: Analytic engine for the digital power plant, 2016. Describes physics-based and AI model integration in Digital Twin applications for power plants. https://www.ge.com/sites/default/files/ge_webcast_presentation_06232016_1.pdf

103 Dassault Systèmes. Virtual twin experiences - the next generation of digital twins. Webpage / white paper, Dassault Systèmes. https://www.3ds.com/virtual-twin,2025. [Online; accessed October 7, 2025].

104 American Institute of Aeronautics and Astronautics (AIAA). Digital twin implementation white paper. White paper, American Institute of Aeronautics and Astronautics, 2025. https://aiaa.org/resources/digital-twin-implementation-white-paper/

105 Riccardo Marini, Francesa Conserva, Maurizio Fodrini, Simone Bizzarri, Marco Becattini, Antonio Iera, Enrico Vicario, Gianluca Cena, Stefano Scanzio Francesco Linsalata et al. Network digital twin: white paper. 2025. https://fondazione-restart.it/wp-content/plugins/download-attachments/includes/download.php?id=7817, [Online; accessed 7 October, 2025].

106 Open Geospatial Consortium (OGC). Urban digital twins: integrating infrastructure and natural systems. https://docs.ogc.org/dp/24-025.html, 2020.

107 Mahmoud Abdelrahman, Edgardo Macatulad, Binyu Lei, Matias Quintana, Clayton Miller, and Filip Biljecki. What is a Digital Twin anyway? Deriving the definition for the built environment from over 15,000 scientific publications. *Building and Environment*, 274:112748, 2025.

108 Alexander Barbie. *Agile Continuous Integration Testing of Embedded Software Systems with Digital Twin Prototypes*. Number 2025/2 in Kiel Computer Science Series. Dissertation, Faculty of Engineering, Department of Computer Science, Kiel University, 2025. https://doi.org/10.21941/kcss/2025/2.

109 James Moyne, Yassine Qamsane, Efe C Balta, Ilya Kovalenko, John Faris, Kira Barton, and Dawn M Tilbury. A requirements driven digital twin framework: specification and opportunities. *IEEE Access*, 8:107781–107801, 2020.

110 Fabian Wilking, Christopher Sauer, Benjamin Schleich, and Sandro Wartzack. SysML 4 digital twins–utilization of system models for the design and operation of digital twins. *Proceedings of the Design Society*, 2:1815–1824, 2022.

111 Eduard Kamburjan, Nelly Bencomo, Silvia Lizeth Tapia Tarifa, and Einar Broch Johnsen. Declarative lifecycle management in digital twins. In *Proceedings of the ACM/IEEE 27th International Conference on Model Driven Engineering Languages and Systems*, pages 353–363, 2024.

112 Mohsin Raza. *Consistency Matters: Building a Consistent Digital Twin as a Virtual Counterpart of a Physical Asset*. PhD thesis, Eindhoven University of Technology, 2025. ISBN: 978-90-386-5838-5.

113 Yifan Tang, Mostafa Rahmani Dehaghani, and G Gary Wang. Capturing lifecycle system degradation in digital twin model updating. *arXiv preprint arXiv:2503.08953*, 2025.

114 Javier Conde, Andres Munoz-Arcentales, Alvaro Alonso, Sonsoles López-Pernas, and Joaquin Salvachua. Modeling digital twin data and architecture: a building guide with fiware as enabling technology. *IEEE Internet Computing*, 26(3):7–14, 2021.

115 Graeme Simsion and Graham Witt. *Data Modeling Essentials*. Elsevier, 2004.

116 Salvatore T March. Data modeling: the entity-relationship data model. In Sushil Jajodia, Tok Wang Ling, and Yang Wang, editors, *Handbook of Databases and Information Systems*, pages 25–50. Springer, New York, NY, 2013. ISBN 978-1-4614-8255-8.

117 Harry Chen, Tim Finin, and Anupam Joshi. An intelligent broker for context-aware systems. In *Adjunct Proceedings of Ubicomp 2003*, pages 183–184, 2003.

118 Boris Moltchanov and Oscar Rodriguez Rocha. A context broker to enable future IoT applications and services. In *2014 6th International Congress on Ultra Modern Telecommunications and Control Systems and Workshops (ICUMT)*, pages 263–268. IEEE, 2014.

119 Roberto Minerva, Faraz Malik Awan, and Noel Crespi. Exploiting digital twins as enablers for synthetic sensing. *IEEE Internet Computing*, 26(5):61–67, 2021.

120 Yahui Yi, Chengyu Xia, Chao Feng, Wenjing Zhang, Chenlong Fu, Liqin Qian, and Siqi Chen. Digital twin-long short-term memory (LSTM) neural network based real-time temperature prediction and degradation model analysis for lithium-ion battery. *Journal of Energy Storage*, 64:107203, 2023.

121 Lu Wang, Tianhu Deng, Zeyu Zheng, and Zuo-Jun Max Shen. Explainable modeling in digital twin. In *2021 Winter Simulation Conference (WSC)*, pages 1–12. IEEE, 2021.

122 Shu Liu, Siwei Ren, and Hongliang Jiang. Predictive maintenance of wind turbines based on digital twin technology. *Energy Reports*, 9:1344–1352, 2023.

123 ETSI. SmartM2M; digital twins. Technical Specification TS 103 846 V1.1.1, European Telecommunications Standards Institute, 8, 2024. Describes behavior models for Digital Twins. https://www.etsi.org/deliver/etsi_ts/103800_103899/103846/01.01.01_60/ts_103846v010101p.pdf

124 Mica R Endsley. Toward a theory of situation awareness in dynamic systems. *Human Factors*, 37(1):32–64, 1995.

125 Stefano Perna. Riconoscimento e tracciamento di oggetti nelle smart city tramite general-purpose sensing ed intelligenza artificiale. Master's thesis, Dipartimento di Ingegneria Informatica, Modellistica, Elettronica e Sistemistica, Universita degli Studi della Calabria – Rende (CS) Italy, 2023. https://labs.dimes.unical.it/speme/wp-content/uploads/sites/8/Tesi___Stefano_Perna-1-1.pdf. Supervision: Giancarlo Fortino, Noel Crespi, Roberto Minerva, Claudio Savaglio.

126 Stefano Morrone. Previsione del traffico stradale tramite general-purpose sensing e machine learning. Master's thesis, Dipartimento di Ingegneria Informatica, Modellistica, Elettronica e Sistemistica, Universita degli Studi della Calabria – Rende (CS) Italy, 2023. https://labs.dimes.unical.it/speme/wp-content/uploads/sites/8/tesi_morrone_stefano-1.pdf. Supervision: Giancarlo Fortino, Noel Crespi, Roberto Minerva, Claudio Savaglio.

127 Vincenzo Barbuto. Creating digital twins with general purpose sensing: architecture and initial experiments. Master's thesis, Dipartimento di Ingegneria Informatica, Modellistica, Elettronica e Sistemistica, Universita degli Studi della Calabria – Rende (CS) Italy, 6, 2022. https://labs.dimes.unical.it/speme/wp-content/uploads/sites/8/Tesi_Digital_Twin_Barbuto_final-compresso.pdf. Supervision: Giancarlo Fortino, Roberto Minerva, Claudio Savaglio.

128 Maira Alvi, Hrishikesh Dutta, Roberto Minerva, Noel Crespi, Syed Mohsan Raza, and Manoj Herath. Global perspectives on digital twin smart cities: innovations, challenges, and pathways to a sustainable urban future. *Sustainable Cities and Society*, 126:106356, 2025. ISSN 2210-6707. https://doi.org/10.1016/j.scs.2025.106356.

129 Tianhu Deng, Keren Zhang, and Zuo-Jun Max Shen. A systematic review of a digital twin city: a new pattern of urban governance toward smart cities. *Journal of Management Science and Engineering*, 6(2):125–134, 2021.

130 Manoj Herath, Maira Alvi, Roberto Minerva, Hrishikesh Dutta, Noel Crespi, and Syed Mohsan Raza. Smart city digital twins: a modular and adaptive architecture for real-time data-driven urban management. In *2024 20th International Conference on Network and Service Management (CNSM)*, pages 1–7, 2024. https://doi.org/10.23919/CNSM62983.2024.10814627.

131 Claudio Savaglio, Vincenzo Barbuto, Faraz Malik Awan, Roberto Minerva, Noel Crespi, and Giancarlo Fortino. Opportunistic digital twin: an edge intelligence enabler for smart city. *ACM Transactions on Sensor Networks*, 2023.

132 Maira Alvi, Roberto Minerva, Praboda Rajapaksha, Noel Crespi, and Umna Alvi. Traffic flow prediction in sensor-limited areas through synthetic sensing and data fusion. *IEEE Sensors Letters*, 8(4):1–4, 2024.

133 Vincenzo Barbuto, Claudio Savaglio, Roberto Minerva, Noel Crespi, and Giancarlo Fortino. Towards an edge intelligence-based traffic monitoring system. In *2023 IEEE International Conference on Systems, Man, and Cybernetics (SMC)*, pages 3434–3439, 2023. https://doi.org/10.1109/SMC53992.2023.10393907.

134 Manoj Herath, Hrishikesh Dutta, Roberto Minerva, Noel Crespi, Maira Alvi, and Syed Mohsan Raza. An AI-driven, scalable, and modular digital twin framework for traffic management. In *IEEE Wireless Communications and Networking Conference*, 2025.

135 Sylwia Werbińska-Wojciechowska, Robert Giel, and Klaudia Winiarska. Digital twin approach for operation and maintenance of transportation system—systematic review. *Sensors*, 24(18):6069, 2024.

136 Almasan Paul, Ferriol-Galmés Miquel, Paillisse Jordi, Suárez-Varela José, Perino Diego, López Diego, Perales Antonio Agustin Pastor, Harvey Paul, Ciavaglia Laurent, Wong Leon, et al. Network digital twin: context, enabling technologies, and opportunities. *IEEE Communications Magazine*, 60(11):22–27, 2022.

137 Syed Mohsan Raza, Roberto Minerva, Noel Crespi, and Mehdi Karech. Definition of digital twin network data model in the context of edge-cloud continuum. In *2023 IEEE 9th International Conference on Network Softwarization (NetSoft)*, pages 402–407. IEEE, 2023.

138 Syed Mohsan Raza, Roberto Minerva, Noel Crespi, Maira Alvi, Manoj Herath, and Hrishikesh Dutta. Exploiting the efficient data modeling in network digital twin to empower edge-cloud continuum. In *2024 20th International Conference on Network and Service Management (CNSM)*, pages 1–4. IEEE, 2024.

139 Yujia Lin, Liming Chen, Aftab Ali, Christopher Nugent, Ian Cleland, Rongyang Li, Jianguo Ding, and Huansheng Ning. Human digital twin: a survey. *Journal of Cloud Computing*, 13(1):131, 2024.

140 Wei Shengli. Is human digital twin possible? *Computer Methods and Programs in Biomedicine Update*, 1:100014, 2021.

141 Greyce N Schroeder, Charles Steinmetz, Carlos E Pereira, and Danubia B Espindola. Digital twin data modeling with automationml and a communication methodology for data exchange. *IFAC-PapersOnLine*, 49(30):12–17, 2016.

142 Matteo Torzoni. *Model-Based and Data-Driven Methodologies Toward Predictive Digital Twins of Structures*. Phd thesis, Politecnico di Milano, 2023.

143 Moritz von Stietencron, Karl Hribernik, and Klaus-Dieter Thoben. How data models can contribute to linking real-life assets with their digital twin-a case study in predictive maintenance. In *I-ESA Workshops*, 2020.

144 Toh Yen Pang, Juan D Pelaez Restrepo, Chi-Tsun Cheng, Alim Yasin, Hailey Lim, and Miro Miletic. Developing a digital twin and digital thread framework for an 'Industry 4.0' shipyard. *Applied Sciences*, 11(3):1097, 2021.

145 AI Vodyaho, NA Zhukova, and V Ya Ananeva. Use of digital threads and digital twin systems in socio-cyber-physical systems. *Automatic Documentation and Mathematical Linguistics*, 58(6):431–440, 2024.

146 Franca Rocco di Torrepadula, Alessandra Somma, Alessandra De Benedictis, and Nicola Mazzocca. Smart ecosystems and digital twins: an architectural perspective and a fiware-based solution. *IEEE Software*, 42(2):38–46, 2024.

147 Juliana Hildebrandt, Dirk Habich, and Wolfgang Lehner. [Vision paper] Digital twin system–from frameworks to a comprehensive system. In *2024 IEEE International Conference on Big Data (BigData)*, pages 2888–2897. IEEE, 2024.

148 Gilles Privat, and Alexey Medvedev. Guidelines for modelling with NGSI-LD. Technical report, ETSI, 2021. https://www.etsi.org/deliver/etsi_gr/CIM/001_099/017/01.01.01_60/gr_CIM017v010101p.pdf. White Paper.

149 Flavio Cirillo, Gürkan Solmaz, Everton Luís Berz, Martin Bauer, Bin Cheng, and Ernoe Kovacs. A standard-based open source IoT platform: fiware. *IEEE Internet of Things Magazine*, 2(3):12–18, 2020.

150 Ulrich Ahle and Juan Jose Hierro. Fiware for data spaces. *Designing Data Spaces*, 395,2022.

151 Martin Bauer. Fiware: standard-based open source components for cross-domain IoT platforms. In *2022 IEEE 8th World Forum on Internet of Things (WF-IoT)*, pages 1–6. IEEE, 2022.

152 Amir Reza Jafari, Víctor González, Laura Martín, Luis Sánchez, Jorge Lanza, Syed Mohsan Raza, Maira Alvi, Kanawut Kaewnoparat, Roberto Minerva, and Noel Crespi. Data enrichment toolchain: a use-case for correlation analysis of air quality, traffic, and meteorological metrics in madrid's smart city. *Internet of Things*, 26:101232, 2024.

153 Luis Sánchez, Jorge Lanza, Juan Ramón Santana, Pablo Sotres, Víctor González, Laura Martín, Gürkan Solmaz, Ernö Kovacs, Maren Dietzel, Anja Summa, et al. Data enrichment toolchain: a data linking and enrichment platform for heterogeneous data. *IEEE Access*, 11:103079–103091, 2023.

154 Antonio Manzalini, Roberto Minerva, and Corrado Moiso. Towards an expressive, adaptive and resource aware network platform. *Advances in Next Generation Services and Service Architectures*, 14:43, 2011.

155 Roberto Minerva. On some myths about network intelligence. In *Proceedings of International Conference on Intelligence in Networks-ICIN2008 (October 2008)*, pages 1–6, 2008.

156 André Costa, João Miranda, Duarte Dias, Nuno Dinis, Luís Romero, and Pedro Miguel Faria. Smart maintenance solutions: AR- and VR-enhanced digital twin powered by fiware. *Sensors*, 25(3), 2025. ISSN 1424-8220. https://doi.org/10.3390/s25030845. https://www.mdpi.com/1424-8220/25/3/845.

157 Brahma Dathan and Sarnath Ramnath. *Object-Oriented Analysis, Design and Implementation: An Integrated Approach*. Springer, 2015.

158 Hatice Koc, Ali Mert Erdog˘an, Yousef Barjakly, and Serhat Peker. UML diagrams in software engineering research: a systematic literature review. In *Proceedings*, volume 74, page 13. MDPI, 2021.

159 Emilio Carrión, Óscar Pastor, and Pedro Valderas. Conceptual modelling method for digital twins. In Wolfgang Maass, Hyoil Han, Hasan Yasar, and Nick Multari, editors, *International Conference on Conceptual Modeling*, pages 417–435. Springer, 2024.

160 Kuzma Kukushkin, Yury Ryabov, and Alexey Borovkov. Digital twins: a systematic literature review based on data analysis and topic modeling. *Data*, 7(12):173, 2022.

161 Sujing Zhou. Numerical analysis of digital twin system modeling methods aided by graph-theoretic combinatorial optimization. *Discrete Dynamics in Nature and Society*, 2022(1):8598041, 2022.

162 Manu Sporny, Dave Longley, Gregg Kellogg, Markus Lanthaler, and Niklas Lindström. JSON-LD 1.0. *W3C Recommendation*, 16:41, 2014.

163 Alexander Meijers. *Hands-On Azure Digital Twins: A Practical Guide to Building Distributed IoT Solutions*. Packt Publishing Ltd, 2022.

164 Salvatore Cavalieri and Salvatore Gambadoro. Proposal of mapping digital twins definition language to open platform communications unified architecture. *Sensors*, 23(4):2349, 2023.

165 Michael Jacoby and Thomas Usländer. Digital twin and internet of things—current standards landscape. *Applied Sciences*, 10(18):6519, 2020.

166 Mariana Segovia and Joaquin Garcia-Alfaro. Design, modeling and implementation of digital twins. *Sensors*, 22(14):5396, 2022.

167 A Sharma, E Kosasih, J Zhang, A Brintrup, and A Calinescu. Digital twins: state of the art theory and practice, challenges, and open research questions. *Journal of Industrial Information Integration*, 29:100362, 2022. https://doi.org/10.1016/j.jii.2022.100362.

168 Wang Kai, Wang Yamin, Li Yizheng, Fan Xiaohui, Xiao Shanpeng, and Hu Lin. A review of the technology standards for enabling digital twin. *Digital Twin*, 2(4):14, 2022. https://doi.org/10.12688/digitaltwin.17549.2.

169 International Telecommunication Union. Digital twin framework and standards for smart cities. ITU-T Y.4400 series, 2021. https://www.itu.int/rec/T-REC-Y.4400

170 Ege Korkan. Web of things (WoT) thing description 2.0. W3C First Public Working Draft. World Wide Web Consortium, 2025. https://www.w3.org/TR/2025/WD-wot-thing-description-2.0-20251104/

171 Digital Twin Consortium. Digital twin system interoperability framework. https://www.digitaltwinconsortium.org/, 2022.

172 Cyrus Azani and Reza Khorramshahgol. Modular open systems approach: an effective business strategy for building affordable and adaptable architectures. *Journal of Management Systems*, 18(1):66–76, 2006.

173 Giselle Bonilla-Ortiz and Dinesh Verma. The need for a secure modular open systems approach (MOSA): Building the case using systems thinking methodologies. In *2020 IEEE Systems Security Symposium (SSS)*, pages 1–4. IEEE, 2020.

174 Gavin Pearson, Richard Smith, Howard Tripp, and Olwen Worthington. A systems approach to achieving the benefits of open and modular systems. In *Open Architecture/Open Business Model Net-Centric Systems and Defense Transformation 2015*, volume 9479, pages 39–47. SPIE, 2015.

175 Milan Groshev, Carlos Guimaraes, Jorge Martín-Pérez, and Antonio de la Oliva. Toward intelligent cyber-physical systems: digital twin meets artificial intelligence. *IEEE Communications Magazine*, 59(8):14–20, 2021.

176 Luca Buonocore, Jim Yates, and Riccardo Valentini. A proposal for a forest digital twin framework and its perspectives. *Forests*, 13(4):498, 2022.

177 Kai Guo, Xiang Wan, Lilan Liu, Zenggui Gao, and Muchen Yang. Fault diagnosis of intelligent production line based on digital twin and improved random forest. *Applied Sciences*, 11(16):7733, 2021.

178 Ian H Witten and Eibe Frank. Data mining: practical machine learning tools and techniques with Java implementations. *ACM SIGMOD Record*, 31(1):76–77, 1999. https://doi.org/10.1145/343048.343058.

179 Roberto Minerva. On the art of creating services: Do different paradigms lead to different services? *Journal of Telecommunications Management*, 1(1): 33–47, 2008.

180 Inès Mouakher, Fatma Dhaou, and J Christian Attiogbé. Event-based semantics of UML 2.x concurrent sequence diagrams for formal verification. *Journal of Computer Science and Technology*, 37(1):4–28, 2022.

181 Yuanjie Lu, Zhimin Liu, Zhixiao Sun, Miao Wang, Wenqing Yi, and Yang Bai. Research on behavior modeling and simulation of complex UAV based on SysML state machine diagram. In Daniel Krob, Lefei Li, Junchen Yao, Hongjun Zhang and Xinguo Zhang, editors, *Complex Systems Design & Management: Proceedings of the 4th International Conference on Complex Systems Design & Management Asia and of the 12th Conference on Complex Systems Design & Management CSD&M 2021*, pages 401–409. Springer Nature, 2021. https://doi.org/10.1007/978-3-030-73542-5_32

182 Marlon Dumas and Arthur HM Ter Hofstede. UML activity diagrams as a workflow specification language. In *International Conference on the Unified Modeling Language*, pages 76–90. Springer, 2001.

183 Wenjie Jia, Wei Wang, and Zhenzu Zhang. From simple digital twin to complex digital twin Part I: a novel modeling method for multi-scale and multi-scenario digital twin. *Advanced Engineering Informatics*, 53:101706, 2022.

184 Anro JH Redelinghuys, Karel Kruger, and Anton Basson. A six-layer architecture for digital twins with aggregation. In *International Workshop on Service Orientation in Holonic and Multi-Agent Manufacturing*, pages 171–182. Springer, 2019.

185 Edward Glaessgen and David Stargel. The digital twin paradigm for future NASA and US air force vehicles. In *53rd AIAA/ASME/ASCE/AHS/ASC Structures, Structural Dynamics and Materials Conference 20th AIAA/ASME/AHS Adaptive Structures Conference 14th AIAA*, page 1818, 2012.

186 Jay Lee, Edzel Lapira, Behrad Bagheri, and Hung-an Kao. Recent advances and trends in predictive manufacturing systems in big data environment. *Manufacturing letters*, 1(1):38–41, 2013.

187 K Agalianos, Stavros T Ponis, Eleni Aretoulaki, George Plakas, and Orestis Efthymiou. Discrete event simulation and digital twins: review and challenges for logistics. *Procedia Manufacturing*, 51:1636–1641, 2020.

188 Christos G Cassandras and Stéphane Lafortune. *Introduction to Discrete Event Systems*. Springer, 2008.

189 Charles M Macal and Michael J North. Agent-based modeling and simulation. In *Proceedings of the 2009 Winter Simulation Conference (WSC)*, pages 86–98. IEEE, 2009.

190 Areli Orozco-Romero, Claudia Yohana Arias-Portela, and JosE Antonio Marmolejo Saucedo. The use of agent-based models boosted by digital twins in the supply chain: a literature review. In *Intelligent Computing and Optimization: Proceedings of the 2nd International Conference on Intelligent Computing and Optimization 2019 (ICO 2019)*, pages 642–652. Springer, 2020.

191 Hongbin Qiu, Yong Chen, Huaxiang Zhang, Wenchao Yi, and Yingde Li. Evolutionary digital twin model with an agent-based discrete-event simulation method. *Applied Intelligence*, 53(6):6178–6194, 2023.

192 Ayman AboElHassan, Ahmed H Sakr, and Soumaya Yacout. General purpose digital twin framework using digital shadow and distributed system concepts. *Computers & Industrial Engineering*, 183:109534, 2023.

193 MohammadReza EffatParvar, Nasser Yazdani, Mehdi EffatParvar, Aresh Dadlani, and Ahmad Khonsari. Improved algorithms for leader election in distributed systems. In *2010 2nd International Conference on Computer Engineering and Technology*, volume 2, pages V2–6. IEEE, 2010.

194 Diego Ongaro and John Ousterhout. In search of an understandable consensus algorithm. In *2014 USENIX Annual Technical Conference (USENIX ATC 14)*, pages 305–319, 2014.

195 Dastan Maulud and Adnan M Abdulazeez. A review on linear regression comprehensive in machine learning. *Journal of Applied Science and Technology Trends*, 1(2):140–147, 2020.

196 Pratap Chandra Sen, Mahimarnab Hajra, and Mitadru Ghosh. Supervised classification algorithms in machine learning: A survey and review. In *Emerging Technology in Modelling and Graphics: Proceedings of IEM Graph 2018*, pages 99–111. Springer, 2020.

197 Absalom E Ezugwu, Abiodun M Ikotun, Olaide O Oyelade, Laith Abualigah, Jeffery O Agushaka, Christopher I Eke, and Andronicus A Akinyelu. A comprehensive survey of clustering algorithms: state-of-the-art machine learning applications, taxonomy, challenges, and future research prospects. *Engineering Applications of Artificial Intelligence*, 110:104743, 2022.

198 G Thippa Reddy, M Praveen Kumar Reddy, Kuruva Lakshmanna, Rajesh Kaluri, Dharmendra Singh Rajput, Gautam Srivastava, and Thar Baker. Analysis of dimensionality reduction techniques on big data. *IEEE Access*, 8:54776–54788, 2020.

199 Ashish Kumar Shakya, Gopinatha Pillai, and Sohom Chakrabarty. Reinforcement learning algorithms: a brief survey. *Expert Systems with Applications*, 231:120495, 2023.

200 Bryan Lim and Stefan Zohren. Time-series forecasting with deep learning: a survey. *Philosophical Transactions of the Royal Society A*, 379(2194):20200209, 2021.

201 Qaisar Abbas, Mostafa EA Ibrahim, and M Arfan Jaffar. Video scene analysis: an overview and challenges on deep learning algorithms. *Multimedia Tools and Applications*, 77(16):20415–20453, 2018.

202 Aung Kaung Myat, Roberto Minerva, Attaphongse Taparugssanagorn, Praboda Rajapaksha, and Noel Crespi. Traffic intensity detection using general-purpose sensors. Master's thesis, Télécom SudParis, Institut Polytechnique de Paris, Évry-Courcouronnes, Essonne, France, 2023.

203 Aung Kaung Myat, Roberto Minerva, Attaphongse Taparugssanagorn, Praboda Rajapaksha, and Noel Crespi. Traffic intensity detection using general-purpose sensing. *IEEE Sensors Letters*, 7(11):1–4, 2023. https://doi.org/10.1109/LSENS.2023.3315251.

204 Ivano Lauriola, Alberto Lavelli, and Fabio Aiolli. An introduction to deep learning in natural language processing: models, techniques, and tools. *Neurocomputing*, 470:443–456, 2022.

205 Lyle Regenwetter, Amin Heyrani Nobari, and Faez Ahmed. Deep generative models in engineering design: a review. *Journal of Mechanical Design*, 144(7):071704, 2022.

206 Gergő Dávid Monek and Szabolcs Fischer. Expert twin: a digital twin with an integrated fuzzy-based decision-making module. In *Decision Making: Applications in Management and Engineering*, pages 1–21, 2025.

207 D Hüsener and J Roßmann. Integrating rule based expert systems into a simulation framework for digital twins. In Tareq Ahram and Redha Taiar, editors, *Human Interaction & Emerging Technologies (IHIET 2023): Artificial Intelligence & Future Applications*, volume 111 of *AHFE International Conference*, AHFE Open Access, USA, AHFE International, 2023. https://doi.org/10.54941/ahfe1004066.

208 Patrick Klein. *Combining Expert Knowledge and Deep Learning with Case-Based Reasoning for Predictive Maintenance*. Springer Nature, 2025.

209 Kassi Muhammad, Teef David, Giulia Nassisid, and Tina Farus. Integrating generative AI with network digital twins for enhanced network operations. *arXiv preprint arXiv:2406.17112*, 2024.

210 McKinsey. Digital twins and generative AI: a powerful pairing. https://www.mckinsey.com/capabilities/quantumblack/our-insights/digital-twins-and-generative-ai-a-powerful-pairing, 2024. [Online; accessed May 1, 2024].

211 Fei Tao, Qinglin Qi, Ang Liu, and AYC Nee. Digital twins and cyber–physical systems toward smart manufacturing and industry 4.0: correlation and comparison. *Engineering*, 5(4):653–661, 2019. https://doi.org/10.1016/j.eng.2019.01.014.

212 Alan W. Biermann and Jerome A Feldman. On the synthesis of finite-state machines from samples of their behavior. *IEEE Transactions on Computers*, C-21(6):592–597, 1972. https://doi.org/10.1109/T-C.1972.223477.

213 Johannes Fürnkranz. Separate-and-conquer rule learning. *Artificial Intelligence Review*, 13(1):3–54,1999. https://doi.org/10.1023/A:1006524209794.

214 Jerzy W. Grzymala-Busse. Rule induction. In Lior Rokach, Oded Maimon, and Erez Shmueli, editors, *Machine Learning for Data Science Handbook: Data Mining and Knowledge Discovery Handbook*, pages 55–74. Springer, 2023. https://doi.org/10.1007/978-3-031-24628-9_4

215 Neeraj Kumar and Upendra Kumar. Comparative analysis of CN2 rule induction with other classification algorithms for network security. *Multimedia Tools and Applications*, 81(26):37119–37135, 2022.

216 Trupti A Kumbhare and Santosh V Chobe. An overview of association rule mining algorithms. *International Journal of Computer Science and Information Technologies*, 5(1):927–930, 2014.

217 Sébastien Salva and Elliott Blot. Cktail: Model learning of communicating systems. In *15th International Conference on Evaluation of Novel Approaches to Software Engineering*, pages 27–38. SCITEPRESS-Science and Technology Publications, 2020.

218 Raghavendran Gunasekaran, Boudewijn R Haverkort, and Loes Kruger. Behavioral analysis of a digital twin using logging and model learning. *Journal of Object Technology*, 24(2):1–14, 2025.

219 Sushmita Mitra and Yoichi Hayashi. Neuro-fuzzy rule generation: survey in soft computing framework. *IEEE Transactions on Neural Networks*, 11(3):748–768, 2000.

220 Ayush K Varshney and Vicenç Torra. Literature review of the recent trends and applications in various fuzzy rule-based systems. *International Journal of Fuzzy Systems*, 25(6):2163–2186, 2023.

221 Tim Kreuzer, Panagiotis Papapetrou, and Jelena Zdravkovic. Artificial intelligence in digital twins—a systematic literature review. *Data and Knowledge Engineering*, 151:102304, 2024. ISSN 0169-023X. https://doi.org/10.1016/j.datak.2024.102304.

222 Rong Gao, Lei Wang, and Jian Li. Artificial intelligence in digital twins-a systematic literature review. *Information Systems*, 92:101522, 2020.

223 Amina Adadi and Mohammed Berrada. Peeking inside the black-box: a survey on explainable artificial intelligence (XAI). *IEEE Access*, 6:52138–52160, 2018.

224 Ming Zhou, Wei Li, and Fang Chen. Hybrid modeling for explainable digital twins: integrating AI and behavior models. *Journal of Systems Architecture*, 123:102456, 2022.

225 Feiyu Xu, Hans Uszkoreit, Yangzhou Du, Wei Fan, Dongyan Zhao, and Jun Zhu. Explainable AI: a brief survey on history, research areas, approaches and challenges. In *Natural language Processing and Chinese Computing: 8th CCF International Conference, NLPCC 2019, Dunhuang,* China, October 9–14, 2019, *Proceedings, Part II, 8*, pages 563–574. Springer, 2019.

226 Haitham Y Adarbah, Mehdi Sookhak, and Mohammed Atiquzzaman. A digital twin-based traffic light management system using BIRCH algorithm. *Ad Hoc Networks*, 164:103613, 2024.

227 Senthil Kumar Jagatheesaperumal, Quoc-Viet Pham, Rukhsana Ruby, Zhaohui Yang, Chunmei Xu, and Zhaoyang Zhang. Explainable AI over the Internet of Things (IoT): overview, state-of-the-art and future directions. *IEEE Open Journal of the Communications Society*, 3:2106–2136, 2022.

228 Tim Kreuzer, Panagiotis Papapetrou, and Jelena Zdravkovic. AI explainability methods in digital twins: a model and a use case. In Jose Borbinha, Tiago Prince Sales, Miguel Mira Da Silva, Henderik A. Proper, and Marianne Schnellmann, editors, *Enterprise Design, Operations, and Computing: 28th International Conference, EDOC 2024, Vienna, Austria, September 10–13, 2024, Revised Selected Papers*, pages 3–20. Springer Nature Switzerland, 2025. https://doi.org/10.1007/978-3-031-78338-8_1.

229 Alexander Timms, Abigail Langbridge, Antonis Antonopoulos, Antonis Mygiakis, Eleni Voulgari and Fearghal O'Donncha. Agentic AI for digital twin. In *Proceedings of the AAAI Conference on Artificial Intelligence*, 2025.

230 Xu Haowen, Sun Yulin, Tupayachi Jose, Omitaomu Olufemi, Zlatanova Sisi, and Li Xueping. Towards the autonomous optimization of urban logistics: training generative AI with scientific tools via agentic digital twins and model context protocol. *arXiv preprint arXiv:2506.13068*, 2025. https://arxiv.org/pdf/2506.13068.pdf

231 Growth Cues. Agentic AI and digital twins: the future of autonomous business, 2025. https://www.growthcues.com/blog/agentic-ai-and-digital-twins [accessed September 2025].

232 TechAhead Corp. Agentic AI and digital twins in telecom operations. https://www.techaheadcorp.com/blog/agentic-ai-digital-twins-in-telecom-industry/, 2025. [Online; accessed September 2025].

233 Hitesh Narayana Atreya and Sathyajith Sridhar. Using discrete event simulation as a step towards creating a digital twin: a pre-study for creating digital twins in a highly labor-intensive production system using simulation modelling. Master's thesis, Chalmers University of Technology, Gothenburg, Sweden, 2019. Department of Industrial and Materials Science. Supervisor: Jesper Birberg, SAAB AB, Linköping, Sweden. Supervisor: Daniel Nåfors, Department of Industrial and Materials Science. Examiner: Björn Johansson, Department of Industrial and Materials Science.

234 Andrew Stuart Hahn, Jenna deCastro, Minami Tanaka, and Christopher Lamb. Evaluation of digital twin modeling and simulation. Technical report, Sandia National Lab. (SNL-NM), Albuquerque, NM (United States), 2023.

235 Peter Fritzson. The openmodelica environment for building digital twins of sustainable cyber-physical systems. In *2021 Winter Simulation Conference (WSC)*, pages 1–12. IEEE, 2021.

236 Bahar Biller, Xi Jiang, Jinxin Yi, Paul Venditti, and Stephan Biller. Simulation: the critical technology in digital twin development. In *2022 Winter Simulation Conference (WSC)*, pages 1340–1355. IEEE, 2022.

237 Moussa Amrani, Dominique Blouin, Robert Heinrich, Arend Rensink, Hans Vangheluwe, and Andreas Wortmann. Multi-paradigm modelling for cyber–physical systems: a descriptive framework. *Software and Systems Modeling*, 20(3):611–639, 2021.

238 Zijin Wang, Ou Zheng, Liangding Li, Mohamed Abdel-Aty, Carolina Cruz-Neira, and Zubayer Islam. Towards next generation of pedestrian and connected vehicle in-the-loop research: a digital twin co-simulation framework. *IEEE Transactions on Intelligent Vehicles*, 8(4):2674–2683, 2023.

239 Damien Bouchabou, Juliette Grosset, Sao Mai Nguyen, Christophe Lohr, and Xavier Puig. A smart home digital twin to support the recognition of activities of daily living. *Sensors*, 23(17):7586, 2023.

240 Oleg Maryasin. Home automation system ontology for digital building twin. In *2019 XXI International Conference Complex Systems: Control and Modeling Problems (CSCMP)*, pages 70–74. IEEE, 2019.

241 Minrui Xu, Dusit Niyato, Junlong Chen, Hongliang Zhang, Jiawen Kang, Zehui Xiong, Shiwen Mao, and Zhu Han. Generative AI-empowered simulation for autonomous driving in vehicular mixed reality metaverses. *IEEE Journal of Selected Topics in Signal Processing*, 17(5):1064–1079, 2023.

242 Nishat Anjum and Balwant Prajapat. ANN-based predictive state modeling of finite state machines. In *Data Science and Big Data Analytics: ACM-WIR 2018*, pages 389–400. Springer, 2019.

243 Elias Montini, Andrea Bettoni, Michele Ciavotta, Emanuele Carpanzano, and Paolo Pedrazzoli. A meta-model for modular composition of tailored human digital twins in production. *Procedia CIRP*, 104:689–695, 2021.

244 Xiaolang Yang, Xuemei Liu, Heng Zhang, Ling Fu, and Yanbin Yu. Meta-model-based shop-floor digital twin architecture, modeling and application. *Robotics and Computer-Integrated Manufacturing*, 84:102595, 2023.

245 Tim Kreuzer, Panagiotis Papapetrou, and Jelena Zdravkovic. AI explainability methods in digital twins: A model and a use case. In José Borbinha, Tiago Prince Sales, Miguel Mira Da Silva, Henderik A Proper, and Marianne Schnellmann, editors, *Enterprise Design, Operations, and Computing*, pages 3–20. Cham, Springer Nature Switzerland, 2025. ISBN 978-3-031-78338-8.

246 Iqbal H Sarker, Helge Janicke, Ahmad Mohsin, Asif Gill, and Leandros Maglaras. Explainable AI for cybersecurity automation, intelligence and trustworthiness in digital twin: methods, taxonomy, challenges and prospects. *ICT Express*, 4(4):935–938, 2024.

247 Olayinka Akinbolajo. Predicting equipment failures using artificial intelligence: a proactive approach. *International Journal of Advances in Engineering and Management (IJAEM)*, 7(1):513–521, 2025. ISSN 2395-5252. www.ijaem.net

248 Luis F Rivera, Miguel Jiménez, Norha M Villegas, Gabriel Tamura, and Hausi A Müller. The forging of autonomic and cooperating digital twins. *IEEE Internet Computing*, 26(5):41–49, 2021.

249 Shohin Aheleroff, Xun Xu, Ray Y Zhong, and Yuqian Lu. Digital Twin as a Service (DTaaS) in Industry 4.0: an architecture reference model. *Advanced Engineering Informatics*, 47:101225, 2021.

250 Roberto Minerva and Noël Crespi. Digital twins: properties, software frameworks, and application scenarios. *IT Professional*, 23(1):51–55, 2021.

251 Fei Tao, Fangyuan Sui, Ang Liu, Qinglin Qi, Meng Zhang, Boyang Song, Zirong Guo, Stephen C-Y Lu, and Andrew YC Nee. Digital twin-driven product design framework. *International Journal of Production Research*, 57(12):3935–3953, 2019.

252 Aidan Fuller, Zhong Fan, Charles Day, and Chris Barlow. Digital twin: enabling technologies, challenges and open research. *IEEE Access*, 8:108952–108971, 2020.

253 Calin Boje, Annie Guerriero, Sylvain Kubicki, and Yacine Rezgui. Towards a semantic construction digital twin: Directions for future research. *Automation in Construction*, 114:103179, 2020.

254 Juuso Autiosalo, Joshua Siegel, and Kari Tammi. Twinbase: open-source server software for the digital twin web. *IEEE Access*, 9:140779–140798, 2021.

255 Ronny Seiger, Lukas Malburg, Barbara Weber, and Ralph Bergmann. Integrating process management and event processing in smart factories: a systems architecture and use cases. *Journal of Manufacturing Systems*, 63:575–592, 2022.

256 Angelo Croatti, Matteo Gabellini, Sara Montagna, and Alessandro Ricci. On the integration of agents and digital twins in healthcare. *Journal of Medical Systems*, 44(9):161, 2020.

257 Gerardo Pardo-Castellote. OMG data-distribution service: architectural overview. In *23rd International Conference on Distributed Computing Systems Workshops, 2003. Proceedings*, pages 200–206. IEEE, 2003.

258 Wael Alghamdi and Emad Albassam. Synchronization patterns for digital twin systems. *Journal of Applied Data Sciences*, 5(3):1026–1037, 2024.

259 Seongjin Yun, Jun-Hong Park, and Won-Tae Kim. Data-centric middleware based digital twin platform for dependable cyber-physical systems. In *2017 Ninth International Conference on Ubiquitous and Future Networks (ICUFN)*, pages 922–926. IEEE, 2017.

260 Carmen Carrión. Kubernetes scheduling: taxonomy, ongoing issues and challenges. *ACM Computing Surveys*, 55(7):1–37, 2022.

261 Davide Borsatti, Walter Cerroni, Luca Foschini, Genady Ya Grabarnik, Lorenzo Manca, Filippo Poltronieri, Domenico Scotece, Larisa Shwartz, Cesare Stefanelli, Mauro Tortonesi et al. Kubetwin: a digital twin framework for Kubernetes deployments at scale. *IEEE Transactions on Network and Service Management*, 21(4):3889–3903, 2024.

262 Alexandre Gustavo Wermann and Juliano Araujo Wickboldt. KTWIN: a serverless Kubernetes-based Digital Twin platform. *Computer Networks*, 259:11095, 2025.

263 Kim Hyun Woo, Mungroo Adrian, and Lewe Jung-Ho. From data lake to digital twin: a data management framework for BEM and BAS interoperable buildings. *ASHRAE Transactions*, 130:607–615, 2024.

264 Athira Nambiar and Divyansh Mundra. An overview of data warehouse and data lake in modern enterprise data management. *Big Data and Cognitive Computing*, 6(4):132, 2022.

265 Kendrik Yan Hong Lim, Pai Zheng, and Chun-Hsien Chen. A state-of-the-art survey of digital twin: techniques, engineering product lifecycle management and business innovation perspectives. *Journal of Intelligent Manufacturing*, 31(6):1313–1337, 2020.

266 Viviana Lopez and Aditya Akundi. A conceptual model-based systems engineering (MBSE) approach to develop digital twins. In *2022 IEEE International Systems Conference (Syscon)*, pages 1–5. IEEE, 2022.

267 Tim Weilkiens. *Systems Engineering with SysML/UML: Modeling, Analysis, Design*. Elsevier, 2011.

268 Gierad Laput, Yang Zhang, and Chris Harrison. Synthetic sensors: towards general-purpose sensing. In *Proceedings of the 2017 CHI Conference on Human Factors in Computing Systems*, pages 3986–3999, 2017.

269 Seth Gilbert and Nancy Lynch. Brewer's conjecture and the feasibility of consistent, available, partition-tolerant web services. *ACM SIGACT News*, 33(2):51–59, 2002. https://doi.org/10.1145/564585.564601.

270 Lorenzo De Lauretis. From monolithic architecture to microservices architecture. In *2019 IEEE International Symposium on Software Reliability Engineering Workshops (ISSREW)*, pages 93–96. IEEE, 2019.

271 Babak Bashari Rad, Harrison John Bhatti, and Mohammad Ahmadi. An introduction to docker and analysis of its performance. *International Journal of Computer Science and Network Security (IJCSNS)*, 17(3):228, 2017.

272 Gigi Sayfan. *Mastering Kubernetes: Master the Art of Container Management by Using the Power of Kubernetes*. Packt Publishing Ltd, 2018.

273 Syed Mohsan Raza, Roberto Minerva, Barbara Martini, and Noel Crespi. Empowering microservices: a deep dive into intelligent application component placement for optimal response time. *Journal of Network and Systems Management*, 32(4):84, 2024.

274 Skan AI. How enterprise digital twins elevate efficiency and ROI, 2025. https://www.skan.ai/blogs/redefining-success-how-digital-twins-elevate-enterprise-business-metrics

275 K Worden, EJ Cross, RJ Barthorpe, DJ Wagg, and P Gardner. On digital twins, mirrors, and virtualizations: frameworks for model verification and validation. *ASCE-ASME Journal of Risk and Uncertainty in Engineering Systems, Part B: Mechanical Engineering*, 6(3), 2020.

276 Gabriella Waters. Testing, evaluation, verification and validation (TEVV) of digital twins: a comprehensive framework. 2025. https://arxiv.org/abs/2507.04555. *arXiv preprint arXiv:2507.04555*. [Online; accessed September 2025].

277 Michael Grieves. Digital twin certified: employing virtual testing of digital twins in manufacturing to ensure quality products. *Machines*, 11(8):808, 2023.

278 INCOSE. Model-based test and evaluation. https://www.incose.org/docs/default-source/insight/insight_vol26-1_0329.pdf, 2023. [Accessed September 2025].

279 Thomas H-J Uhlemann, Christian Lehmann, and Rolf Steinhilper. The digital twin: realizing the cyber-physical production system for industry 4.0. *Procedia CIRP*, 61:335–340, 2017.

280 Zhihan Lv and Shuxuan Xie. Artificial intelligence in the digital twins: state of the art, challenges, and future research topics: [version 2; peer review: 2 approved]. *Digital Twin*, 1(1):12, 2024.

281 Edward M Kraft. The air force digital thread/digital twin-life cycle integration and use of computational and experimental knowledge. In *54th AIAA aerospace sciences meeting*, page 0897, 2016.

282 Jan Van Os. The digital twin throughout the lifecycle. In *SNAME Maritime Convention*, page D023S003R002. SNAME, 2018.

283 Shimin Liu, Pai Zheng, and Jinsong Bao. Digital twin-based manufacturing system: a survey based on a novel reference model. *Journal of Intelligent Manufacturing*, 35(6):2517–2546, 2024.

284 Maggie Mashaly. Connecting the twins: a review on digital twin technology & its networking requirements. *Procedia Computer Science*, 184:299–305, 2021.

285 Enxhi Ferko, Luca Berardinelli, Alessio Bucaioni, Moris Behnam, and Manuel Wimmer. Towards interoperable digital twins: integrating SysML into AAS with higher-order transformations. In *2024 IEEE 21st International Conference on Software Architecture Companion (ICSA-C)*, pages 342–349. IEEE, 2024.

286 Blake Ives, Iris Junglas, and Mohamed Tazkarji. On the road to an automotive digital twin. *Communications of the Association for Information Systems*, 54(1):1079–1093, 2024.

287 Alexandre Vallee. Digital twins for personalized medicine require epidemiological data and mathematical modeling: viewpoint. *Journal of Medical Internet Research*, 27:e72411, 2025. https://doi.org/10.2196/72411. [Online; accessed September 13, 2025].

288 Andrea Chiarini, Marco Frosolini, and Marco Ugolini. Deploying digital twins in complex engineering systems: challenges and enablers. *Journal of Systems Engineering*, 28(2):123–145, 2025.

289 Kenneth M Rosen and Krishna R Pattipati. Operating digital twins within an enterprise process. In *The Digital Twin*, pages 599–659. Springer, 2023.

290 Amazon Web Services (AWS). AWS IoT twinmaker: optimize operations by easily creating digital twins of real-world systems. https://aws.amazon.com/iot-twinmaker/, 2025. [Online; accessed September 13, 2025].

291 Microsoft Corporation. Azure digital twins documentation. https://learn.microsoft.com/en-us/azure/digital-twins/, 2025. [Online; accessed September 13, 2025].

292 ESRI. How NASA mapped and modeled Langley's digital twin. https://www.esri.com/about/newsroom/blog/nasa-langleys-digital-twin, 2025. [Online; accessed September 13, 2025].

293 SAP. Digital twins at work: 9 examples. https://www.sap.com/uk/blogs/digital-twins-at-work, 2023. [Online; accessed September 13, 2025].

294 Russ Hoffman, Paul Friedman, and Dave Wetherbee. Digital twins in shipbuilding and ship operation. In *The Digital Twin*, pages 799–847. Springer, 2023.

295 Toobler. The best digital twin examples transforming industries. https://www.toobler.com/blog/digital-twin-examples, 2025. [Online; accessed September 13, 2025].

296 Eric Green. Digital twins across manufacturing. In Noel Crespi, Adam T Drobot, and Roberto Minerva, editors, *The Digital Twin*, pages 735–771. Springer International Publishing, Cham, 2024. In press, accessed September 13, 2025.

297 Joseph J Salvo. Welcome to the complex systems age: Digital twins in action. In *The Digital Twin*, pages 559–575. Springer, 2023.

298 Pascal Lünnemann, Carina Fresemann, and Friederike Richter. The digital twin for operations, maintenance, repair and overhaul. In *The Digital Twin*, pages 661–675. Springer, 2023.

299 Bryan R Moser and William Grossmann. Digital twins of complex projects. In Noel Crespi, Adam T Drobot, and Roberto Minerva, editors, *The Digital Twin*, pages 677–702. Springer International Publishing, Cham, 2024. In press, accessed September 13, 2025.

300 Friederike Richter et al. The role of the digital twin in oil and gas projects and operations. In Noel Crespi, Adam T Drobot, and Roberto Minerva, editors, *The Digital Twin*, Springer International Publishing, 2024. Cham, In press, accessed September 13, 2025.

301 Matteo Perno, Lars Hvam, and Anders Haug. Implementation of digital twins in the process industry: a systematic literature review of enablers and barriers. *Computers in Industry*, 134:103558, 2022. ISSN 0166-3615. https://doi.org/10.1016/j.compind.2021.103558.

302 Zhu Hanjing, Hwang Bon-Gang, Tan Yu Zhen, and Wei Feiyang. Building on digital twin: overcoming barriers and unlocking success in the construction industry. *Journal of Construction Engineering and Management*, 150(10):04024142, 2024.

303 Nand Kochhar. Leading the transformation in the automotive industry through the digital twin. In Noel Crespi, Adam T Drobot, and Roberto Minerva, editors, *The Digital Twin*, pages 773–797. Springer International Publishing, Cham, 2024. In press, accessed September 13, 2025.

304 De-Graft Joe Opoku, Srinath Perera, Robert Osei-Kyei, and Maria Rashidi. Digital twin application in the construction industry: a literature review. *Journal of Building Engineering*, 40:102726, 2021.

305 Flávia Pires, Ana Cachada, José Barbosa, António Paulo Moreira, and Paulo Leitão. Digital twin in industry 4.0: technologies, applications and challenges. In *2019 IEEE 17th International Conference on Industrial Informatics (INDIN)*, volume 1, pages 721–726. IEEE, 2019.

306 Faraz Malik Awan, Roberto Minerva, and Noel Crespi. Improving road traffic forecasting using air pollution and atmospheric data: experiments based on LSTM recurrent neural networks. *Sensors*, 20(13):3749, 2020.

307 Faraz Malik Awan, Roberto Minerva, and Noel Crespi. Using noise pollution data for traffic prediction in smart cities: experiments based on LSTM recurrent neural networks. *IEEE Sensors Journal*, 21(18):20722–20729, 2021.

308 Harry B Weiss. The Scarabaeus of the ancient Egyptians. *The American Naturalist*, 61(675):353–369, 1927.

309 Moayad Aloqaily, Ouns Bouachir, Fakhri Karray, Ismaeel Al Ridhawi, and Abdulmotaleb El Saddik. Integrating digital twin and advanced intelligent technologies to realize the metaverse. *IEEE Consumer Electronics Magazine*, 12(6):47–55, 2022.

310 Saeed Banaeian Far and Azadeh Imani Rad. Applying digital twins in metaverse: user interface, security and privacy challenges. *Journal of Metaverse*, 2(1):8–15, 2022.

311 Zhihan Lv, Wen-Long Shang, and Mohsen Guizani. Impact of digital twins and metaverse on cities: history, current situation, and application perspectives. *Applied Sciences*, 12(24):12820, 2022.

312 Zhihan Lv, Shuxuan Xie, Yuxi Li, M Shamim Hossain, and Abdulmotaleb El Saddik. Building the metaverse using digital twins at all scales, states, and relations. *Virtual Reality & Intelligent Hardware*, 4(6):459–470, 2022.

313 Dimitris Mourtzis. Digital twin inception in the era of industrial metaverse. *Frontiers in Manufacturing Technology*, 3:1155735, 2023.

314 HanSeong Lee, SeungTaek Ryoo, and SangHyun Seo. A comparative study on the structure and implementation of unity and unreal engine 4. *Journal of the Korea Computer Graphics Society*, 25(4):17–24, 2019.

315 Maria Lavinia Cappa. From Web 2.0 to the Metaverse: analyzing the evolution of platform-based business models and the creator economy. Tesi di laurea magistrale in management engineering - ingegneria gestionale, Politecnico di Milano, 2023.

316 Naveed Ahmed, Imad Afyouni, Hamzah Dabool, and Zaher Al Aghbari. A systemic survey of the omniverse platform and its applications in data generation, simulation and metaverse. *Frontiers in Computer Science*, 6:1423129, 2024.

317 Md Ariful Islam Mozumder, Muhammad Mohsan Sheeraz, Ali Athar, Satyabrata Aich, and Hee-Cheol Kim. Overview: technology roadmap of the future trend of metaverse based on IoT, blockchain, AI technique, and medical domain metaverse activity. In *2022 24th International Conference on Advanced Communication Technology (ICACT)*, pages 256–261. IEEE, 2022.

318 VV Vikhman and MV Romm. “Digital Twins” in education: prospects and reality. *Vysshee Obrazovanie v Rossii= Higher Education in Russia*, 30(2):22–32, 2021.

319 Baolin Deng, IpKin Anthony Wong, and Qi Lilith Lian. From metaverse experience to physical travel: the role of the digital twin in metaverse design. *Tourism Review*, 79(5):1076–1087, 2024.

320 Giacomo Barbieri, David Sanchez-Londoño, David Andres Gutierrez, Rafael Vigon, Elisa Negri, and Luca Fumagalli. Digital twin and education in manufacturing. In *The Digital Twin*, pages 1113–1134. Springer, 2023.

321 AltexSoft. Digital twins: components, use cases, and implementations. https://www.altexsoft.com/blog/digital-twins/, 2025. [Online; accessed August 6, 2025].

322 Zhao Tang, Dayuan Zhuang, and Jianjun Zhang. Evaluation framework for domain-specific digital twin platforms. *Scientific Reports*, 15(1):10544, 2025.

323 Sebastian Richard Newrzella, David W Franklin, and Sultan Haider. Methodology for digital twin use cases: definition, prioritization, and implementation. *IEEE Access*, 10:75444–75457, 2022.

324 Corrado Moiso and Roberto Minerva. Towards a user-centric personal data ecosystem the role of the bank of individuals’ data. In *2012 16th International Conference on Intelligence in Next Generation Networks*, pages 202–209, 2012. https://doi.org/10.1109/ICIN.2012.6376027.

Index

Printed and bound by CPI Group (UK) Ltd, Croydon, CR0 4YY
26/04/2026
14868063-0001